**Why
We
Fight**

Shane
Burley

Why
We
Fight

Essays

on

Fascism,

Resistance,

and

Surviving

the

Apocalypse

FOREWORD BY NATASHA LENNARD

"Shane Burley was one of the very first to take the Alt Right seriously as the emerging new face of White Nationalism, and he has remained one of its closest watchers. This collection is a clear and concise history of its ups-and-downs under the Trump administration."

—**Spencer Sunshine,** researcher of far-right movements

"Shane Burley is a journalist and thinker for our time, a time challenged by fascists in the streets and in the White House. With this essential book, Burley reports on the eye of the storm, so that we may better understand it, stop it, and build a better world. He sheds a necessary light on a dark, toxic corner of American politics and culture, and reports on the hopeful organizing efforts to dismantle fascism today."

—**Benjamin Dangl,** author of *The Five Hundred Year Rebellion: Indigenous Movements and the Decolonization of History in Bolivia*

"Shane Burley is one of our best chroniclers of the fascist resurgence today. More than simply *why* we fight, this book is essential for grasping *what* we are fighting and *how*. With a topographer's precision, Burley charts the contours of the motley fascisms of the present, showing us why they must be crushed and the best weapons we have for doing so."

—**George Ciccariello-Maher,** author of *Decolonizing Dialectics*

"Burley's meticulously observed, fluidly written collection is a must-read for anyone interested in the far-right's evolution during the Trump era, and its opposition. A collection that delves into the howling abyss and emerges with aplomb."

—**Talia Lavin,** *Culture Warlords: My Journey Into the Dark Web of White Supremacy*

"Shane Burley's work is invaluable to understanding fascism and the far-right in the U.S., as well as parsing the challenges facing the working class and political activists in our current moment. His reporting is thorough and imbued with critical nuance as well as deep compassion for the people whose stories he illuminates, and a principled commitment to the greater struggle for liberation. This collection of essays is a must for every radical bookshelf."

—**Kim Kelly,** *Teen Vogue*

"Shane Burley is a literal antifa ideologue."

—Andy Ngô

"The 21st century has brought, and will continue to bring, fresh political horrors for working people around the world. In the U.S., the decrepit dream of sustained neoliberal order has died, and we are now witnessing monstrous, reactionary forces emerging—from digital cellars to corporate board rooms and Fox News, from right-wing think tanks and militia groups to astroturfed Political Action Committees—to replace it. With a centrist political establishment that is either unwilling to fight for us or, more frequently, perfectly willing to capitulate to our illiberal enemies, we, the people, are on our own. It is for this reason that Shane Burley's work is so vital and, frankly, indispensable right now. While mainstream media outlets devote all their energy and oxygen to hand wringing over 'civility' and drawing false equivalences between the 'political extremisms' on the left and the right, Burley has regularly put himself in harm's way to bear witness to the fascist creep in America. With an inexhaustible commitment to the struggle for justice, compassion for working people, and care for his readers, Burley's writing provides us with thoughtful but clear-eyed analysis of the forces we're up against and with coverage of the many brave people and organizations who are fighting for what's right."

—**Maximilian Alvarez,** host of *Working People* podcast

"From the streets of Charlottesville to the bleachers of Major League Soccer, Burley's *Why We Fight* is a clear-sighted and utterly compelling collection of stories of fascist creep and organized resistance. Beyond its chronicling of the bumbling and violent rise of white-supremacist groups during the last few years, Burley's most important lesson is this: Fascism will come for us all if we let it, but we are neither alone nor powerless to fight it. Read this book then give it to a friend and then organize."

—**Vegas Tenold,** author of *Everything You Love Will Burn*

"Shane Burley is one of the most important, thoughtful, and moral chroniclers of American fascism working today. The collected works in *Why We Fight* are invaluable, at once a vivid and accessible account of the origins and rise of the Alt Right, and an urgent call to antifascist action in the Trump era. Read this book."

—**Christopher Matthias,** Senior Reporter at *Huffington Post*

Why We Fight: Essays on Fascism, Resistance, and Surviving the Apocalypse

© 2021 Shane Burley
© Foreword 2021 Natasha Lennard
This edition © 2021 AK Press
ISBN: 978-1-84935-406-6
E-ISBN: 978-1-84935-407-3
Library of Congress Control Number: 2020946103

AK Press	AK Press
370 Ryan Ave. #100	33 Tower St.
Chico, CA 95973	Edinburgh EH6 7BN
USA	Scotland
www.akpress.org	www.akuk.com
akpress@akpress.org	akuk@akpress.org

Please contact us to request the latest AK Press distribution catalog, which features books, pamphlets, zines, and stylish apparel published and/or distributed by AK Press. Alternatively, visit our websites for the complete catalog, latest news, and secure ordering.

"Disunite the Right" was first published by Political Research Associates, September 18, 2017; "Lawsuits are Not Enough to Stop the Far-Right" was first published by *Truthout*, December 7, 2017; "The Fall of the 'Alt Right' Came from Antifascism" was first published by *Truthout*, April 7th, 2018; "25 Theses on Fascism" was first published by The Institute for Anarchist Studies, December 2017; "The Kult of Kek" was first published by A Beautiful Resistance, 2017; "The 'Free Speech' Cheat" was first published by *The Baffler*, May 3, 2019; "We're Being Played" was first published by *Commune*, August 1, 2019; "Wolf Age" was first published by *Commune*, August 12, 2019; "A History of Violence" was first published by *Commune*, December 23, 2019; "Contested Space" was first published here"; "How Racists Dream" was first published by *Full Stop*, February 24, 2020; "Introduction to Armageddon" was first published by *A Beautiful Resistanc*e, July, 2020; "Blackface is the Story of White Identity" was first published by *Splice Today*, February 26, 2019; "Because of Their Violence" was first published by *Revolution by the Book* (AK Press blog), June 19th, 2018; "Living Your Life in a State of War," "The Continuing Appeal of Antisemitism," and "Chase the Black Sun" are published here for the first time.

Cover photograph by Daniel Vincent, www.danielvmedia.com
Cover design by Crisis
Printed in the United States on acid-free, 100% recycled paper

For my wife, Alexandra Burley, who showed me how to build a home out of love and kindness and is at the heart of everything I have ever written. And for Yaka aka Armeanio Lewis aka Sean Kealiher, who will live forever in our hearts, without hope and in total rebellion

CONTENTS

Foreword

In an August 2020 essay, published some months after this collection was first compiled, Shane Burley took us back to Charlottesville in 2017. "Though the Trump presidency is marked by an assiduous march of horrors, Charlottesville still stands out as a key moment in which the stakes and severity of the situation came into focus," he wrote.

It speaks to Burley's point, when we speak of the intolerable events of the Unite the Right Rally in Virginia, we speak in synecdoche: we need only say "Charlottesville." It was there, that White supremacists marched Klan-like with burning torches and Nazi salutes while chanting "Jews will not replace us!"—a gruesome pastiche of nineteenth century American and twentieth century European race hate, now adorned with MAGA hats. It was there that a neo-Nazi plowed his Dodge Charger into a crowd of antifascist counter-protesters, killing Heather Heyer and injuring many. A young Black man was viciously beaten by racists with metal poles in a parking lot by a police station. Charlottesville was where the flimsy veil of plausible deniability about the violent fascism of the Alt Right had been ripped off. And, in response, the contemporary shape of antifascist rebellion began to emerge.

In the years that have followed, as Burley traces in these pages, the specific coalition of the far-right that constituted "Charlottesville"

I

has all but collapsed. Richard Spencer, in many ways the father of the Alt Right, is now a failed drunk without a movement to lead. Even his neologism, "Alt Right," has fallen out of popular parlance. Yet key to understanding the threat of fascism's proliferation today is to reckon with the ways in which a fascist politics has exceeded its embodiment in the Alt Right shock troops. Burley's collected essays offer perhaps the clearest and most incisive study available into how the rise and implosion of a neo-fascist movement can coalesce with fascism's broader rise.

Burley's interrogation into the drives, mythologies, and habits of today's fascist movements in the U.S.—and their contradictions and failures—is as much a document of history as it is an antifascist intervention. To follow his analysis of how the far-right *works*, which he situates in extensive research and reporting, is to understand why a retreat to liberal centrism and reason is no solution at all. It's of note, that when Spencer canceled his college tour—a major inflection point in his demise—he did not blame his defeat on losing out in the so-called marketplace of ideas. He blamed antifa.

Establishment commentators and politicians looked aghast at the violent spectacle of Charlottesville: the event, like the rise of Trump, was digestible to them only as an aberration in history's mythic arc of progress. "This is not my country," and "this is not my president," cried liberal Americans of their country and their president. As if fascist rule, with its techniques forged in colonialism, were not always continuous with modernity. Bertolt Brecht wrote in 1935, "Those who are against Fascism without being against capitalism, who lament over the barbarism that comes out of barbarism, are like people who wish to eat their veal without slaughtering the calf. They are willing to eat the calf, but they dislike the sight of blood." In the same critical vein, Burley's essays refuse to let racial capitalism—the perennial condition for fascism—off the hook.

In 2016, a media cottage industry emerged, dedicated to defining fascism in order to prove that we are not faced with it. But now, in the midst of the worst public health and economic crisis in a century, federal troops are kidnapping antiracist protesters in the streets, ICE concentration camps are a normalized fact of border policy, and the State has named "antifa" as its enemy, while the deadly reality of far-right extremist violence is all but ignored if not sanctioned. Meanwhile, the state's response to the Coronavirus pandemic made ever clearer its racist, classist necropolitical governance: make work and let die.

As antiracist uprisings swept through the United States in the summer of 2020, following the police execution of George Floyd, far-right violence escalated in turn. The vast federal law enforcement apparatus oriented its efforts—including vicious arrests, raids, overreaching prosecutions and authoritarian crowd control—to quash left-wing rebellion and the struggle for Black lives. Meanwhile, the scattered forces of right-wing militiae amassed in the streets from Oregon to Arizona, armed with military grade weapons. Kyle Rittenhouse, a seventeen-year-old Trump enthusiast, crossed state lines from Illinois to Kenosha, Wisconsin, where he shot dead two Black Lives Matter protesters. He is a conservative hero now; prior to his killing spree, law enforcement officers thanked him and his fellow vigilantes for their presence at the protests. There has never been a time in American history when the State has abandoned its alignment with white supremacy. In 2020, as a pandemic raged, poverty soared, and a righteous rebellion erupted, the fascistic allegiances between State forces and far-right gangs stood in plain sight. Burley makes clear: we face Trump-emboldened fascist constellations, which neither began with his presidency, nor will be felled simply by virtue of his unseating.

"White supremacy and social hierarchy are implicit in class society, but fascism seeks to make it explicit," Burley writes. "The only thing that will end fascism in perpetuity is to destroy the mechanisms that allow it to arise in the first place." For myself, there is no doubt that it is appropriate to deploy the term "fascism" when speaking of today's far-right constellations: from the heavily armed militia groups hounding immigrants on the Southern border, to the cops extinguishing Black life after Black life, to every corner of the Trump administration. We deploy that weighted term, fascism, not only as an accurate label for certain political tendencies, but as a way to invoke an unambiguous antifascist response: a refusal to give fascism an inch.

Yesterday's Alt Right may be a fractured and fumbling mess, in large part thanks to the effective and disruptive "deplatforming" work taken up by antifa participants. But antifascist struggle is not simply a game of whac-a-mole, aimed at shutting down each neo-fascist assemblage that pops up. Burley invokes a more profound fight, against fascism and the racial capitalism that breeds it, and for each other and our mutually dependent survival and flourishing. As he reminds us, "We have never won anything on our own, and so in the face of repression from above, the only antidote is solidarity from below."

Natasha Lennard
October 2020

Introduction

A Home at the End of the World

"We have always lived in slums and holes in the wall. We will know how to accommodate ourselves for a while. For you must not forget that we can also build. It is we who built these palaces and cities, here in Spain and America and everywhere. We, the workers. We can build others to take their place. And better ones. We are not in the least afraid of ruins. We are going to inherit the earth; there is not the slightest doubt about that. The bourgeoisie might blast and ruin its own world before it leaves the stage of history. We carry a new world here, in our hearts. That world is growing in this minute."

—Buenaventura Durruti (1936)

"We live in our language like blind men walking on the edge of an abyss. This language is laden with future catastrophes. The day will come when it will turn against those who speak it."

—Gershom Scholem

"There is no act of love toward one's neighbor that falls into the void. Just because the act was realized blindly, it must appear somewhere as effect. Somewhere."

—Franz Rosenzweig, *The Star of Redemption*

"Did you know that we are in the Earth's last days?"

I was used to Clay's breaks with normality, but this was strange even for him. My Mom often reminded me that Clay's family was a little different than ours, closer to what she had grown up in. Inside of a Swedish immigrant farming community in Central California, my Mom grew up in an ecstatic Pentecostal church where the End of Days was the primary feature of scripture. Every week they would drag out a giant banner that served as Earth's timeline. On one end was the Creation of the world (six thousand years ago), then the exit from Eden, the cultures of pre-antiquity, the arrival of Jesus, the destruction of Rome, the Middle and Modern Ages. Far to the right was the destruction of the world, bathed in a fire that was premeditated by our collective sinfulness. The goal, each Sunday, was to locate exactly where they were on the timeline, always somewhere just encroaching the fiery end.

Clay's family may not have been so extreme, but they weren't that far off. My Mom was hesitant to let me go to with Clay to his church, which was different than our granola and Birkenstock variety. It was a town over and what we now call a "megachurch," complete with raised hands and sacred languages. Despite Clay's family being desperately poor, particularly after his father was diagnosed with an inoperable brain tumor, I saw his mother writing out the largest check I had ever seen to put in the offering. She told me it was a required Tithe, and besides, our money wouldn't be much use soon anyway.

"Revelation says that towards the end we will see the Blood Red Moon, that will be a sign that the Rapture is soon to come. And I saw the Red Moon just last week!" Clay told me, pleased as could be. That was absolutely all the evidence I needed.

This would have been around 1994, and the apocalypse was all the hot gossip. In advance of the new millennium, pulp media was desperate to pump out end-of-the-world content. There were docuseries mining Biblical prophecy, a revival of Nostradamus's predictions, movies with Schwarzenegger battling renegade demons, and a collective effort to calculate a possible date. I remember students debating what year the Anti-Christ, the harbinger of the end, would be born. Is it 1999? 2000? How long do we have from then? Is he supposed to live as long as Jesus did? Will the world confuse him for the true Messiah? I did not live in a tremendously fundamentalist area, but this was the cultural obsession, and it wasn't a new one.

The United States has always been obsessed with the coming apocalypse. The dispensationalism my Mom was raised on was just one brand of the millennialism that the country has been baking for generations, the feeling that the end is just around the corner. Millennialism imbues our actions with significance, the sense that even the mundane is sacred because of its proximity to our culmination. Millennialism is an eschatological idea from the Book of Revelation (Christ's coming thousand-year reign), but it broadly means an apocalypticism whereby this world comes to an end, and in its toil and strife it will be redeemed. This millennialism flowed through most of America's Christian history, particularly its trends towards fanatical Protestantism, leading to one pastor after another embarrassing himself when his End Times predictions fell flat. As a scholar of conspiracism, Michael Barkun identified a new form of millennialism, starting in the eighteenth century: the secular kind.[1] This new form took the essential millennial script, the battles of Armageddon, the tipping society, the possible messiah, and brought it down to the world. Secular millennialism has led to a shifting sand of apocalypticism in the American mind, sometimes religious, sometimes only seeming religious, and oftentimes disconnected from even the last fragments of a coherent ideology. In the twentieth century, apocalypticism went into overdrive as people began picking and choosing how they built this road to the end: a little bit of Christian theology, some UFO stories, mix in a secret government, and add a dose of crystal healing. Barkun labeled this Improvisational Millennialism; it wasn't bound by any past tradition, and it had the ability to replicate itself beyond ideology, class, and religion.[2] "Such belief systems can flourish only in an environment in which two conditions are present. The first requirement is that a wide range of potential material—motifs that might be incorporated into a belief system—be easily accessible. The second is that existing authority structures be sufficiently weakened so that novel combinations of ideas can be proposed and taken seriously," writes Barkun.[3]

The U.S. was founded by fundamentalist fanatics. Our history has witch trials and failed predictions of Christ's return, yet we never cease to look to the skies and, more than anything, to wait, always certain it will happen. This history is foundational to what Richard Hofstadter called the "Paranoid Style in American Politics." It's our ability to piece together radically complex, though patently untrue narratives about power, commerce, and government. The puritans lived with the imminent return of Christ, the World Wars led to a sense of impending collapse, and eschatology became the way that New Religious Movements made their mark in America. In the 1960s, the Christians became increasingly obsessed with the apocalypse and its Illuminati minions, with hit franchises like the *Late Great Planet Earth* leading to the Satanic Panic and the signs of the Devil's imminent capture of our youth.[4] Our secondary religion is the quest to reveal our shadow selves, the conspiracy that undergirds every significant moment of history. Assassinations must have resulted from a coordinated campaign, the grand movement, the machinations of Masons or Jews or sacred bloodlines, never just the obvious aboveground conspiracy of capital and statecraft. Our religious identity and political paranoia have a chicken-and-the-egg quality, one informs the other in a self-reinforcing cycle. They find their unity in what they are waiting for: an end by either fire or ice.

I kept thinking about Clay as the smoke from summer 2020 wildfires blotted out the Portland sun. Over 10 percent of Oregon was blanketed in untamed wildfires that forced thousands to flee from their homes.[5] The smoke blanketed the entire state so profoundly that we had to trade in our Kn95 masks, which we had gotten used to wearing because of the pandemic, for respirators. This was fine because I already owned several; they were what I had used to attend the Black Lives Matter protests that were being teargassed nightly by baton-happy police. The sky shifted in hues: gray turned to orange to blood red, a nauseating shade, like a slaughterhouse. The air quality in Portland became the worst in the world, but at least it cut down on COVID-19 transmission for a few weeks. We didn't see a dramatic upsurge in fatal cases until a couple months later.

The uptick of COVID cases happened amidst a culture that not only refused to acknowledge the reality of the virus but fought the transmission of basic epidemiological facts. The most striking image at the beginning of the pandemic was a screaming, red-hatted woman leaning out of her truck while a man in scrubs, and a mask, blocked her path. She was screaming at this front line health worker that he might as well be a "communist" since the disease was a hoax by Soros or the liberals or antifa or whoever. Even as the Coronavirus started to spread, and the death toll started to climb in places like New York City, almost half the country did not see it as a real threat. Almost a third of people in the summer reported not regularly wearing masks, and as the crisis continued even the most committed started venturing into public gatherings.[6] Some people didn't even believe there was a pandemic.[7]

"Folks delaying seeking care or, taking the most extreme case, somebody drinking bleach as a result of structural factors just underlines the fact that we have not protected the public from disinformation," said Dr. Duncan Maru, a doctor and epidemiologist in Queens, New York, one of the areas hit hardest by the virus.[8] This led to a backlash as right-wing "anti-mask" protests—basically mass spreader events that led to large bowls of potential infection—started around the country. Protesters agreed that mask laws and "shelter in place" orders around the country—which were necessary to stop mass infection and hold explosive death counts back—were a liberal plot. Some even were starting to use militia contacts to pressure local sheriffs to refuse to enforce the orders, and many law enforcement leaders obliged.[9]

According to a Pew Research poll conducted in the summer of 2020, almost half of the country thought that there was some truth to the idea that the novel coronavirus was a *planned* virus.[10] About the same time, one-third of Americans thought that less people had actually died than was being reported.[11] Huge numbers were refusing to wear masks, and a study found that this was largely because of a misunderstanding about how the virus spread, something that became even more dire as misinformation became the status quo in the media cycle.[12] Huge figures in "alt medicine" jumped into action, including high profile figures promoting theories that it was actually 5G towers (which were targeted with arson) and vaccines that were responsible.[13] Even as the second wave came into full effect in places like South Dakota, patients positive with the virus were denying its existence right up to their own death—nothing would break the narrative.[14]

Populist narratives about cabals and secret actors are partially a working-class attempt to unpack the real conspiracy of inequality that we live with, a world where they can never seem to get on top no matter how hard they try and how much they sacrifice. The real apocalypses of foreclosed homes and lost generations is ignored, and instead we turn towards the only real ideological training we have had: the theological kind.

And we all agree on this. "We are already deep into the trajectory towards collapse," said a majority of Australia's top climate scientists in the summer of 2020, noting that we reached a "global tipping cascade" that was likely to bring down civilization.[15] A million species are now threatened with extinction, and that could catastrophically disrupt the biosphere and lead to the dissolution of ecological stability.[16] A new wave of "preppers," people who prepare to survive during a collapse, have readied for a coming climate apocalypse.[17] The atmosphere will become toxic, heat-related deaths will rise as will the oceans, and a mass die off will take most of the planet's life. We are entering a period where fish will mostly go extinct, where wildfires will consume more and more vegetation each year, and where wars will rage over who controls water. These are not the paranoid delusions of religious fanaticism, this is promised weekly in reports on the accelerating climate apocalypse.

Climate apocalypse is, in part, what has led to the COVID-19 pandemic, which killed millions in 2020 and is likely just the start of what could be a dangerous hot-house effect of rising temperatures that leads to more and more pandemics. The health crisis threw us, collectively, into an immediate economic crunch, yet this was also expected. As global capitalism continues its reckless march forward, we are seeing the increasingly chaotic nature of the economic system as the rich pilfer the natural resources and working classes in a systematic transfer of wealth to the top. Global economic inequality is only skyrocketing as speculation increases and markets teeter on the edge. I grew up in the 1980s and 1990s, when the perpetual growth paradigm seemed forever content (at least for white middle-class families), but we were living on borrowed time: the shock and awe of crisis is the new status quo.

False Prophets

The various pieces of this collapse, from accelerating economic turmoil the ecological ruin, are factors that have led to insurgent movements, including the far-right. "Capitalism in crisis invites the reaction that racism readily provides: criminalization of the exploited and the oppressed, subject to heavily militarized control and containment, as well as scapegoating by the corporate media," writes Brendan O'Connor in *Blood Red Lines*, his history of "border fascism" in the U.S.[18] Trumpism rose in 2015 and washed over the United States, which shouldn't be a surprise if understood in the context of a global return of nationalism. The national populist surge brought in the Alternative for Deutschland in Germany, the authoritarian ultra-right of Orbán's Fidesz in Hungary, the Law and Justice Party in Poland, and even the "post-fascist" rebranding of the Front National that came within an inch of the sun in France. Britain pulled out of the European Union, a last stand was made in Crimea, the BJP took over India, and Bolsanaro has a new vision for Brazil. From sea to shining sea it is, well, not exactly a new world, but more of a hyperreal re-enactment of the old one—one that we thought, in full hubris, we had escaped.

And I predicted none of this. I started writing about fascism toward the end of 2014, after lingering over research for some years before. At the time, it was hard to get anyone to publish work on fascism. One publication I pitched to said that, while the article was a nice idea, the "real issue" was systemic white supremacy—white nationalism was not on the radar. Part of me agreed, which led me to write one of my early articles on the subject. I called it "Why We Fight" in an attempt to unpack what the real threat of fascism was. After talking about some foiled "white genocide" action that failed to materialize in Portland in 2015, I said that fascists "certainly are not going to sway electoral politics in any meaningful way" before going on to say that the threats were things like insurgent violence, pushing open the "Overton window," and capturing radicalism by reframing what dissent looks like. Those threats were real, but my white naivete missed something that is so painfully obvious today: fascists could win the whole thing too. It's not just their terrorism that threatens us, it is the fact that they emerged from the American colonial project and they can further radicalize the existing organs of power by taking over the State. What's even scarier, they may even do it through the mass consent of the white working class.

Shortly after, the #Cuckservative hashtag trended, marking the first coalescence of "Alt Right 2.0." The Alternative Right had been a clever rebranding of fascism, attempting to string together threads like American paleoconservatism, the European New Right, and other fascist philosophers into a pseudo-intellectual form of white nationalism. By 2015, it had reached a tipping point, and it spilled out into mass activism with groups like Identity Evropa (later renamed as the American Identity Movement) and the Traditionalist Workers Party. The Alt Right rolled into the public consciousness along with what was called the Alt Light, a slightly more moderate far-right current based on civic nationalism, populism, conspiracy theories, and more rhetoric and action than ideas. This led to the massive groundswell that became Trump's base, the most radical of which formed into fascist street gangs like the Proud Boys or was funneled into "Patriot" organizations.[19] This, as far as anyone can tell, was another sign of the cracks in neoliberalism (it's paradoxical veneration of liberal representation politics mixed with international capitalism), yet with a reactionary populism rather than a liberation from below. There was anger and instability as our consensus reality crumbled in the midst of fake news and institutionalized conspiracy theories, where the very understanding of meaning and politics was called into question. By the time of the 2020 election, almost two-dozen Republican political candidates subscribed to the antisemitic conspiracy theory Q-Anon, which posits that Trump is fighting a Satan-worshiping cabal of pedophile Democrats who control the government.[20]

The dominant feature of the far-right in the Trump era is not the uniformity of ideology, or even the proposed extremism of the platform, but its commitment to the propaganda of the attack. The four years of the Trump presidency have been marked by a series of rallies designed to be little more than vessels to initiate attacks on leftist demonstrators and marginalized communities. Across the country, cars were rammed into protesters, firearms were drawn, antifascists beaten with bats and pipes, and actual conspiracies abounded as right-wing fringe actors prepared to kidnap governors, kill politicians, and gun down activists.[21] By the time I wrote *Fascism Today* in 2017, the kind of fascism that was possible was in full view.

The Alt Right started to see a period of decline in 2017, a combination of effective antifascism and their own incompetent hubris, and this moment of decline unleashed the fury of the fringe of the fringe.[22] The crisis of the surrounding culture was then framed around an even more profound feeling of Armageddon: the accelerationist. Built on the idea that the current society is doomed to failure and that it must crash down around us for their white utopia to be built, the politics of fascist accelerationism are built around hastening the collapse. Places like the Iron March online forums led to the explosive growth of groups like the Atomwaffen Division, which based their vision of revolution on the writings of James Mason who wanted to hasten the end through terroristic guerilla war. "Mason believed that regular legal political activity was doomed to failure. Instead, he sought a vaguely defined political and social collapse, hoping that in the vacuum—one example he gives is a war between Leftists and the State—the Nazis could swoop in and become victorious. His infamous advocacy of random racist murders was also an attempt to spread social anxiety that would facilitate this collapse," says Spencer Sunshine, a researcher who has done work on Mason.[23]

White nationalist cells like The Base plotted attacks around the country.[24] Alt Right subcultures emerged, like the "Bowl Patrol," which idolized Dylann Roof, the shooter who killed nine parishioners in Charleston, South Carolina, in 2015.[25] It was the extremity of the violence that bound them together; the only vision they had for a future was through a wall of suffering that would necessarily tear society apart at the seams. Their white Zion was post-apocalyptic; they would deliver their people to the promised land only after the horrors (started by multiculturalism and ended by their bombs) were wiped away.

The growth of the fascist right came, in large part, because the feeling of white apocalypse permeated the culture as frightened whites saw their demographic majority slip. This was typified by the White Genocide meme, the idea that the white race was being purposely exterminated.[26] The exact narrative of this concept (also called the "Great Replacement") differs depending on the audience telling it: sometimes it is about demographic replacement, sometimes it is about actual industrial-scale murders, sometimes it is "the Jews" responsible, sometimes it is proxies like George Soros. The theory of White Genocide emerged from South Africa, where the phenomenon of violence in rural areas was filtered through a post-Apartheid lens of white anxiety and a common notion, filtered through right-wing politics, that white Boer farmers were being ethnically cleansed. The narrative of farm murders, which is a manipulation of both the crime statistics and a misunderstanding of rural crime in South Africa, was simply a hyperbolic way for whites to express their fear of displacement.[27] In the final days of Rhodesia, the white supremacist colony that later became Zimbabwe, whites tried desperately to shore up the white population, and shared the same rhetoric that their ancestral home, Britain, did as they tried to stop non-white immigration. They talked of being consumed by invaders, overwhelmed by alien cultures, and having their whiteness erased by a sea of color.[28] After legal segregation was lost (somewhat) in the southern United States, the anti-integration Confederates looked to South Africa and Rhodesia as their brothers in arms, with their shared experience of trying to preserve white sovereignty.[29] Their paranoid delusion is that anything other than white supremacist rule would delete whites from the planet. Their identity depended only on subjugation; there is nothing other than whiteness, whiteness without end.

Anxiety over white genocide has fueled the return of eco-fascism, exterminationist nationalism phrased in the language of environmental conservation. Here, population becomes the center of all things, particularly those racialized groups that are posed as being external to the nation. They are then the coercive force that swamps our resources and pillages our forests, and it requires a "law of nature" mentality to restore order and hierarchy and create borders to preserve the sanctity of our world. This concept of populations external to the nation has underscored a great amount of the obsessive American "border fascism" ingrained into law by organizations founded by white nationalist John Tanton, who was possessed by a fear of an invading "Other" who could possibly destroy his beautiful planet. Tanton's organizations, including the Federation for American Immigration Reform, the Center for Immigration Studies, and NumbersUSA, are now the driving force in American immigration policy, and are all founded on discredited ideas about race and IQ and a guttural obsession with ensuring white apartness.[30] The Christchurch shooter, who killed fifty-two people at a New Zealand mosque, echoed the same thinking in his manifesto, in which he positioned his anger about non-white immigration in line with the impending climate crisis. The same concept ran through the letter by Patrick Crusius, the man who murdered twenty-two people in a Walmart in El Paso, Texas.[31] The story of environmental doom is told in the same frame as the artificial narrative about white displacement, their story about climate collapse actually a declaration of racial terror. The fascist mind is obsessed with justifying their rage through externalization, whether economic or religious or, in this case, melting ice caps.

While 2020 felt like apocalypse from start to finish, nothing was quite as terrible as its election season. From the start, President Trump suggested there was a coup by the "deep state," and he pushed forward conspiracies and scapegoating that led to real world violence as far-right attacks multiplied on antiracist demonstrators. Hundreds of attacks dotted the summer months as Trump supporters and far-right hooligans went to "intervene" on the uprising against police murders that took place in the wake of George Floyd's killing.[32] The aggressive repression from the police, and their unwillingness to intervene on fascist attacks only reinforced the case the protesters were trying to make, which only increased their numbers, keeping people in the streets for months in high profile standoffs with federal officers and sweeping riots that tore apart luxury commercial districts.[33] Trump returned to the law-and-order rhetoric that got him elected, reframing reality as a conspiratorial revolution, poised to bring about a prophetic implosion of this country, unless vigilantes and supporters would emerge to defend it. When Kyle Rittenhouse, an seventeen-year-old gunman, rode into Kenosha, Wisconsin, with white supremacists, and murdered two protesters, the Trump movement was ready to venerate him as a martyr and to send the message that this is how proper Americans handle a threat.[34] When Michael Reinoehl shot a member of the far-right group Patriot Prayer (he claimed in self-defense), he was summarily killed by law enforcement, which Trump then celebrated, saying "that's how it has to be."[35] The lines were clearly drawn in a battle between good and evil, and no canister of tear gas or bear mace would be spared.

After Trump lost in a clear electoral outcome, he escalated his rhetoric, saying the count was rigged and that he had won. His followers heard the message loud and clear, heading out into the streets in violent armed rallies where reporters and activists were beaten and stabbed in incidents around the country. On November 7th, I went to the "Stop the Steal" rally in Vancouver, Washington, just over the river from Portland, Oregon, to cover the event. Upon walking up, I was approached by three men who were holding baseballs bats and had AR-15s strapped to their bodies. "I know who you are," said one of them, unclear if he means me personally or some vague category like "reporter" or "antifa." "Why don't you try going into the rally and see what the fuck is going to happen." I asked another attendee how long the rally was going to last. He laughed, "As long as it takes to kill them all." There was one lone Black Lives Matter protester standing silently, refusing to move or make eye contact with any of them. Before I left, she stopped me to tell me they were reading people's license plates into a CB radio so that others could stop them down the road, presumably for some kind of threat of violence.

Comparisons to the Weimar Republic have been a constant liberal reaction to the Trump era, and that continued as Trump signaled a possible coup attempt. Historian Benjamin Carter Hett's description of Weimar as "the result of a large protest movement colliding with complex patterns of elite self-interest, in a culture increasingly prone to aggressive mythmaking and irrationality" makes a pressing comparison.[36] It was always built to spill.

Trumpism continued in the coming weeks without interruption, which was to be expected because his power was never just located in the office he held. Trump was the voice for a new ground-up movement that transposed the demographics of conventional conservatism into something more insurgent, more racial. He had mobilized a base with the energy that only comes from populist answers to all relevant problems, with black-and-white enemies and clear figureheads to blame.

"We have a really large contingent of radicalized folks out there who believe that the election was actually stolen," said David Neiwert about the persistence of Trumpism after the election. "I think we can expect to see a significant increase in domestic terrorism over the next four years."[37] Trump is the boldest face of the political right in America. He has eclipsed all other trends and figures and has centralized a movement entirely on explicit nativism and conspiracism, which are now part of the new status quo.

The Antifa Scare

This nativist far-right dynamic has created another permanent state of being: Antifascism has become a mass movement. "Antifa" was one of those radical brands you would often see on t-shirts at anarchist book fairs, like Earth First! or the Industrial Workers of the World, but it was hardly a household name beyond those circles. More than this, it was likely to be one of the movements least to raise eyebrows—it was Nazis they were dealing with, after all. Since 2015, antifascism has moved far past subcultures and has become an intersecting movement with different strains, strategies, cultures, tactics, identities, and personalities, with none defining it as a singular movement. Antifascism called to question what most European and American countries said they were: publicly opposed to inequality and celebrating democracy, at the same time as white identity extended the violence of colonialism into modernity. Now everyone has a hand in fighting fascism, with groups popping up around the country, some using the "antifa" branding, some going with larger non-profits, and all finding a certain common language in the mass action. The Trump presidency brought the return of massive, city shuttering, street-blocking protests, from the Women's March to anti-Trump mobilizations to the fight against racist police violence in 2020. These are all under the banner of antifascism, implicitly or explicitly, but it made sense to almost everyone because the impending threat of fascism was no longer ephemeral. People were collectively responding, not only to the seemingly impulsive violence of small white nationalist groups, but also to the massive growth of Trumpism as a street-level movement with violent potential, the growth of massive far-right organizations training for war, and a potentially captured State set on border imperialism, mass incarceration, and the validation of white supremacy.

Even more, "antifa" itself became a buzzword, and less for what the term actually meant and more because of the fears right-wing pundits could place on it. Because of far-right grifters like Andy Ngô and Tucker Carlson, the word *Antifa* has been divorced from its meaning (militant antifascist organizing) and has now become the default word for all left-wing protests with an antiracist edge. Black Lives Matter, labor actions, mutual aid networks, immigration protesters, and abortion clinic defense have now all been painted as "antifa," and antifa is a proxy for every fear that the right has conjured up about what an insurgent left is capable of. The violence of the right, which is itself a lethal pandemic that touches all of our lives, is reframed as defense when paired with a hollowed-out image of antifa. Reality has become malleable, and just as "Fake News" stole our shared understanding of events, so has edited video footage, viral tweets, and dishonest testimonials. Antifa is everywhere and nowhere, bringing down society and composed of nothing but lazy millennials. Antifa is now a stand-in for every cultural trend the right finds frightening. This would be ridiculous if it didn't have such dire consequences, as senators and attorneys general vie to label antifascism as terrorist criminality, potential prosecutions become a viable threat, and the far-right is egged on to murderous attacks.[38]

"At this moment the people are a real threat to their power and they're desperate to discredit the movement because it's growing and spreading so rapidly they can't contain it," says Effie Baum, an organizer with the antifascist group Pop Mob.[39]

Given the public perception and stigma that already exists against antifascists, we are an easy scapegoat. This scapegoating also works to create division between those who are outraged by the police violence but may choose different tactics to show it. An authoritarian administration is always going to villainize those most opposed to the rising tide of fascism in the U.S. and internationally. By shifting the narrative away from police brutality and the rampant murder of Black and brown people by police, they can get public support from both sides who are clutching their pearls over broken windows, instead of focusing on the brutal police violence that we've seen over the last few days or the countless murders of Black men and women like George Floyd.[40]

Antifascists spent the years after 2016 fighting off accusations and innuendo, and the directionless attacks only expanded to journalists, politicians, community leaders, and the clergy. No one was spared from being discredited as another "antifa," putting them outside the bounds of polite company. This labeling happened while antifascist groups continued to grow and meet the far-right in event after event, even after absurd lawsuits and baseless criminal investigations attempted to dull their effectiveness. "Our community stands up to protect those who are targeted by white nationalists," said David Rose of Rose City Antifa. "In this unity, comes the only sure defense against fascism and similarly violent nationalist ideologies. As a community, we need to say that this is unacceptable, that we will not allow immigrants, minorities, and activists to be attacked in our city."[41]

To see antifascism—from liberal NGOs to radical groups—come to the forefront, for antifascism to become the default language for any mass resistance to the politics of this moment, is significant. The current crises, from economic to ecological, are confronted in relation to antifascism, a coalition effort of the entire left pushing against an insurgent right-wing backlash. The implicit understanding is that, as this crisis widens, fascism will become even more persistent, and that all of the intersecting social movements will have to reckon with it. The "all hands on deck" approach will persist because there can be no success while the threat looms, and it is not going away anytime soon. The crisis, a vague notion we seem to apply to all forms of instability, is now defined in the mass consciousness as laced with fascist potential. Economic instability, the response from landlords and bosses as working people organize, the absolute decimation of wild lands... all of it is assumed to have *fascism* stamped on top of it as we have seen how capital will use nationalism to protect its interests.

Antifascism is the stopgap to very real and potential outcomes of the current crisis. To curb the crisis, to fight back against the destruction of our communities, to imagine a different future—these are now being recognized as requiring some degree of antifascism. There is no vibrancy without it, no grand vision of a different world is realistic without the awareness that defense against their preferred future is necessary. Crisis breeds the "mobilizing passions" to turn this way or that, towards one radical solution or another, and it requires an intervention to stop the borders and nativism from becoming the result.[42] Fascism is the worst possible scenario. It's an approach to crisis that intervenes on the most catastrophic features of humanity, a false promise (prophet) that will lead to a perversion of peace and reconciliation. This crisis is an End Times narrative of its own, a kind of millennialism, as entire generations reckon with the fact that widespread fascism could become our reality. We are all millennialists now.

Antifascism is now the language we use to confront this tidal wave of misery. This "final battle" is now phrased in the most black and white of terms—us versus them—because fascism looks to transform diverse intersecting communities into tribal allegiances bent on confronting one another in desperate battle. If the apocalypse is now defined by fascism, our survival is built on antifascism, our ability to stave off the worst outcomes so something new is possible in its stead.

This presents a strange challenge to antifascism then, to not just be a resistance to a possible future, but to be a future in its own right.

How We Survive

A great deal of ink has been spilled about the horrors of the 2010s, and even more about the Trump presidency and the dumpster fire of 2020, and with good reason. Travel bans have targeted marginalized people, while the Trump administration herded children into concentration camps on the border. Police murder became a spectacular marker for racist cruelty, and as the Coronavirus swept city after city, the death toll only more accurately captured the violence that oppressed communities face as a standard course.

However, there is also an inverse to this story, which focuses on what everyone did collectively not just in response but also in many cases, to simply survive. Mass revolts became the new status quo and the overwhelming of public space became a common language, from the streets of cities to the entrance of airports. As 2020 really hit its stride, and most states went into some degree of quarantine, mutual aid networks formed in many, many cities.

"Mutual aid is important because it normalizes and reminds us how to be in community again, how to look out for our neighbors and how to recenter ourselves in the values of justice, service, and relationship," says Stephanie Noriega of Tucson Mutual Aid, a group from Tucson, Arizona, that was creating systems of support during the height of the pandemic. "As a social worker for the past sixteen years, we have become too reliant on state and/or social service systems to serve those in need or under-resourced."[43]

A sort of alternative to the charity model of servicing, with mutual aid, communities provide systems of care out of a mutually beneficial relationship, with *solidarity* as the operative term. This mutual aid intends to transform disconnected relationships into real, working, and personal community bonds, creating an alternative to the often disjointed neighborhoods we come from. The U.S. government was immediately ill equipped to respond to the Coronavirus crisis, and the far-right mobilized racism to sow divisions, so mutual aid networks were an effort to root a different approach to the crisis, which brought us together into working relationships.[44]

The biggest uprising in half a century was also part of this, when cities erupted spontaneously in solidarity actions after George Floyd was murdered by police in Minneapolis. These widespread protests acting as tributaries to a larger police abolition movement. These mass mobilizations in the U.S. followed those in regions around the world: Chile, Belarus, Rojava, Hong Kong, Bolivia, the world is seeing a return to history. All over the world, people flooded the streets in confrontational protests, rioters burned down police stations and looted luxury businesses, and the number of people in the streets multiplied as militancy became a starting point.

In Portland, where I am, the protests went on for months and Trump ordered in federal officers for protracted street warfare with protesters, including using military grade CS gas and running "snatch and grab" operations.[45] The presence of the feds only fueled the anger, and a Wall of Moms came out to block federal officers from brutalizing the demonstrators. The nightly police assaults, which left many hospitalized with lasting injuries, kept the protests going.[46] As I write this, huge portions of the city are still boarded up, the result of an uprising that will only continue as the underlying conditions that brought it fail to be addressed. On Halloween night, an anti-capitalist march tore through the Northeast commercial district of the city, with demonstrators taking hammers to the windows of Starbucks, Verizon, and commercial banks. Just across the river, an array of Trump supporters armed to the teeth amassed to taunt and heckle a vigil for Kevin Peterson, a man who was killed by Vancouver, Washington, police just days before. They were eventually drowned out by counter protesters, who are able to pull together hundreds or thousands with almost no notice simply because mass resistance is now a common sense community function. While the country had been recoiling from lost jobs and potential infection, in towns and streets where we barely know our neighbors, these protest spaces became familial, as people came together in an ecstatic mix of grief, rage, and joy. The protest is the new home, borne of catastrophe, and yet, it is a space of its own where the rules of social relationships are being rewritten.

This is part of why these protests became the center of mutual aid work as the wildfire smoke descended on Oregon and people fled their homes. To only add to the feeling of apocalyptic doom, a conspiracy theory floated around the state (and the country) that it was "antifa"—whatever they mean that to be—who was responsible for the fires, rather than exurban sprawl and climate change. Militias created checkpoints, and armed patrols looked for looters and arsonists, yet it was mutual aid groups from the Left that offered the foundation of the aid that was necessary. "[We] believe in a more just and generous world, and we are trying to live that," said Stella Fiora, a member of a pagan collective, The Witches, who had been providing resource support to the Portland protests and shifted to bring resources to people affected by the fires.[47]

Like everyone, we despair about it much of the time, but more so we feel compelled to respond. So we want our response to be not just sowing justice, but generosity—not just righting wrongs, but seeking to create abundance and joy in their place. I think we see all human injustices as related: the protests are about racial injustice, seeking to defund police and dismantle a system that has been designed since the beginning to hunt, murder, and imprison Black people. And more broadly, justice will require we dismantle white supremacy, which brutalizes all BIPOC. We see these fires through a lens of justice as well—climate justice and racial justice are deeply intertwined, both because POC are suffering first and most from the collapse of our climate and the capitalist exploitation that got us here, and because Indigenous people, whose stolen land we live on, already know how we could have prevented these fires, and cultivated that practice for centuries.[48]

Mutual aid has become a key factor in our future, both in our day-to-day survival and the social reproduction necessary to actually build social movements. Organized labor has recently seen one of its largest flash increases of the last thirty years, both in general unionization and militancy. This has come, in part, because of a new generation's inability to survive in the crushing economic precarity of the twenty-first century. Militant labor unions like the Industrial Workers of the World have expanded to support low-wage freelance workers (as have the National Writers Union), and as service sector jobs see solidarity unionism on a mass scale, they are building in mutual aid mechanisms to care for workers facing uncertainty from the pandemic.[49] Teachers started wildcat strikes around the country and in 2020 alone there were hundreds of strikes, pickets, and direct actions across every sector.[50] Instead of despair, this crisis was met with a consummate fight, one result of years of preparation so that when a real wave came it could not drown us.

The amalgamation of these crises is known not just in its detrimental effects, the lost jobs and unpaid bills, but in the parallel experiences that happen. As the protests occur, as mutual aid networks are formed, as people join together with their coworkers to build a vibrant spiritual community or build affinity, a "space" of its own is created. These new formations are created by a situation, a crisis that pressed people to respond, but they have their own social relationships as well. Inside of a protest space, even the most outwardly disruptive, there is a social fabric, a way of relating between people. The dialectic of this current crisis is that it continues to build this space, night after night, in situation after situation, because people are being crushed. Our day-to-day life is slowly creeping away from us, our old lives seem as distant as a stable job or an unburdened mind, and new walls are being erected as we try to find solutions. The old world is quite literally dying, and the ways in which we get by as its rotting corpse stinks and seeps, is not just how we deal with the death: it is quite literally the new world struggling to be born.

This new "resistance society" is built as much by utility as it is by circumstance, but it offers people something more than the sum of its parts. Our struggle to simply survive is a kind of revolution of its own because, as the State and the old mechanisms of support dissipate under years of privatization, the only thing we can rely is each other. This type of relationship is new to us because togetherness was so alien before.

The Common Ground Collective came together in New Orleans in 2005 after Hurricane Katrina decimated every piece of the community, from houses to infrastructure, and the void in public services and stability was being filled by white vigilante militias on the hunt for their Black neighbors. An opening was created where what the Common Ground Collective had to offer, anarchist networks of solidarity and mutual aid, were actually useful, and they could build something new to meet the needs of the community. Common Ground came from a dynamic approach to crisis, to confront the insurgent fascism of white militias and to create something organic. They made mistakes along the way, particularly as the project grew and white activists flooded in from around the country, but mutual aid was at its heart.[51] "Mutual aid is the antidote to fear, despair, and isolation," says scott crow. "What it does is it makes you not think about the fear of the future."[52]

"If we work together to build these networks of autonomy and collective ideas. . .they have liberatory foundations," says crow. The way we survive now is not just a pathway to something else, or the promise that we will be delivered to a new world after the catastrophe. Instead we are actually building the new world in the moments we create. This is because there is no great revolution to wait for, only us and what we decide to do. "I don't want revolution on the other side. I don't want 'Capital R' revolution. I want it now, man," says crow. "What I have come to is: just what would it look like to take care of ourselves?"[53] Our revolution is in our everyday life, the ways when we break with the norm by building a new reality, based on kindness and support, mutual aid, and solidarity. Any new society is the result of the tipping point, when the old world is subsequently crushed by the weight of what we have already replaced it with.

There is a cultural obsession with collapse. Movie after blockbuster movie shows humans surviving in the ruins of vegetation-reclaimed cities, as if through the destruction of past society we will be freed from the everyday horrors of our jobs and lives. This societal collapse is at the heart of the far-right Boogaloo Movement, which surfaced in 2020 as an accelerationist project trying to push for the collapse of the American government to open a window for their libertarian hellscape.[54] Collapse itself is painful and awful, and something we should try to halt the progress of as much as we can.

But as institutions fail and the government is unable, or unwilling, to help those most affected, their absence allows people to replace the dead functions with something entirely new. Mutual aid and solidarity-based organizing, the real meat of which is caring human relationships, are not a window to a new society: they are the new society. The question is instead how to bring them to capacity so that they can directly challenge the failures of our stale empires. If the survivalists and Klansman reign in the ruins of our failed civilization, then there was really no collapse of the old order. The revolution wasn't a failure, it just didn't occur. Instead, the only cataclysmic shift is in the fundamental fabric for how we build social relationships, without this no level of collapse could ever lead to a new world. Dual power is the battle for hegemony between social systems, and the only thing a social crisis does is potentially clear the playing field. An apocalypse only occurs when you can decisively say that the previous world has come to an end, when it can be said to have been replaced.

A Messianic Age

The word *apocalypse* actually comes from a Greek word for "revelation" or a "disclosure," meaning the disclosure of what is to come. The modern interpretation tying it to a cataclysmic event, is a more recent one. We have a sense that "something" might happen in our world, some profound change, and likely we will have had a hand in it in some way. The question is not whether the oceans will rise, or another demagogue will come along, but when. The last few years have been overwhelmed with a feeling of the apocalypse, some kind of end of the world, but it is unclear exactly what that will be, and the story of that uncertainty has been soaked in a cataclysmic feeling of dread.

One of the failures of the oh-so-secular left is the refusal to discern the folk language that many people use to understand the world, and which still informs the thinking of even the most hardened atheist. The millenialism of the far-right is built on a prophetic spiritual framework, one that attempts to re-interpret social forces through a story that sits well with their gut instincts of bigotry and rage. There is also a prophetic vision of egalitarianism and liberation, one that makes itself an enemy of the fascists and tries to bring together the mind and the heart in how it tells the story of our path to a new world. There are echoes of this in the radical environmental movement, the Christian pacifists and Quakers, neopagans like Starhawk, artists, poets, musicians, and outsiders.

One of the things that set Judaism apart from other religions is that it sanctifies time. A lot of spiritual traditions sanctified space—they had holy ground or sacred groves or blessed temples—but Jews made sacred time by separating it from the day to day of regular life (it becomes sacred specifically because it is not profane). This is where the idea of the Sabbath, the seventh day, which is sacred and holy, comes from. The Sabbath is separated from the rest of the week, defined by the space of commerce and careers, where we sacrifice our time to build the space of the modern world. The Sabbath is the reprieve from this, where we give up something to experience a completely different way of life, if only briefly. The Sabbath then may be a sign of *olam ha-bah* (The World to Come), the paradise that will arrive not at a precise location but a specific time, after the Messianic Age when humans can be redeemed from the crisis of their world.[55] "The Sabbath is the day on which we learn the art of surpassing civilization," wrote Abraham Heschel in his famous 1951 treaty on the Sabbath.[56] "The Sabbath is a metaphor for paradise and a testimony to God's presence; in our prayers, we anticipate a messianic era that will be a Sabbath."[57]

The Sabbath is a window into what the world after time might be: where the complicated mess of our working world, commerce, and countries, concludes. The Messiah brings the story of human beings to the end, what happens after the Messiah is something else entirely. The Messiah is not a signal that the world is ending, the Messiah *is* the world ending. The West has been shaped heavily by Christian eschatology, the return of Christ with the rapture, the tribulation, and the showdown with the Anti-Christ.[58] The Jewish messiah is conceived of differently, with less clarity around how and when they will arrive. The ambiguity has inspired some to question what agency people have in bringing the messiah: is it totally without our control? A sixteenth century rabbi named Isaac Luria grappled with this question. Luria believed that because the world was flawed, likely since it was formed, and therefore it likely "emerged broken from God's very hand," and that god's created impulse was shattered and spread throughout the universe, the world's brokenness was part of god that we shared.

When I was at Zuccotti Park in 2011 for Occupy Wall Street there were some Hasidic Jews standing nearby offering flowers and prayers for passersby. I overheard a man talking with one of them, and then responding to what I assumed was the prayer's lack of concern with the afterlife. "Then what is all of this for?" he asked, pointing around. The man in the black hat laughed, "To save the world, of course," he replied. "Probably the same as you."

G-d is immanent in the world, and both G-d and humans need to be repaired, and so humans can help this process of healing with their day-to-day actions (*mitzvot*) combined with inner intentions. The term for this healing is called *tikkun*, which people likely know from the particularly popular modern phrase *tikkun olam*, to heal the world. Many years later, in the early-twentieth century, the founder of Reconstructionist Judaism, Mordecai Kaplan, believed that God was actually more like the creative power in the universe and drives us more and more toward a better world. This was not supernatural—it was more like the beauty that pervades all things, broken, but it is that unidentifiable thing in us that strives to heal it always toward perfection (the intention is more important than the destination). Together, we work with G-d toward a better world.[59] This reflects an idea that has come to pervade some branches of Judaism that understands the Messiah less as an individual coming to save Israel and more as a Messianic Age when we simply are saved and the world changes so fundamentally that the old world could be said to have come to its end. Jewish mystic Martin Buber said what set Judaism apart was that it "teaches that what a man does now and here with holy intent is no less important, no less true—being a terrestrial, but none the less factual, link with divine being—than the life of the world to come."[60]

It could be that our worldly actions, the kindnesses we bare and the challenges we make to power, could be the work it takes to bring about this Messianic Age, one that exists after the toil and cruelties of everyday life has been eradicated.

"There is no document of civilization which is not the same as a document of barbarism. And just as such a document is not free of barbarism, barbarism traits also the manner in which it was transmitted from one owner to another," wrote Walter Benjamin, in his treaty on the end of history.[61] Our human civilization is so completely tied to the oppression we face, what would it be like to live in an era when those hierarchies, victimizations, and humiliations have come to an end? Perhaps we can instead not simply live bound to the past, the rise and falls of revolutionary movements that attempt to free us from this oppression ("nourished by the image of enslaved ancestors") and instead look to our "liberated grandchildren," the people of a future world we hope to build.[62] Our past haunts us with warnings of how we did it wrong, how a liberatory movement turned repressive or how we simply gave up a utopian vision for a practical one, but we also have a profound tradition of looking forward, of letting the image of what could be just as powerfully motivate us as the story of what was. Benjamin likely thought that a profound break had to come and shatter consensus reality, to tear apart our world since we were not necessarily able to free ourselves from the bonds of history on our own. The past is important, but the future has to be something different, not just the culmination of historical processes, ancient stories, and failed attempts at liberation. "The Torah and the prayers instruct them in remembrance, however. This stripped the future of its magic, to which all those succumb who turn to the soothsayers for enlightenment. This does not imply, however, that for the Jews the future turned into homogeneous, empty time. For every second of time was the strait gate through which the Messiah might enter," wrote Benjamin to close his Twenty Theses.[63] The past was important, our histories of failed attempts at liberation, but only in as much as we acknowledged that a break with the past had to come. We had to end the cycles with a revolution like none other.[64]

Erich Fromm saw it slightly differently. Instead of the Messianism only being seen as a cataclysmic break with the past, he saw human agency as leading to the Messianic Age and, as with the Lurianic

Kabbalah of the sixteenth century, cumulative of our human actions. The age itself was brought about when our actions compounded and we entered a new paradigm (socialism) where the dialectic of history, defined by its toil, had come to an end.[65] What could be called "catastrophic messianism," which abandoned a hopeful perspective about a Messianic Age, was the result of failed revolutions and the executions of revolutionaries, a cultural pessimism come accelerationism. That catastrophic thinking required a *deux ex machina*, someone or something "from the heavens" to save us (perhaps a strong leader) to tear the old world asunder so the new could be born. Instead, Fromm challenged this "catastrophic messianism" and believed we could be the agents of our own salvation.

> Man creates himself in the historical process which began with his first act of freedom—the freedom to disobey—to say "no." The "corruption" lies in the very nature of human existence. Only by going through the process of alienation can man overcome it and achieve a new harmony. This new harmony, the new oneness with man and nature, is called in the prophetic and rabbinic literature "the end of the days," or "the messianic time." It is not a state predetermined by God or the stars; it will not happen except through man's own effort. The messianic time is the historical answer to the existence of man. He can destroy himself or advance toward the realization of the new harmony. Messianism is not accidental to man's existence but the inherent, logical answer to it—the alternative to man's self-destruction.[66]

We may not determine all of the conditions, but we can choose how we respond, with the hopeful messianism Fromm calls "prophetic messianism;" or with the passivity and isolation of the accelerationism of "catastrophic messianism." Only when we transform our conditions does the old world truly end because we have built something new and have chosen to live in it.

An apocalypse can mean different things to different people, it can happen on a microscale (for one group of people) or affect all of society. For millennialist cults like the Branch Davidians, their

obsessive search for Armageddon ended with an eschatological battle with ATF agents, and their small world was eventually consumed
by fire. If people, even just a person, believe fully that an apocalypse
is imminent, it is their actions that could bring about that apocalypse
for a widening collection of others. The apocalyptic feeling from the
far-right has brought about mass shootings, terroristic bombings,
car attacks, all of which create an experience of apocalypse, even if is
just for the direct victims and their families. Together, these attacks
have created one of the foundations for the era of cultural panic we
are entering. The other foundations are accelerated by our failing social systems, which are hastening economic and ecological collapse.
They bring about another vision of the apocalypse, one where the
society we built is no longer able to function and suffering grows exponentially. Just as with our vision of what a "messianic" new society
could look like, our apocalypse is based on us, how we view it, what
agency we take in it, and how the end will come.

Our world is composed of us, imperfect pieces that fit together
better and better as we try to reimagine what a healed society would
look like. We are now living through an era where it would be naive
to believe that full scale fascist revolutions are impossible. We see the
scattered escalation of police violence, repression of dissent, the attack on reason and truth, melting ice caps and sheets, the eradication
of species, the "death of birth," as it were. The subjectivity we have is
how we respond to that, and the choices we make to survive. Contrary to the assumption that history plays out with predetermined
dialectics, there are actually a great deal of choices involved, where
ideas and people intervene. "We can be redeemed only to the extent
to which we see ourselves," said Martin Buber.[67]

The struggle is responsive: it responds to the break in history,
the total collapse that we see (or feel), but the choices are our own.
Antifascism suggests a possible future; through the total negation
of white supremacy, this new future is made. The resistance that is
forming in every corner of the world is this new world in utero, small
acts fixing our broken selves.

"Today, we face the choice exactly as Friedrich Engels foresaw it
a generation ago: either the triumph of imperialism and the collapse

of all civilization... Or the victory of socialism, that means the conscious active struggle of the international proletariat against imperialism and its method of war," wrote Rosa Luxembourg in 1915, birthing the phrase "socialism or barbarism."[68] The crisis was inevitable, out of our control as capitalism hurdles chaotically through history, tearing life from limb, branch from tree. But how the story resolves, or ends, comes from how we heal the world. Humans generally know how to survive a collapse; they naturally turn to mutual aid, they experience solidarity in their shared experience, or they choose a lonely, selfish individualism. Becoming a prepper, stocking up on ammo and toilet paper and abandoning the world is no way to live.

In the choice between antifascism and barbarism, the clash draws out who we are. The opposite of this horror is the magic moments that come when we reject the programming and care for one another, the flowers in the cracks, the mutual aid networks, the walls of protesters bearing the teargas, the vigils in memoriam. The crisis can expand outward, seeming to consume the old world, but that is the mirage. It is us, resisting the call of nations and borders, that is eating the decay. It is hard to see the entirety by looking at the pieces on their own—a food distribution site or a rent strike blockade feels only localized and isolated, but it is a piece of how we are reinterpreting and responding to the crisis. It is when we internalize resistance as our methodology that each act helps to rearrange the scattered pieces. The world only ends when we replace it with something else, something a little less broken, the shared commitment to healing more each day. This Messianic Age will not arrive on its own, and it may not arrive with a bang, but we will know it when we look around and start to see the world we have been dreaming of. We can save ourselves.

* * *

What I pulled together here is a collection of essays, some previously published and some that I wrote over 2020 trying to capture the Trump years, the rise of antifascism, and the desperate feeling of the unknown that weighs on us. They say that somebody else can look at your work, particularly from a moment in time, and they will see something that you didn't notice. Most of my work is on fascism and antifascism, but it became obvious that, in each piece, the elephant in the room was the crushing mystery of what comes next. When looking at the memetic rise of the mass shooter, the accelerationist turn, the crisis of modern antisemitism, Alt Right street violence, and systemic police killings, it felt like we had reached a turning point. What I think binds these essays is that they attempt to stay in the moment we are living through and they feel what it means to fight like we have no choice.

Both of my parents died within a few months of each other, both fighting an uphill battle against illnesses that couldn't be cured. My wife took a necklace of my father's and attached a pendant made from a medieval mold of St. Jude, the patron saint of lost causes. Some fights we have because we have to win, some fights we take on because the struggle itself is victory. We fight because we have been pressed into a corner, a choice between two types of world. We fight because the cost would be too great if we didn't, we have a whole world to lose. We also fight because the fight itself has value, the method of the fight is not just the window to the new world, it is its entirety.

I would like to think that the experiences of the past few years would naturally feed the movements on the ground, swell their numbers and multiply tactics, but I don't know that. The same forces that radicalize people can also move them to despair, and so much about the world is outside of our control. But we can control the little things. We can build something.

One of the persistent realities of crisis is that people help each other, almost without exception. Panic is rare among working-class people, but the rich and those in power are infected with what is often called "elite panic," and they are unable to believe that we can take on the functions of society and run it better ourselves.[69] The catastrophic failures of the state and corporations to help with the Coronavirus, to stabilize the economy, to stop police violence, to halt the climate catastrophe, to do any of the functions that our collective consent is predicated on brings up a bigger question altogether: Is this the best we can do? The future of our survival depends on our ability to come together in community and social bonds, and in doing so we will undermine the entire complex that is crumbling around us.

I spent most of my youth absolutely obsessed with the apocalypse, mostly as a coping mechanism for the crushing religious terror that kept me up nights. I am back at it, though it is filled with nihilistic news reports about environmental terror and the ever-increasing reality of armed far-right rallies. It would be negligent to ignore it, but not to reframe it, to tell the story not just on the terms of the terrorists but instead from the vantage point of our resilience. There is no reason that the story of strife, or even tragedy, has to exist only in that framework. Tragedy can instead be the story of our resistance. We can define the crisis by how we launched our way forward. To do so will be to give into apocalypticism, to decide fully and completely the old world is dead—not because the rich killed it with their hubris, but because we did.

Disunite the Right

How Divides Formed in the Pepe Coalition

By the time Richard Spencer, the man responsible for coining and popularizing the term Alt Right, made his way to the front of the crowd on the steps of the Lincoln Memorial and took the microphone, anger was already brimming among his supporters. While barely a hundred Alt Right acolytes amassed for this June 25, 2017 "free speech" rally in Washington, D.C., they represented the hardcore adherents of a movement demanding a white "ethnostate"—a nation for whites only. Standing in front of banners for white nationalist organizations like Vanguard America, the Traditionalist Workers Party, and Identity Evropa, Spencer issued the sort of romantic call for struggle that had once made him a leader:

> We are fundamentally fighting to be part of something that is bigger than ourselves. We are fighting to be part of a family together. We are fighting to be strong again. To be beautiful again. We are fighting to be powerful again in a sea of weakness and hopelessness. That is our battle. Our greatest enemies will tell us that there is nothing to fight for, that it is all over. All you have to do is go to the voting booth or go purchase some cute new product or watch some cute new video. We are

going to fight for meaning. We are going to make history all over again.[1]

Spencer's passionate appeal came after a falling out with Jack Posobiec and Laura Loomer, who had denounced Spencer's presence at the rally and opted to hold their own competing event across town.[2] As Spencer became the focal point of broader divisions, the far-right was sent into a tailspin, with Spencer leading his explicitly White nationalist faction of the Alt Right against the more moderate "Alt Light." "We need to attack the Alt Light in the most ruthless manner possible," Spencer declared in a rant on the podcast *Alt Right Politics* on the eve of what were now two rallies. "They are objectively the immediate enemy, they must be destroyed."[3] What might have appeared to outsiders as simple subcultural rivalry had more definitive consequences: Spencer was declaring war against the Alt Light—a group peripheral to the core Alt Right, which Spencer appeared to see as his access point to mainstream conservatism. As the man who developed staple Alt Right institutions such as the National Policy Institute, the *Radix Journal*, and AltRight.com, Spencer had spent 2016 and 2017 scrambling to capitalize on the increased exposure the Trump campaign brought to his rebranded White nationalist movement. The Alt Light, which served as the next ring around Spencer's core movement organs, weren't committed to the harder-edged ideology of the Alt Right, but as a collective of right-wing provocateurs, they had helped popularize Spencer's talking points.

Now, Spencer's "Free Speech" rally became purer but far smaller: a parade of White nationalist celebrities, who came at the cost of the rally's potential to influence more mainstream conservatives.

A Fragile Coalition

In 2008, the Alternative Right was born as a concept, which triggered a movement, after Richard Spencer's time working among paleoconservatives led him into the "dissident right": those who reject liberal values of human equality and multiculturalism. The Alternative

Right, and the eponymous web journal Spencer would launch in 2010, brought together a range of Rightists loosely defined by racial identitarianism and their belief in human inequality. While the GOP still rhetorically rejects racism and inequality, the Alternative Right embraced these ideas, redefining fascism for a twenty-first century U.S. context. When their nascent movement collided with Internet troll culture, their name was shortened to Alt Right and their flag-bearers adopted the racially abusive personality we know today.

The Alt Light came later—its supporters mobilized largely around the celebrity of former Breitbart Tech Editor Milo Yiannopoulos, and also including former *Rebel Media* star Lauren Southern, online "manosphere" leader Mike Cernovich, and Infowars conspiracy baron Alex Jones. Though their agendas weren't identical, they served a purpose for the Alt Right. Fascists who have difficulty entering the public stage have always required crossover figures and institutions that can help pave the way for more ideologically pure leaders to come—a "stopover" point on the road to authoritarianism. In earlier generations this included figures like Pat Buchanan and the paleoconservative movement, but as public trust in party politics has waned, that role has fallen to online cultural leaders who sway social networks. In the age of the Alt Right, it was the less radical representatives who guaranteed the movement broader popular appeal.

But the relationship between the Alt Right and the Alt Light, as well as "patriot" organizations like the Oath Keepers, has often been more pragmatic than cordial. And maintaining this coalition has not been easy, requiring compromises on language, targets, and allies. To the Alt Right, compromise on core principles threatens the ideological purity they were founded to uphold.[4] The Alt Right already constituted a coalition, linking together the "race realist" pseudoscientists, racial pagans, European New Rightists, male tribalists, classic White nationalists, paleoconservatives, and others who defined themselves by essentialized identity and inequality. This point of agreement was enough to initially bring them together, but disagreements over issues like Ukrainian independence, Brexit, and culture led to splits, which were papered over when Trump ran, demonstrating to them again that they could be stronger if they suppressed their differences and rode the wave.

It was the need to find a more palatable vessel for their politics that led the Alt Right to embrace the Alt Light in the first place, although both camps had different intentions from the start. To Alt Light figures hoping to parlay movement celebrity into lasting careers, the Alt Right's overt white nationalism threatened to become a toxic association. In both camps, strong personalities combined with murky ideological boundaries became a recipe for explosive fractures, undermining the potential of a unified front. That disintegration provides insights into the organizing process of the Alt Right, and how the Left can challenge their growth before it becomes a populist wave.

Free Speech Light

A nineteen-year-old student named Colton Merwin began planning the June 25 "free speech" rally in Washington, D.C., weeks in advance. It was the latest in a series of rallies, hosted by Alt Right and Alt Light figures alike, in response to public clashes between the far-right and anti-racist organizers that had started in December 2016 and escalated in early February 2017, after an appearance by Milo Yiannopoulos at the University of California, Berkeley was canceled amid mass protests. The later cancellation of Ann Coulter at Berkeley prompted Lauren Southern to host the inaugural "free speech" rally in the city of Berkeley in April.[5]

While Yiannopoulos and Southern were both Alt Lightists, Southern opened her rally to Alt Right speakers as well, inviting Brittany Pettibone, a contributor to websites like *AltRight.com* and *Red Ice Creations*. After Southern's Berkeley event descended into violent attacks on counter-protesters—a media spectacle that played heavily in the news cycle, leading to greatly increased media exposure for both the Alt Light and Alt Right—"free speech" protests spread across the country. The rallies became popular enough that Spencer and the Alt Right had the opportunity to use them as recruitment opportunities.

Later in the spring, the movement continued to make headlines, as Alt Light leaders Jack Posobiec and Laura Loomer gained notoriety for derailing multiple Shakespeare in the Park performances in New York City. Colton Merwin invited both as speakers at the rally in D.C., alongside Mike Cernovich, author of *The MAGA Mindset*.

But when Richard Spencer's name was floated as a fellow speaker, Posobiec and Loomer declared that they wouldn't share a stage with him, instead announcing a simultaneous rally across town, targeting the "political violence" of the shooting attack on a congressional baseball team that left House Majority Whip Steve Scalise in critical condition. (This rally focused on blaming the broad Left, suggesting that the shooter's brief support of Bernie Sanders was evidence that the shooting amounted to political terrorism.[6])

After the Alt Light abandoned the Lincoln Memorial rally—splitting the crowd and depriving Spencer of the big platform he sought—Alt Right trolls swarmed, with one prominent commentator, Baked Alaska, harassing Loomer with violent antisemitic images. While Spencer had long sought to present an above-the-fray tone for his new brand of white nationalism, he quickly joined in, tweeting, "The Alt Light is a collection of outright liars (Posobiec and Cerno), perverts (Milo, Wintrich), and Zionist fanatics (Loomer)."[7]

Tensions had been growing for months. The Alt Right had bristled at Milo Yiannopoulos's refusal to fully adapt to the Alt Right through his rejection of "identity politics"; at Trump's Syrian intervention, which struck the Alt Right as capitulation to GOP "globalism"; and Spencer's earlier ostracism from Alt Light events like the DeploraBall.[8] But after D.C., it appeared that the face of the Alt Right had tired of his moderate counterparts.

Alt Identities

While the break in Washington stemmed from particular complaints—denying the Alt Right a recruitment platform at crossover events—the underlying issues were deeper conflicts over rhetoric and ideology. The Alt Right is an "identitarian" movement that can accurately be described as fascist and White nationalist: they seek to create a "traditionalist" society in the form of a pan-European ethnostate. That is specific and concrete. The Alt Light, on the other hand, seeks to create a bigger tent, including a range of "Independent Trumpists" who generally ally themselves with a looser type of nationalism—"American" or "Civic Nationalism," which tempers its ideas about race yet still utilizes national chauvinism, protectionism, and isolationism.[9] (To be sure, in effect Civic Nationalism manifests many of the same bigotries as its more explicit counterpart.)

Similar movements outside the U.S., like Nigel Farage's UK Independence Party (UKIP) and its push toward Brexit, are in the same vein as this Civic Nationalism, as is Donald Trump's brand of populism. Steve Bannon, the *Breitbart* alumnus and former chief strategist for Trump, has defined his role in Trump's campaign and administration as an expression of Civic Nationalism, viewing Trump's "us-versus-them" language as a means to overturn establishment politics.[10] (Unlike leftist expressions of populism, Civic Nationalism seeks to reestablish a mythic version of a stable and hierarchical America.)

The Alt Right has often identified Trump and the Alt Light, as well as older figures like Pat Buchanan, as Civic Nationalists. As "free speech" events proliferated, and organizations like the Proud Boys—a "Western chauvinist" group associated with the Alt Light— rose to prominence within them, some coalition members broke with the Alt Right in favor of vocal expressions of Civic Nationalism. At a June 4 rally in Portland, Oregon, Kyle "Based Stickman" Chapman, a movement celebrity allied with the Proud Boys, did just that. Although Chapman had become famous within the Alt Right for attacking anti-racist protesters with a large wooden rod, he distanced himself from the Alt Right's racial politics, noting his Asian-American girlfriend and biracial child. Speaking to a line of news cameras, he declared himself a patriot, not a racist: "I consider myself an American nationalist. . . It's a type of nationalism specifically applied to America, where we come together under Americana, 1776, the embrace of our beautiful country . . . Western Civilization. Regardless of race, regardless of sexual identity, we all come together to embrace America, American values, and put Americans first in all the dealings of this country."[11]

Chapman had already been condemned by Nathan Damigo, who recently resigned as head of the White nationalist group Identity Evropa, for his social media posts "denouncing racism" and suggesting that the "founding fathers" had created the U.S. as a country centered on ideals rather than ethnicity.[12] But what appeared to be Damigo and the Alt Right's larger complaint was that Chapman had legitimized the accusations of racism in the first place, by calling "for a rejection of white interests" and, effectively, denouncing white nationalism.[13] The Alt Light's separate rally later that month in Washington, D.C., reinforced this rejection: that the Alt Right's "White identitarianism" was so toxic that they had to hold their own nationalist rally somewhere else.

The Alt Light wasn't motivated by conscience alone; there were financial considerations at stake. Mike Cernovich has made a career peddling his books and videos, and with the growth of crowdfunding websites and donation appeals, Alt Light organizing against the Left has become a money-making prospect for many movement leaders. Kyle Chapman, for example, has parlayed his "Based Stickman" persona into a clothing line that promotes the Fraternal Order of the Alt-Knights, using incendiary language to promote his brand and create a financial base for himself. (Chapman, who has served ten years in prison for a litany of crimes including grand theft, was able to make a reported $87,000 for his legal defense and $40,000 for a graphic novel that he is pitching at Comic Con through crowd source websites.) Websites like WeSearchr also cashed in, raising money through crowd-sourcing to deliver "bounties" for different right-wing causes, like paying money to people who successfully doxxed antifascists.

But while edgy language and fighting postures have helped bring Alt Light leaders some acclaim, they seem to rightly suspect that open white nationalism is still a bridge too far for anyone seeking to build a lucrative career. Leading Alt Light website *The Rebel* has raised over a $1 million in its three years, almost entirely in crowd-sourced small donations. And while sites like GoFundMe are often off-limits to the Alt Right, since openly racist appeals violate their Terms of Service, the coded language of the Alt Light—using Civic Nationalist rather than "identitarian" talking points—can and does pass the bar.[14]

The Alt Right has also taken hits when it comes to movement branding. In the heyday of the big Alt Right tent in 2015 and 2016, *Gateway Pundit*'s Lucian Wintrich told *The New Yorker* the movement name "was adopted by libertarians, anti-globalists, classical conservatives, and pretty much everyone else who was sick of what had become of establishment conservatism." But after "Richard Spencer came along, throwing up Nazi salutes and claiming that he was the leader of the alt-right," Wintrich continued, "He effectively made the term toxic. . . We all abandoned using it in droves."[15] Wintrich's summary was ahistorical: the broader use of the term Alt Right during the long election season was ideologically inconsistent with how it had been used for years by Spencer and his crew of "identitarians," and Spencer's efforts to reclaim the term, as explicitly signifying white nationalism, were really what the Alt Right had always been about. But the larger point remained—the bigger coalition Spencer had sought was falling apart.

There was further splintering within the Alt Light. Lauren Southern released a video message, "The Alt-Lite vs Free Speech," arguing that blocking Spencer's participation was capitulation to Leftist suppression of free speech. But despite this show of support for Spencer and the Alt Right, other Alt Right figures criticized her. In a long post at *AltRight.com* in late June, writer Michael Driscoll took Southern to task for what he saw as her lackluster opposition to immigration, arguing that "Something more is needed. That something is *identity*."[16]

While further alienating their depleting number of allies may be a tactical misstep for the Alt Right, many, like Driscoll, see the popularity of more moderate voices like Southern as an impediment to the Alt Right's goal of mobilizing anti-immigrant sentiment into support for open White identitarianism. As Driscoll wrote: "Southern is the focal point between the 'Alt-Lite' and the Alt Right and is one of the few new media figures aware that 'classical liberalism' is not synonymous with Western Civilization, nor is it sufficient to defend that civilization's existence. For that reason, where she goes from here is important."[17]

Taking the Oath

The tensions arose on other fronts as well, sometimes spilling over into violent confrontations between Alt Right white nationalists and Alt Light "Patriot" groups. On June 10, 2017, far-right groups including the Oath Keepers, a prominent Patriot movement organization, protested the removal of a Houston statue depicting former Texas President Sam Houston. The Oath Keepers, seeking to disassociate themselves from the white nationalist element of the Alt coalition, openly tried to keep the Alt Right from attending. But they came anyway, including an associate of the neonazi website *The Daily Stormer*, who arrived bearing a Nordic "Black Sun" flag and shouting antisemitic slogans. After event organizers asked protesters affiliated with *The Daily Stormer* and Vanguard America to leave, a scuffle broke out. When the man brandishing the flag was confronted, he began to repeat a line that would have seemed nonsensical before 2016—"What about the memes?"—until a rally attendant placed him in a chokehold. It was an absurdist image of a movement disconnected from most people's political experiences, but within the fractious Alt coalition, it signaled another marked break.

The various Patriot militia organizations, headed primarily by the Oath Keepers and the more decentralized III%ers, can mobilize a large base for public events like the "free speech" rallies. While much of the Alt Right, and even the Alt Light, have little experience with public protest, the militia movement has frequently relied on displays of community pressure and intimidation. Starting with the first Bundy siege in 2014 and the Malheur Wildlife Refuge in Southeastern Oregon in January 2016, Patriot groups' visible presence has led to an increase in membership numbers not seen since their 2008 surge in response to the election of President Obama.[18] But while often lumped together with other players on the far-right, Patriot groups' stated ideology often excludes open white nationalism. Instead, they could easily be seen as the hard edge of the Republican Party, mixing extreme libertarian economics with anti-federal conspiracy theories, opposition to environmentalism, and a denial of the reality of racism, sexism, and other forms of oppression.

Due to their experience and numbers, Patriot groups have assumed a deciding role in strategizing some "free speech" events, as at the June 4 rally in Portland, Oregon, where militia organizations planned the entire security and structure of the event, outlining their efforts with local police and the Department of Homeland Security.[19] But Patriot groups also represent the most consistent right-wing voice against the ideological platform of the Alt Right. While the Alt Right attempts to destigmatize "White racial consciousness," the militias hope to avoid accusations of racism entirely. During the Portland rally, Patriot Prayer organizer Joey Gibson appealed to attendees "to make this day positive, with no hate and no violence," and the speaker lineup included a trans woman and a security team member with Pacific Island heritage who performed a traditional "warrior dance."[20]

These gestures towards diversity may seem surprising. Patriot groups' rhetoric is well known for racialist dog whistles, decrying everything from communism to "illegals," but the image the organizers of the Portland rally sought to create was of a united Right unburdened by "identity politics."

While major racialist groups like Identity Evropa have participated in the "free speech" rallies, there has been increasing pressure for the militia movement to take a stand against their presence. In June, Oath Keepers founder and president, Stewart Rhodes, distanced his organization, saying: "We're not white nationalists. We're not racists of any kind. And if they show up [at our rally], I am going to personally, physically remove them. Because they are trying to co-opt what we're trying to do."[21]

The subsequent Alt Right backlash to Stewart trended the hashtag #OathCuckers, recalling the popular Alt Right #Cuckservative hashtag used to denigrate Republicans perceived as weak on immigration during the 2016 campaign season. When the Oath Keepers then condemned the Alt Right organizations that came to the Houston rally, seemingly hoping to exploit conservative anger over the destruction of Confederate monuments to drum up recruits, the divide deepened.

AltRight.com immediately ran a story claiming that the Oath Keepers "showed their true colors." *The Daily Stormer* published a series of articles denouncing them that focused heavily on the age of their membership and the fact that they allow non-White members, and suggesting that the attack on the flag-bearing "Nazi" was an affront to free speech.[22] Robert Ray, an Alt Right attendee at the Houston rally who goes by the handle "Azzmador," scolded the Oath Keepers for their treatment of the flagbearer and their "color blind" politics; he would later appear on the white nationalist podcast *The Daily Shoah*, using antisemitic slurs as he said, "I had been predicting before we went to this thing that antifa was not going to be our main problem there, it was going to be these 'Cucks.'"[23]

Unite the Right?

In August of 2017, some of these divisions appeared to begin healing, as the various factions of the Alt Right coalesced around planning for an August 12 rally in Charlottesville, Virginia. The rally, "Unite the Right," sought to bring together all organizations to the right of the Alt Light in protest of the planned removal of Confederate monuments. Organizer Jason Kessler saw the rally as a formal break with movement moderates and an effort to start harvesting the energy of the previous two years. Among the invited groups were the National Socialist Movement, the Traditionalist Workers Party and other street-level organizations associated with skinheads or explicit neonazism that Spencer had avoided in the past.[24] It was a decisive move for the Alt Right: associating with openly violent Nazi and KKK organizations, but not with those who cite Civic Nationalism and acknowledge the concept of racism. They anticipated high attendance—anywhere from 400 to more than 1,000 protesters—since the annual American Renaissance conference in Tennessee had sold out just two weeks before. And while counterprotests at American Renaissance were larger than in years past, the event went on largely uninterrupted, demonstrating that even at an explicitly white nationalist event the Alt Right could draw a crowd without the aid of the Alt Light or Patriot groups.[25]

The movement converged on Charlottesville on the evening of August 11, 2017. Alt Right protesters, including figures like Christopher

Cantwell, the racist "libertarian" known for his foul-mouthed Internet rants, and Richard Spencer, marched from the University of
Virginia to surround a church hosting Union Theological Seminary
professor Dr. Cornel West, kicking off a two-day frenzy of violence.
When the Alt Right came upon people chanting and holding signs
with Black Lives Matter slogans, they started punching the coun-
terprotestors, spraying mace, and hitting them with torches in full
view of the press.[26] The next day, a Black counter-protester, Deandre
Harris, was beaten with metal poles in a parking garage, and dozens
of others were pepper sprayed or beaten.[27] Just after 1:00 pm, a man
who had been seen protesting alongside Vanguard America, and car-
rying a shield bearing its logo, drove a Dodge Challenger into the
counter-protesters, killing one woman, Heather Heyer, and injuring
nineteen more.[28]

Across the political spectrum, the melee was roundly repudiated,
along with the movement itself (though not by President Trump,
who refused for two days to condemn white nationalism by name,
and suggested that "many sides" shared blame for the violence).[29] At
a subsequent press conference intended to "disavow" the violence,
Unite the Right organizer Jason Kessler was chased off by protesters.[30] And while *The Daily Stormer* published a ghoulish celebration of
Heather Heyer's death, many other Rightists, such as Alt Light leader
Laura Loomer spent the weekend tweeting about the Alt Right's connection to neonazis.[31]

Aside from constituting a national tragedy, the moment marked
a decisive turn in the Alt Right's position: granting them credibility
with the further reaches of the Nazi Right, but also severing any access they had to the more moderate Trumpian Right, and likely other
militia and Alt Light organizations. This had a profound effect on the
Alt Right's status, as they were subsequently deplatformed from most
of social media, antifascists interrupted their live events, and they
were firmly kicked out of their mainstream associations. Cantwell,
for his part, faced charge after charge as he continued to threaten
and attack people associated with the events in Charlottesville, and
is now facing a heavy prison term for extortion and threatening sexual assault.[32]

What Next?

There have been massive social shifts on the Right following Trump's election, including a mainstreaming of nativism. And yet, despite this cultural change, the social toxicity of open white supremacy has prevented the Alt Right from finding mainstream support for explicit white nationalism.

To overcome this, the Alt Right would need to find critical wedge issues—problems that appear insurmountable to those feeling them—that provide communities in crises with systemic answers. That has been, until recently, the Alt Right's remaining avenue for growth: to present themselves as the answer to "problems" like crime, immigration, terrorism, and a range of perceived social ills like political correctness. But to gain access to those crowds they need more accepted factions of the Right to give them access to a stage (that they will use for their own reasons). The Civic Nationalists of the Alt Light seemed to offer this opportunity, but to keep this coalition intact, it has to be a mutually beneficial relationship, offering something that the Alt Light doesn't already have.

This task is even harder in the wake of Charlottesville. In the days immediately following the Charlottesville riot, a number of Alt Right participants had their identities made public, and were subsequently arrested, fired, or denounced by embarrassed family members. *The Daily Stormer*'s web hosts at GoDaddy canceled their contract and forced the website offline (although they soon reemerged on a website only available through the Tor web browser).[33] They, along with multiple other Alt Right accounts, have been banned on Twitter, and PayPal is cleaning out many profiles used by white nationalist projects, denying AltRight.com a major funding channel.[34] Within days of the tragedy in Charlottesville, two of Richard Spencer's planned events—a "white lives matter" rally at Texas A&M University and a speaking engagement at the University of Florida—were unceremoniously canceled.[35]

AltRight.com has claimed that the showdown in Charlottesville will prove to be the "beginning of the White Civil Rights movement." But facing nearly universal condemnation by the public, it's likely that the existing divisions between the Alt Right and the Alt Light will only grow.

While the Trumpist moment was too advantageous for them to ignore, the avenue for growth it offered also exposed a key disconnect between the Alt Right's ambitions and its reason for being—that is, its radicalism, and its reduction of politics to identity. Other conservatives, including Civic Nationalists, argue for ideological principles, and semi-universal policy positions that outline a worldview. The Alt Right's principles, by contrast, all flow downstream from identity—a politics that are ordered entirely around their perceived "White interests." While they've battled over tone and optics, the divide between the Alt Right and Alt Light is not just a disagreement about intensity, but about their core understanding of the world. And while they may find these partners useful in attacking the Left or targeting mass immigration, when it comes time for the Alt Right to define its perspective, it must finally alienate its crossover supporters, who simply will not agree on the fundamentals.

Trump's populist banner gave the Alt Right access to the broader culture but by not compromising they've hampered their ability to grow. The increased violence at events like Unite the Right further widen the divide, as their radicalism is shown to have bloody consequences, and it will force even the revolutionary side of their movement to take sides. In a post-Charlottesville world, they may be too toxic for the Alt Light to touch, making the benefits of their earlier coalition moot.

For anti-racist organizations looking to stem the rise of the Alt Right, these divides illustrate an opportunity to pressure the crossover organizations, from *Rebel Media* to the Oath Keepers, to draw a line between themselves and open white nationalists. The Alt Right needed some hold on mainstream cultural institutions if they were to ever to see critical mass that can result in effective, self-sustaining organizing. Ensuring further breaks in the coalition they seek helped to disrupt their growth and led to the profound decline they saw from the end of 2017 onward.

Lawsuits are Not Enough to Stop the Far-Right

The sleepy holiday town of Whitefish, Montana, had been Richard Spencer's part-time home for years, though he rarely wanted to talk about it. Spencer, the founder of the "Alt Right" movement, had been living there off and on since taking over the National Policy Institute in 2010, staying close to his parents and the private ski resort he frequented. As his profile rose, so did attention from a local affiliate of the Montana Human Rights Network, Love Lives Here. His mother, Sherry Spencer, had been investing in real estate around the town, including condos and retail space. After pressure was put on Sherry by local activists to sell her properties and distance herself from her son, Richard and his mother exploded in anger, and the "Alt Right" embarked on a fear campaign targeting Whitefish residents in December 2016.[1]

Led by neo-Nazi Andrew Anglin of *The Daily Stormer*, online trolls threatened residents' families so severely that some went into hiding, and Anglin promised that armed protesters would target the town's Jewish residents.[2] While his physical presence was little more than a bluff, the terror he inflicted brought a massive response both from the community and his neo-Nazi supporters. The Southern Poverty Law Center (SPLC), a nonprofit known for supporting survivors of hate crimes, filed a lawsuit against Anglin on April 18, citing Anglin's responsibility for the campaign of harassment against real estate agent Tanya Gersh and her twelve-year-old son. Gersh had, from her statements, offered to help Sherry sell her properties, which Sherry and her son Richard interpreted as a threat.[3]

The strategy the SPLC is employing is well-traveled for them: Use incidents of white nationalist violence to sue white nationalist organizations, destabilizing them into nonexistence. While the acts of violence are often done by so-called Lone-Wolf combatants (a term that negates their connection to the larger white nationalist movement) that are not acting on formal orders from an organization, those organizations set the priorities and behavior of members through their internal praxis.

This strategy has been highly successful in bringing down some of the largest and most violent racialist organizations in U.S. history. In the 1960s we witnessed the "Third Era" of the Ku Klux Klan, where the Klan resurfaced during the battle over segregation. One of the largest and most violent of the disparate Klan organizations was the United Klans of America (UKA) under the leadership of Robert Shelton. Even after being associated with major terror attacks throughout the South—like the famous bombing of the Birmingham, Alabama, church that resulted in the death of four young girls—the UKA still was not brought down, and seemed untouchable. That was until the 1981 lynching of a teen boy, Michael Donald. After the criminal proceedings, Morris Dees, the founder of the SPLC, brought a "wrongful death" suit against the UKA. The court awarded Donald's family seven million in damages, which forwarded all the resources of the UKA directly to the family, including the building that the UKA had operated out of for years.[4]

A similar case played out when members of the Portland, Oregon white supremacist skinhead gang East Side White Pride murdered Ethiopian immigrant Mulugeta Seraw in 1988. The SPLC argued that the gang had gotten its praxis from the neo-Nazi organization White Aryan Resistance (WAR), which had been linking up skinhead gangs around the country in the 1980s. After the criminal trial, the SPLC, along with the Anti-Defamation League, filed a lawsuit against WAR founder Tom Metzger and his son John Metzger, arguing they had set the young skinheads up for racist attacks like the one that took Seraw's life. The courts agreed and all of Metzger's assets, including his home, were seized and transferred to the Seraw estate. WAR, and by extension the racist skinhead movement, was significantly weakened.[5]

In northern Idaho, the Aryan Nations' compound was once the center of the most violent wing of the white supremacist movement. A beacon for survivalists and the racist Christian Identity church, it had relationships with dozens of white supremacist terrorists from the 1970s to the 1990s. In July 1998, several security guards at the compound opened fire on a Black woman, Victoria Keenan, and her son when they had car trouble nearby.[6] After the guards riddled their car with bullets and ran them off the road, the Keenans were held at gunpoint by Nazi militiamen.[7] The SPLC again filed a civil lawsuit, this time against the Aryan Nations, and a jury awarded the Keenan family $6.3 million. This destroyed the compound entirely, ending its years as a center for the most revolutionary-minded neo-Nazi formations.

Each one of these cases shows an incredibly effective strategy for responding to acts of racist violence. However, this strategy is missing a connection to the larger community, relying instead on a team of attorneys from a well-funded nonprofit. Without this larger community component, there is no social movement base to rely on once the well-paid experts have left the incident. While effectively dissolving the offending organization, a lawsuit does not necessarily translate to a larger anti-racist community project that can continue to do the work of confronting these organizations once the court case is closed.

What this shows is not that legal solutions aren't valuable—they have proven incredibly effective—but instead that they provide ample additional organizing opportunities. Instead of relying on these lawsuits on their own, they should be points at which community organizations are empowered through educational programs, workshops, and larger external organizing strategies so that the neighbors who have witnessed the terror that racist organizations inflict can become active in combatting them as well. Instead of creating a format where only experts from an external entity are enlisted to solve the problem of white supremacy, we should create formats where the entire community is equipped with the same agency. If these lawsuits are paired with real grassroots community engagement, and organizing solutions are also prioritized, then the win that comes in the legal setting can help launch community groups that can continue organizing for years afterward.

Since the lawsuit against Anglin was filed, he raised over $150,000 to fight the SPLC's claim, and has essentially gone into hiding from the legal petitions.[8] After the disaster of Unite the Right in Charlottesville on August 12, Anglin lost his web hosting platforms, effectively pushing *The Daily Stormer* to the "dark web."[9] While the lawsuit and the platform denials will do a lot to limit his reach, it will take more than that to really end his ability to recruit more young people to his particularly brutal brand of neo-Nazism.

Without engaging the larger community and equipping community members to actively continue the work, these momentary, if effective, blasts to neo-Nazis infrastructure will not have as long-term of an effect as they could otherwise. As incidents of "Alt Right" violence increase, large nonprofits should be mindful of how they can shape their efforts to fuel long-term, broad-based community organizing.[10]

The Fall of the Alt Right Came from Antifascism

Richard Spencer, the infamous founder of the white nationalist Alt Right movement, already knew his group of racists was making a public nosedive even before the recent catastrophe at Michigan State University.

"I think the movement is in a bad state right now, I'm not going to lie about it," Spencer said to his millennial sidekick Gregory Conte during a March 3 episode of his podcast. "We're going to have to figure out how to build institutions in the era of rapid—and rabid—de-platforming. Which is really hard."[1]

Spencer has been the figurehead for the Alt Right since its evolution from the backwoods of esoteric web blogs, within private conferences, and then, finally, attaining public recognition as part of a national political conversation. No one could have seen the highs that 2015 and 2016 would bring to white supremacy, and they thought their boom in numbers and exposure would be a permanent incline. But even after Donald Trump's election, the antifascist movement has detonated like a bomb, with Spencer seeing one devastating hurdle after another. Conferences have been shut down, Alt Right violence has been publicly exposed, and opposition has been so explosive that he can't even buy a cup of coffee without a mob chasing him down the street.[2]

Publicly, though, he has claimed he would never back down in the face of opposition and has pushed forward on a series of high-profile college appearances. On March 5, 2018, he was set for yet another, this time at Michigan State University, in a move that was so unpopular with the student body and administration that it took a lawsuit from a supporter of Spencer to get him into a university building.[3] This had become the usual pattern over the last nine months for the Alt Right, following the disastrous Unite the Right rally in Charlottesville, Virginia. Since then, the movement's public outreach has been punctuated by canceled venues, dropped web platforms, and the exposing of deception.[4]

At this point, it is safe to say the Alt Right is in a period of extreme decline. The term "Alt Right," short for "alternative right," was applied to the growing movement when Spencer developed a webzine in 2010 using the term to link up various strains of pseudo-intellectual far-right nationalist ideologies with which he was mingling. White nationalists of various stripes became the center of his movement, and over the next five years, they worked hard to create an intellectual foundation and narrative structure they could use to argue for open fascism: white identity meets human inequality.

By 2015, their rhetoric was picked up by the angry trollosphere, where it transformed into a world of memes, harassment, and multimedia content—all while they struggled to move from the virtual world of message boards into street action. The high point of this rise was Trump's election, but since then, even their more relatively "moderate" counterparts have abandoned them and every project they launch has seemed to fail.

This is not an unusual story for white nationalism in the U.S. Strong personalities mixed with instability and inadequate know-how has created a series of catastrophic disasters for organizations focused on building a "white ethnostate," and we have watched groups, from the Ku Klux Klan (KKK) to the Aryan Nations, burn out in violent spectacles. The most common narrative that media outlets have picked up on is that it is the ineptitude of the racists themselves that has collapsed their movements, and reporters often stereotype them as poor and ignorant "rednecks" against actual demographic information about these movements. While the white nationalist ability for self-sabotage can be impressive, it misses the most critical factor in the story of every white supremacist loss: They failed because of effective antifascist organizing.

Stop Spencer

Back in 2016, Spencer had decided to launch himself onto state-school campuses in what he labeled the "Danger Zone Tour." The idea here was that government-owned institutions would be more likely to host him against the pressure of antifascists than private institutions. There is some merit to his logic. After both the 2010 and 2011 conferences for the "race realist" organization American Renaissance were canceled by pressure campaigns from the antifascist community organization One People's Project, the Alt Right settled into a long-term relationship with Montgomery Bell State Park just outside Nashville, Tennessee. Since then, they have not had to move, and even though they have annual protesters, the state-managed venue has not cowed to pressure. Spencer assumed the same would be true on campuses.

Michigan State is only the latest in a string of these, and even though a mass campaign from students at multiple campuses formed to stop him, the school administration caved to a lawsuit leveled against it and offered him a farm building on the outskirts of their Lansing campus during spring break.[5]

The organizing for what was branded the "#StopSpencer" campaign began toward the end of 2017. The timing of the campaign—taking shape during the period in which Spencer could be granted his platform—allowed for the student body and surrounding communities to organically build a solid base of opposition. By the time Spencer's March 5, 2018 talk happened, there had already been escalations with student walkouts and informational actions.[6]

The existence of the Alt Right has given impetus to the idea of antifascist organizing, which goes back decades, even while remaining on the margins of the American left. Anti-fascist work, however, was given more urgency with the rise of Trumpism, and therefore grew as an organizational priority. When the Alt Right plans a public event—especially with a high-profile face like Spencer's—that impetus hits the periphery of those organizers like a lightning bolt, and all of a sudden, it moves from the confines of committed activists to a movement composed of huge swaths of the community. Spencer himself, as with the rest of the "Alt Right's" all-star bench, can be considered the catalyst and injection of adrenaline into an already angry community.

The resistance against Spencer has not just emerged during the past twelve months. Years before the Alt Right became a household name, Spencer was being brought to campuses by groups like the now defunct Youth for Western Civilization. Anti-fascists often disrupted Spencer's talks against affirmative action, mirroring what we saw later in the high-profile actions against Milo Yiannopoulos. The Alt Right's attempts to focus on college campuses because of access to affluent, young, professional-class men has also put them in proximity to student activist culture, and the fires outside the University of California, Berkeley and the clashes at the University of Washington, among many others, were the result. The insistence of people like Yiannopoulos and Spencer to force their way onto campuses only escalated things and prompted antifascist organizations to be ready to mobilize.

Spencer generally ignored the fact that his appearances were becoming demilitarized zones, with his December 2016 event at Texas A&M drawing hundreds in a spectacle comparable to a football game.[7] He used, what he claimed as "success" there, to go on to Alabama's Auburn University on April 19, 2017, employing former Klan attorney Sam Dickson to sue his way into the college. The same strategy took him to the University of Florida, Gainesville, on October 19, where a massive coalition pushed back on him and his followers. At each location, organizations of students and community members were formed, battling the white nationalists showing up, rendering the events barely functional, and creating permanent connections for ongoing organizing work.

This activity was only an extension of what was taking place anytime Spencer—or white supremacist groups like Identity Evropa or the Traditionalist Workers Party—attempted to hold a public conference or rally. Police barricades, last-minute venue cancelations, and public brawls overshadowed the Alt Right's message, and as members were doxxed and fired from their jobs, it became harder and harder to make their movement attractive to recruits. In the wake of Charlottesville, they were forced off social media, web hosting, podcast platforms, and just about every outreach tool available, leaving them only to the back alleys of the Internet.

The situation over the course of Spencer's campus tour, which was intended to be a victory lap for the Alt Right, ended up a death spiral. Charlottesville was intended to be their high-water mark, where they brought out nearly 1,000 fully-committed white nationalists, but it now seems like a ghost they only wish they could hold onto.

On March 4 and 5, 2018, there was a planned Alt Right conference in Detroit. Anti-fascist organizers got wind of the location and the Alt Right were banned from one venue after another, including private restaurants that wouldn't even serve them drinks. Under pressure, Spencer's attorney and host of the conference, Kyle Bristow, publicly distanced himself from the white nationalist movement. It just wasn't worth it anymore.

Spencer still had high hopes for his use of the campus, but since students were gone and the building provided to him was used primarily by farm animals, it wasn't looking good. Hundreds were brought out by the #StopSpencer campaign, which was coordinating in multiple locations to block audience members from entering the hall. The Traditionalist Workers Party, led by the now-disgraced leader Matthew Heimbach, was stopped by a flash mob of protesters, and Gregory Conte was arrested and ended up as a ranting meme in a million YouTube clips. In the end, only a handful showed up despite the 150 tickets he offered. About twenty actually made it in, less than the number of people arrested out front. Those who did show up had more in common with skinhead gangs like the Hammerskin Nation than the suit-and-tie crowd Spencer so desperately wants to recruit.

The bottom line is that coordinated antifascist action like this has made it incredibly difficult for the Alt Right to organize. Major figures like Spencer have had their events turned into platforms for mass opposition, and his speeches shouted down. In 2016, he was able to host a sold out National Policy Institute conference at the famed Ronald Reagan Building in Washington, D.C., but in 2017 the organization got booted from the unheated barn they were forced to rent. All of the tools they had—online outreach, public events and private meetings—have essentially been stolen from them, and an entire infrastructure of doxxing and protest action have made consequence inevitable. This is not how they build "the movement of the future."

In a YouTube video shortly after the Michigan State debacle, Spencer recapped this failure, admitting that antifascist organizers had won and they cannot have public appearances anymore.

"I don't think that it's a good idea for me to host an event that is wide open to the public," Spencer said, lamenting the pressure from antifascist groups. "Things are difficult. We felt that great feeling of winning for a long time. We are now in something that feels a lot more like a hard struggle."

Matt Parrott, a longtime white nationalist and cofounder of the Traditionalist Workers Party, went on "Gab," an alternative to Twitter popular among white nationalists, to place blame for their failure solely on the opposition.

"The antifa has pretty much succeeded in achieving what the progressive left cannot, which is fully and finally de-platforming the hard right," Parrott said. "They demoralized and disabled the majority of the 'alt-right,' driving most of them off the streets and public square."

The major Alt Right blog, *The Right Stuff*, has been organizing private meet-ups that are heavily vetted for their membership, a format they are now presenting as an alternative to "in real life" activism. Spencer agrees, basically giving up on open, public events that can reach the unconverted.

The story of Michigan, and the decline of the Alt Right, is the result of a coordinated campaign of thousands of antifascists who have radicalized in a period of insurgent white supremacy. The goal of antifascist organizing of all stripes is to dismantle the functioning of white nationalist organizations to make white nationalists unable to meet their goals, which range from recruitment to violence.

What Antifascism Means

Even still, the overall narrative in many media outlets has instead been one framed as antifascist violence, minimizing the entirety of antifascist community organizing to snapshots of street fights. The argument made here is that this type of antifascism, narrowly understood, is counterproductive to stopping fascist growth since it makes them appear as victims. The problem with this discourse is that it first misses the actual diversity of antifascist organizing, which has a massive spectrum and is predominantly made up of ordinary people doing traditional organizing work with neighbors and congregants, but also that it misunderstands what actually stops fascist growth.

It is not the vague mysticism of public opinion or the spin from op-eds. What stops white nationalists is activists stopping white nationalists: stopping their project from functioning, from expanding, from making a difference. In this way, the antifascist movement— made up of church groups, student clubs, anarchists, and liberals— has prevented the Alt Right's infrastructure from self-replicating by throwing a monkeywrench into their machine.

We have every reason to believe that the Alt Right could recover from this and any other period of massive decline. The white nationalist movement has seen mass upheavals against it, destabilizing lawsuits from nonprofits like the Southern Poverty Law Center, and projects like the KKK rise to national prominence before dropping to pariah status. What the Alt Right has done over the decades, and will continue to do, is manipulate edge issues that they can use to push conservatives into a more reactionary direction. What matters now is how the left continues to build this movement so that a resurgence is neutralized through competent organizing work that shows community members the stakes of the threat, inoculates them against nationalist lies, and shows them how getting involved can change lives for the better.

The only thing that will really sign the death certificate of the Alt Right is an ever-growing presence of antifascism in all areas of social life, a movement whose vibrancy is overwhelming and whose composition is intergenerational. While Alt Right branding and strategies are new, their ideas are not, and they won't be the last—unless antifascism is not seen as just the hobby of a few.

25 Theses on Fascism

1

Fascism in the twenty-first century has direct continuity to the insurgent movements that tore apart Europe, culminating in the Second World War. The methods, tactics, and strategies have changed, but the potential of the genocidal-racialist machine remains, and the ideologies are linked through history.

Fascism does not necessitate a specific type of statecraft (or a State at all), nor does it require a particular party apparatus, a fixed demographic of finance capital, or economic depression. What it does require is mass politics, popular support, and the ongoing destructive upheaval of class society.

{3}

When inequality is sanctified, identities made to be fixed and essential, and a mythic past is demanded in a distinctly post-industrial, modern world, fascism is the manifestation of the "True Right," a distinct political identity revolting against democracy and equality. This real right-wing exists throughout history, with fascism acting as the "reactionary modernist" version of the tendency towards violent inequality and essentialized identity. Fascism represents the iconic manifestation of the "True Right," which then presents itself as a repudiation of the founding principles of liberal democracy.

{4}

Nihilism, as an apolitical destructive force, is a part of the fascist process, one that requires a destruction of the old infrastructure of morality so that a new mythic one can be built. Fascism often tries to colonize methods used on the Left/post-Left to achieve this creative destruction, disingenuously adopting revolutionary deconstruction.

{5}

The impulsive nature of reactionary violence is stoked by fascist ideology and ideologues in an effort to center an irrationalist response to the unbinding rage of modernity. In a culture that trains the working class in systems of bigotry, energy is forced toward scapegoating rather than directing that alienation at the oppressive institutions that birth it.

{6}

Today, fascism is largely built on metapolitics rather than explicit politics. Fascist projects attempt to influence culture, perspectives, and morality as precursors to politics. This puts much of their work into the realm of art and music, philosophy and lectures, counter-institutions and counterpower. This is the development of a fascist value and aesthetic set, not simply a fascist political program.

{7}

The values set by fascists enable them to use methodologies traditionally associated with the Left, including mass politics, postcolonialism, anti-imperialism, and anti-capitalism. Fascists employ the power of the marginalized classes and redirect their anger against systemic inequality and alienation against other marginalized people, thus reframing the source of the crisis.

{8}

Because of their strategic and revolutionary orientation, fascists have historically been able to draw on disaffected areas of the Left. There is no revolutionary tradition that is free from far-right entry, wherein the flaws in radical Left analysis and practice allow for fascists to present an alternative and recruit.

[9]

Nationalism is itself considered the core motivating vision in fascism, yet it is actually only a subset of the larger identitarian trend. Tribalism, of which nationalism is only one type, is the key component of this assertion of essential identity. Nationalism is a version of this that will always be tied to the nation state, and therefore tribalism placed in a modern context necessitates itself through nationalism, but this is not universal. The modern fascist movement redefines itself consistently in praxis, and reimagining that tribalism means that how they divide up tribe, and the social authorities that reinforce the boundaries of that tribe, can change.

{10}

Ethnic nationalism is a foundational principle of fascism today, a type of racial tribalism, which is not relegated only to white nationalism or the civic nationalism of Western nations. This draws on an ethnopluralist ethic of "nationalism for all peoples," which attempts to ally with nationalist components of Third World national liberation movements, minority nationalist movements, and those resisting Western imperialist powers. When racial nationalism is used as a component solution to confronting oppressive powers, it makes itself the potential ally of a fascist logic that sees the answer to capitalism and imperialism in authoritarian forms of identitarianism.

{11}

Fascism's focus on immigration, founded on the desire for monoracial countries, draws on the anxieties that are often tied to Left organizing. The "offshoring" of jobs due to neoliberal globalization, isolationist rhetoric in the anti-war movement, labor institutions' fears of immigrant workers driving down wages, environmental fears associated with population growth, the scapegoating of Islamic immigrants for supposedly repudiating liberal norms, and the smug liberal secularism of the U.S. coasts, are all well mobilized by fascist movements attempting to use liberal modes of thought for their own anti-immigrant populism.

{12}

The Alt Right is the most coherent and fully formed fascist movement in several decades. The mislabeling of all Trump supporters as true Alt Right adherents, whether those in Patriot or militia organizations, or those in New Right or Alt Lite projects of right populism, has created a fuzzy media spectacle that misses the Alt Right's true motivations. The belief in human inequality, social traditionalism, racial nationalism, and an authoritarian vision founded in the resurrection of heroic mythologies are what distinguish the Alt Right as a self-conscious fascist movement.

{13}

Third Positionism, which draws Left ideas into fascist politics, is the dominant form of open fascism today. True fascist ideologues, the "idea makers" in these movements who currently make up the most radical element, necessarily consider themselves anti-imperialist, anti-capitalist, and opposed to current Western governments.

{14}

Fascism has often been described as a process of multiple stages, in the way that it starts from a radical cadre and develops to the point of acquiring political power. But this is a description of a particular historical moment of fascism, rather than a universal description of its operational trajectory. This understanding should be revised for different periods and countries where power, influence, and social cohesion appear differently. For instance, in interwar Europe, party politics developed coalitions for State power, but in other times and places power could also involve the church, the media, or cultural centers. In modern America, fascists are allying with an online culture that helped the Alt Right grow and take over influential cultural spaces with the ability to influence essential parts of the larger society. In the 21st century U.S., party politicians have waning influence while Internet celebrities are more influential than anyone could have ever dreamed.

{15}

While "The Five Stages of Fascism" described by scholar Robert O. Paxton outline the process by which fascism took power, and then went into decline in Europe before and during the Second World War, both the conditions and movements are fundamentally different now.[1] Predicting the process for power acquisition and possible failure in a period when fascism remains primarily influential in culture and insurgent movements is impossible to predict fully in advance.

{16}

The crisis for fascists today comes from the contradictions in their approach to their own growth. Fascism of the interwar period relied first on political organizing, which then had to consider media representation. The Alt Right of the 21st century developed almost entirely online through a culture of memes and hashtags. While this has given them a huge jump in the expanse of their messaging, they have since had trouble translating this into real-world engagement and subsequent organizing. The vulgarity of their language, the style of their approach, and the demographics of their retweeters does not necessarily extend to radical organization and organizing.

{17}

If fascists see cultural spaces as premeditating political ones, then the movement of fascists into cultural spaces is effectively political. If fascist public speech is intended to recruit and organize, then fascist public expression is indistinguishable from fascist organizing. If fascist organizing results in violence, whether explosions of "seemingly random" street violence, or genocide if they were to take power, then fascist organizing is fascist violence. Unlike other forms of revolutionary politics, fascism seeks to sanctify violence, built directly into their conception of identity and a correctly hierarchical society.

Therefore, even the most muted fascist ideologue holds the kernels of brutality.

{18}

Fascism can only hide its violence for so long. The history of white nationalism has been the history of bloodthirsty terrorism, a point which marks all fascist parties and organizations in all countries in all times. While fascist intellectuals and movement leaders desperately want to decouple the image of identitarian nationalist ideas from street and State violence, this is impossible in the real world. Within a long enough timeframe there will always be killing.

{19}

Fascism could not exist in a period before mass politics. While it is decidedly elitist—it believes that society should be run, in part, by an elite caste—it also requires the mass participation of the public. This means recruiting from large segments of the working class, requiring their complicity in increased oppression. Hannah Arendt described the way this works as the "banality of evil," to characterize the casual complicity and bureaucratic malaise of the German people in the events of World War II and the Holocaust. This banality is a requirement for fascism to take power, for a mass to believe its benefits are worth its cost. This is the unity of populism with elitism, resetting the mentality of the masses so that they can walk themselves to destruction.

{20}

The conditions that breed fascism, the unfinished equation of late capitalism, are only likely to become more ingrained and dramatic. Crisis is essential to capitalism and will increase as global economic markets continue to shake with instability. That penchant for crisis, mixed with the stratification built into capitalism and the State's reliance on bigotry, makes fascist explosions inevitable.

{21}

The Left's inability to provide a real and viable alternative to the current system, and its capitulation to institutions of power, are what give fascism its strongest rhetorical appeal. An effective antifascist movement would do more than simply oppose the fascists in order to then return society to its previous order. Instead, the Left should present a radically different vision that answers the same feelings of alienation and misery to which fascism presents itself as a solution.

{22}

Fascism's ability to adapt to changes in technology, social systems, values, ethics, and the politics and practices of the Left is profound. As progress is made in Left circles toward confronting legacies of colonialism, white supremacy, patriarchy, heteronormativity, and other systems of oppression, fascist ideologues will find ways of manipulating those projects for their own advancement. Preventing this cooptation requires understanding the core ideology and methodologies of fascism while being consistent about the motivating ideas of Left organizing, always striving towards greater freedom and equality.

{23}

Donald Trump rode into the White House on the same kind of right populism that led to Brexit, the U.K.'s exit from the European Union, emboldened Marine Le Pen and the National Front in France, and allowed the anti-immigrant Alternative for Germany party to enter the State. This creates the possible bridge between the mass populace and fascist or proto-fascist ideologues, who want to see a society of enforced inequality and essentialized identity. This bridging is a necessary precondition for a mass fascist societal shift and should be seen as a part of the concentric circles that give fascism its ability to enact mass violence.

{24}

Resistance to fascism must then take on the form of mass politics as well, going after the macropolitics of right populism that bridge mainstream conservatism to the fascist cadre. This cannot be done only by a radical fringe but should be done by mobilizing both the base that fascism recruits from and the mass marginalized communities that it targets (which make up the vast majority of the working class). The most effective counter to fascist recruitment is Left mobilization, and the only thing that stops mass violence is mass refusal.

{25}

White supremacy and social hierarchy are implicit in class society, but fascism seeks to make it explicit. The Left's counter to this can also be to make that oppression explicit, to spell out the underlying hierarchies of civilization so as to undermine the fascist progression. The only thing that will end fascism in perpetuity is to destroy the mechanisms that allow it to arise in the first place. Destroying the impulses of authoritarianism and intrinsic inequality is a requirement for eradicating fascism from collective consciousness. The only thing that can do this is a revolutionary movement that goes far beyond simple reactions to the brutal movements of fascists.

The Kult of Kek

From the multiple available livestreams you could see that things were heading south in Berkeley. On April 15, 2017, Lauren Southern brought together the iconoclastic Trump supporters in her base along with explicit white nationalists and patriot militia members aligned against the resistance forming to the rightward shift in the U.S. What was markedly different about this convergence is that the event was secondary to its goal of antagonisms to the left, specifically to draw antifa into a fight.

While you would expect the nationalist contingent to be flying the usual flags, such as the Confederate Battle Flag or banners of the Third Reich, instead the symbolism skewed towards message board jargon, little known memes, and a comic character that became the unlikeliest hate symbol. The flag for "Kekistan," an ironic locale, was used to identify the edgysphere of the Alt Right, inlaid with a cross-striped pattern that looks remarkably similar to those hung in German beer halls in the late '20s. Various incarnations of cartoon frog Pepe were displayed on signs, along with "Da Goyim Knows" taglines. That iconography took on a life of its own as it signified its own social clique amidst the larger convergence. More than just a proxy for the white nationalism found on 4Chan and made militant on Twitter, Pepe, and now the idea of "Kek" has its own culture that hopes to give white nationalism a unique depth.

The Alt Right's trollstorm on the collective dialogue was best seen on Amazon.com, where various images of frogs, from shirts to idols, are labeled Kek, inscribed with Alt Right in-jokes and racial dog whistles. The meme of Pepe has moved to the next level, even to be touted as religious iconography by some Alt Right loyalists, all reliant on a highly internal counterculture that lacks a clear social connection to much of the "All-American" white nationalism of the 1980s and 1990s. Kek, the word drawn from World of Warcraft and shared by the Egyptian God of Chaos, has become the "next level" symbol of the Alt Right, a meme made flesh. The image they have created of Kek, based on the idea that their current irony could be rooted in something transcendent, was too striking to ignore.

This hit its zenith when a series of pamphlets finally joined the Alt Right swag, presenting its own outline for a "Kek religion." *The Divine Word of Kek* led off several other pamphlets, all of which take the meme culture and intensify it into something that claims an *essential* meaning far beyond the casual in-jokes that birthed the reactionary vengeance of the Chans. This simulacrum hit a point of completeness as the subculture within a subculture, completely self-referential and dependent on esoteric memedom, becoming self-indulgent and losing sight of its original purpose as an avatar for basic ideas of white supremacy.

Inside the Spirit of Chaos

The Kult of Kek is the logical conclusion of the meme culture that gave the Alt Right its popularity. Pepe the Frog became the mascot for the Alt Right, often seen adjacent to talking points about racial nationalism and anti-Jewish hatred, yet snarky and jovial rather than openly genocidal. Many began to argue that Pepe held a remarkable resemblance to the Egyptian God Kek, who is often portrayed in hieroglyphics as sitting in front of something that could be interpreted as a computer. Building on ancient Aryanist occultist ideas of the early twentieth century, as well as the widely discredited thesis that ancient Egyptians were actually white Europeans, their notion is that Kek is a living Aryan pagan god manifesting through the modern Pepe meme. "The Egyptians believe that before the world was formed, there was a watery mass of dark, directionless chaos. In this chaos lived the Ogdoad of Khmunu (Hermopolis), four frog gods and four snake goddesses of chaos."[1] This draws heavily on the Jungian ideas that motivated Aryan-centric versions of paganism starting with German romanticism. In much of folkish heathenry, the notion persists that the gods are ethnically-exclusive archetypes, spiritual metaphors for the motivations, emotions, and modes of thought that humans traverse through. Kek is then the God of Chaos, the troll hurricane that tears down the lies of modernist multiculturalism and egalitarianism so as to reinstate the proper human order of hierarchy and racial exclusivity.

The actual explanation of Kek as a "meme religion" comes largely from their appropriation of Chaos Magick, using ideas such as hypersigils to argue that it was actually "meme magick" that made things like the Alt Right, Donald Trump, and the white identitarian wave come into existence.

By thinking, by dreaming, they upended reality, and Kek is now the chosen deity of a mystical few who's postmodern magickal science will move dreams from the ethereal to the material. Their readings and explanations of these types of mysticism are, as one would expect, often devoid of the deep study that you find in most occultism, often mimicking self-help videos and positive affirmation diatribes.

The pamphlets themselves are of two worlds: one of ironic racism, and the other of finding spiritual connectivity and patterns to make the mundane sacred. Using mostly low-resolution graphics and bad fonts in an amateur collage of nonsense, it mixes in Kek aphorisms, copypasta forum discussions, and simplified explanations of magickal concepts and New Age superstitions, all of which looks as though it was screenshotted from a Geocities homepage circa 1995. Instead of acting as a vessel for concrete white nationalist ideas, as offensive as they are, the "worship" of Kek is a simulacrum of that; hyper intensified in-jokes and cultural artifacts, all built on signaling "in-group" status in the cultish "community" of racialist message boards.

Empires Crumble

Decadence is founded in the aesthetics of decline, the ruinous space of empires past, the nostalgia for an earlier time.

The concept of decadence, the process of civilizational decline, is baked into the imagination of the right—all versions of the right. The garish lectures of Jesse Helms or the dire warnings of *Taki's Mag* signal encroaching decadence, the force that, while acting as a ferocious inferno, consumes that which came before. That decadence is a rot; the destruction of what was once great, what could, if not for failure, be made great again. Decadence is often misapplied, or even used as coloring to describe those articles of disgust that are fashionable for a period. Queerness, fat bodies, egalitarianism, miscegenation, all owe to decadence in that they are seen as a rejection of the proper hierarchical order they assume is natural to European descended people. They are results of a society hitting a point of rupture, losing the identity and values that, they believe, defined them for centuries.

Within a rejection of modernity these can be summed up as distinctly recent concepts that drive us away from an "essential tradition" from which humanity sprang and to which it must return if it is to be healthy. Changes in society are then, in the most classic nostalgia of the right, a movement in the wrong direction, a form of dysgenic degeneration rather than progress.

Defining modernity comes at the intersections of both the romanticism of the past and the future, the inability to fully denounce the world in progress or to determine exactly what previous epoch is preferred. On the one hand, modernity is often determined to be the modern state of Western capitalism, built on colonialism and made homogeneous through its ever expanding consumerism. It is also, as Marshall Berman writes, something that "can be said to unite all mankind" under its promises of ecstasy, yet "threatens to destroy everything we know, everything we are."[2] Modernity is then offered as hedonism, whose allure robs people of their essential identity, their race and nation.

Modernity is the center of the neo-fascist project, an identity set forward by Julius Evola's rejection of the "modern world." Evola's Traditionalism, building on the work of Rene Cuenon, posited a "divine truth" in all spiritual paths, not just in their gods, but in their hierarchies and tyrannies.[3] Using the Vedic Cycle of Ages, he argued that we have long slipped from the Golden Age and are now in the fourth age, the Kali Yuga, the time of dark passions and decadence.[4] The modern world had rejected the racial purity, hierarchy, and spiritual transcendence that had existed naturally in previous generations. This modern world needed "men against time," as Aryan mystic Savitri Devi called them, to resist this modernity as spiritual warriors. Modernity is defined by its state of decline, a false consciousness obscuring the underlying Tradition that puts things in their place through some type of natural law. Fascism is then a distinctly modern concept, something that can only exist in this age of decadence in an effort to return to a fabled place of purity. Jeffrey Herf termed this "reactionary modernism," the state of technological advancement, and attempts to return to the past of memory. Richard Spencer, the enigmatic founder of the "Alt Right," sees fascism as the modern application of an undying spiritual impulse toward order and hierarchy. European New Right theorist Guillaume Faye used the phrase "Archeo-Futurism," to define a world where the effects of materialism, namely technology, will be used towards "anti-materialist" ends of a spiritual connection between race and identity, blood and soil. Fascism, in this way, is modernity turned on itself, a revolution against its own methodology, in hope that decadence will open a window to a nationalist rebirth while it crushes the door to democracy.

Fascism rests its entire identity in this decadence, symbols that, in their decline, have been made aesthetic once again. When Identity Evropa, the white nationalist group of middle class college students blitzed campuses after the 2016 presidential election they did so with a familiar set of images. On photos of classic European sculpture, each worn or broken with time, they had phrases like "Let's become great again" emblazoned in retro-chic fonts overlaid. In 2016 Richard Spencer inspired a series of Roman salutes at the National Policy Institute conference by tying together a motif that has defined his career. "Things can only be normal again when we can become great again," he declared. By this notion Spencer attempted to show the decadence of Western culture, where Europeans supposedly gave up their "Faustian spirit" to explore and create so as to elevate the feelings of non-whites.[5]

Decadence fills their rhetoric, imagery, aesthetics, and art. It is how they have defined their internal logic; one that does not see grand European empires in their actuality, but instead the remnants of what they believe was once there. The fascist project, one that scholar Roger Griffin has labeled "palingenetic ultranationalism" requires a mythic interpretation of the past, one that, while lacking a factual basis, has an emotional quotient through its romantic reinterpretation. The stories that they tell about these pasts are ones that express their hopes for the future, not a place they can actually return to. What they build this narrative through is the pieces they see left behind, weathered by years of storms and the political campaigns of long dead rulers.

Their conception of this past, and the future they believe is inevitable, is built on decadence, the reification of decline, the rebuilding of something now well destroyed.

In the article "Decadent Politics," decadence is put into the political context, the politics of freedom rather than living out the democratic models proposed by previous authorities. "Decadence—the aesthetics of decay, the embodiment of deranged but heightened senses—is an undeniably political stance. The romantic can never find satisfaction in the truly dead worlds of the suburban subdivision or the garish fluorescence of the stripmall . . . Decadent politics is the realization that today's real-politic is in ruins."[6] Decadence then works at two intersections: those in the fragments of modernity and those signaled as moments of decline. Together these put the Alt Right into a point of contraction. As a reader goes through the pamphlets themselves, it is easy to notice that there is almost no mention of race. The Kult of Kek was not a religious concept believed because it was "true" in the literal and fundamentalist sense. This nature is outlined with incredible detail in its own internal understanding of Chaos Magick and other bits and pieces of occult traditions it has chosen to represent its ideas. Racialism was its entire reason for being, the foundation on which the culture of memes and trolling was built. The Kult of Kek is then a tool intended to give that culture a deepening, yet it lacks a clear connection back to its reason to exist. Its battle for substance defined it more clearly as superficial, lacking even its own destructive ideological core.

This simulacrum is itself the defining mode of modernity, the point at which an object or idea and the simulation of that object or idea become invariably the same. The culture of the Alt Right was intended to be one that popularized the hard ideas of white nationalism. The pseudo-academic culture they have been building since the 1960s, starting with the French New Right and heading up through places like *Radix Journal*, need this new pop-culture flavor. In this case all they are left with is the flavor and the actual ideology is slipping.

Kek, their god of chaos, is proving himself real by sweeping through and destroying their entire model for perpetuating a coherent identity. The texts themselves are rested firmly in this decadence, filled with confusion, irrational aphorisms, internalized internet jargon, copy/pasted conversations from message boards, and things outright plagiarized. It has had its ideas brushed away, until only the base structures of a conversation remain. The ruins of a movement.

The Alt Right itself has lost even its own claim to Tradition. Its masculinity is both at odds with the left and even its own mythology about the necessity of the atomic family. Its brutalist language is in direct conflict with the nationalist veneration of chastity, and its sense of national civility is compromised by its unburdened rage. Through avatars and anonymity, a biting synthetic personality is formed, one disconnected from the collective accountability that is central to their ethnic communitarianism. This is based on the non-relationship, interactions done through metaphor and meme, lacking in subtlety, sensuality, and nuance, free of care and concern, which are the foundations for the "high trust society" they persistently signal for. Their culture is one that is distinctly modern, by their own denunciatory definition, one that has become hyper subcultural in the language of consumer capitalism.

This is a culture of crisis, one that presents one of the most well-defined cracks in the growing Alt Right coalition. The Alt Right is white nationalism for the twenty-first century middle class male, and it then creates crossover spaces with Trump Republicans, civic nationalist types, anti-liberal libertarians, and so on. It requires, though, a reason to exist as an autonomous movement with its own ideological purity. With its development of a culture that can recruit it has given up this core, traded it for the self-reflexivity of smug web comics.

While the Alt Right's presence has never been more discussed, this presents a critical failure, a point at which the newly built empire crumbles. Kek's role is to destabilize their order, and if any weight is put on the meme religion by the ideological movement of the Alt Right then it shows its willingness to build politics on unstable ground. This presents the critical juncture for a coming collapse, but not one that is fixed as a dialectical inevitability. Its attempt at depth, the intellectual collaboration of racists that Richard Spencer started building a decade ago, has become its own signal of decline, its capitulation to the game of "modernity." The Alt Right's subsequent decline was met with a return of the Americanist far-right, such as Proud Boys and the invocation of Q-anon (a perhaps even more esoteric prophet), and Kek has been pushed further back to the recesses of the Internet.

As the Kult of Kek intensified, YouTube channels were created, blog posts increased exponentially, and the language of meme magic only became more obscurantist, more ironic. This route outlined where the critical failing of the right was, and outlined the options for the left to exploit, undermine, and destroy. Decadence is the reminder that even the most powerful topple, that structures require capitulation, and that our role in them is often what gives us the ability to undo them. Symbols of decline are a message of the possibility for replacement.

The Alt Right's rise and fall, which only came because antifascist movements pushed it over the edge, shows an internal logic of instability. Their culture, built not through practical organizing but through converting adherents through social media, is founded on obscurantist thinking, and because of this their vulnerabilities are easy to find. Their weaknesses do not make them any less lethal (in fact, it may make them more so), but it does make their Achilles Heel easier to find. While the Alt Right saw a period of decline, white nationalism itself continues unabated in the border and policing policies of the United States, where a sense of divine mission still resonates with the most reactionary elements of the far-right base. As climate collapse creeps even further, the promise of decadence still offers hope to white nationalists looking toward a total assault on communities of color. The only option is to undermine their very capacity by building something new ourselves.

The "Free Speech" Cheat

College Student Senate chambers are not historically hotbeds of nationwide controversy, but Turning Point USA (TPUSA) is set to rewrite the rules of campus politics. The ultra-conservative student group, which could easily be labeled "the youth wing" of Trump Republicanism, has become a legitimized force in campus conservative politics and has gained a reputation for its mix of public shaming and bigoted public statements. Turning Point has staked its claim on changing a college campus culture that they allege leans dramatically to the left. If they can change the political climate for college students, especially on issues like immigration and queer rights, can they change the values of the next ruling generation?

At Texas State University, the clash between TPUSA and the larger student body came to blows in the spring of 2019 when student leadership proposed a bill to ban it as a student group on campus.

"Turning Point USA definitely films students, including graduate students, and tries to get them fired," said Claudia Gasponi, a senior at the Texas State University and the Student Senator who introduced the resolution to bar Turning Point from the campus. "This is not about student organizations. TPUSA is not a student organization, it is a national menace that uses students to mask their hostile and corrupt agenda."

True to their brand of political sadism, TPUSA has reframed the issue of campus safety as a heroic battle to save free speech in the caustic co-ed environment of college life. And, what's more, they have now brought in high-priced friends from the GOP's Southern power base to help them.

With the fragmentation of the GOP during the Obama years, Turning Point was primed to emerge as a leader of a new conservative generation. Based heavily on Donald Trump's national populism and the online right-wing culture of provocation and dog whistles, TPUSA offers something to the post-millennial generation of students that the Brooks Brothers suits at the Heritage Foundation never could: edginess, or at least its appearance.

The group was founded by twenty-five-year-old CPAC-styled luminary Charlie Kirk, a man known primarily for trying to speed-talk over leftists in public venues. Styled on the Ben Shapiro model of "owning the libs," he fashioned TPUSA by drumming up controversy, usually an effort to present leftist opposition as foolish on camera. TPUSA has now become a massive multi-organization right-wing operation with millions of dollars a year as an operating budget and presenting itself as a Trumpian Republican version of a youth-activist institution, uniting everyone from College Republicans to those further to the right in one grand project to support the President and harass anyone to his left. They have since funneled millions in right-wing donations into talk-radio inspired projects like a "Professor Watchlist" of leftist faculty.

This genre of performance politics has helped them open over 1,300 chapters on college campuses; like conservative activists before them, they are now burrowing into student governments through student senatorial elections as a way of shifting campus culture in their favor, singling them out as the most efficacious way to gain advantage with otherwise indifferent college administrations. Recently, left and progressive college activists have gained traction on issues like sexual assault and campus police through grassroots organizing around procedural mechanisms, like trustee votes and Title IX violations—TPUSA would rely on the same mechanisms to produce the opposite results.

At the Texas State University, TPUSA-affiliated students captured the leadership of student government by electing Student Body President Brooklyn Boreing—amid student allegations that Boreing received $2,800 in donations and twenty-five tablets from the Campus Leadership Project, a subsidiary of TPUSA that focuses on campus and fraternity elections.[1] Along these lines, Turning Point has been accused of violating campus campaign finance rules repeatedly.

"I think it was widely believed by the student body that the tablets came from Turning Point," said Claudia Gasponi, a point that led her and her student colleagues to press the issue. "They have a lot of power on our campus."

TPUSA's history of members being caught using racial slurs and making outwardly fascistic statements, for example recently departed Director of Communications Candace Owens's 2018 comments defending Adolf Hitler, turned the tide for Gasponi. (White supremacists have targeted Texas campuses more than those of any other state, according to the Anti-Defamation League, and TPUSA often creates a slippery slope.) On April 11, the student body voted in favor of Gasponi and co-author Trevor Newman's resolution "Calling for the immediate removal and barring of Turning Point USA from Texas State University and suggesting protecting minority and marginalized populations from their negative campus influence."

Named the "Faculty and Student Safety Resolution of 2019," the resolution cited TPUSA's reputation for campus harassment and the need to distance the campus from an organization that could be a threat to students' safety. They mention that the TSU chapter of Turning Point regularly reports to the national organization, and they argue that doing so cancels its status as a student organization. The President of the Texas State University chapter of TPUSA, Stormi Rodriguez, attended the vote and spoke in support of TPUSA. "Do you want this to be your legacy? A legacy of censoring your peers?" she demanded against the sounds of hecklers.[2]

In a move that Gasponi argues was political, Student Body President Alison Castillo issued an immediate veto of the measure, citing it as a violation of free speech. "I have taken time to diligently consider this action and stand firmly by my decision to uphold the First

Amendment to the United States Constitution," said Castillo in her letter, redirecting the issue to TPUSA's talking points.[3]

What happened next was a testament to TPUSA's national political strength, and their ability to set the tone for politically charged discussions at public universities.

After Charlie Kirk fostered resentment about the resolution on Twitter, Texas Governor Greg Abbott entered the mix by retweeting him: "I truly question if taxpayers should still fund schools like this," he wrote.[4] The Governor then cited Texas Senate Bill 18, which would codify support for organizations like TPUSA on campus, applying strict penalties for campus activists who disrupt similar groups. The bill has already passed the Texas State Senate and is now in front of the House of Representatives' Higher Education Committee.

Expectedly, this kneejerk reaction was framed as a defense of conservative speech against censorship by leftist students. Except this was never possible.

"Texas State Student Government has been stripped of all of its power by our Administration," Gasponi pointed out. "Student government resolutions are the University's designated tool to hear student voices. The university doesn't usually listen to our voices, even when we pass a resolution, but it at least stops them from gaslighting us whenever they say, 'Go through the channels! Go through student government.' We go through student government and come directly to their door, demanding our voices be heard."

The case at Texas State University wasn't the first time a student body has attempted to stop Turning Point. At Drake University, the Student Senate denied TPUSA's status as a student organization over concerns of violations of student and faculty privacy. Students at Wartburg College, Santa Clara University, Cornell College, and Hagerstown Community College all took similar measures to stop TPUSA, mostly in the form of student government bans.[5] An Indiana University of Pennsylvania organization, the Pennsylvania Student Power Network, organized throughout 2018 to have TPUSA banned as a "hate group," yet the student government quashed the attempt.[6] This tactic has been used extensively in an effort to raise consciousness and mobilize organizing on the issue.

But the public reaction to the events at Texas State University was, for the most part, an example of political theater, and one that favors a tradition that has made TPUSA dangerous. The interventions of the Governor's office and the Senate allowed for a false characterization of campus activism and legislation that would create massive legal protections for conservative and fascist hate speech. While Turning Point managed to manipulate public perception around the student resolution, the purpose of the resolution was symbolic. It was intended to send a message to the administration rather than act as functional ban, a point that Turning Point had no intention of highlighting.

On April 11, the University of Illinois Student Government issued a statement supporting the Texas resolution, citing their long history of dealing with Turning Point. "Turning Point USA has a long history of harassment on campuses around the country," they wrote. "They have publicly distributed the personal information of undocumented students, repeatedly harassed both fellow students as well as professors, built a wall on our main quad as part of a racist statement against Latinx individuals, and most recently held a 'Hate speech is Free speech' event the same day as the Christchurch Mosque shooting."

"I think we have to use every tool in the shed, so to speak," said Adam Miyashiro, a Medieval Literature professor faculty from Stockton University and organizer with the Campus Antifascist Network, which openly supports the resolutions. "Student resolutions are great, but also at the faculty and administrative level, there are steps we can do, such as make sure that speakers from these groups aren't given a platform on campus, as they don't serve the institution's educational goals."

Turning Point has also been the source of controversies at the University of Illinois at Urbana-Champaign, where Tariq Khan, who was speaking against right-wing policies and confronting TPUSA members, leading to a string of death threats from white supremacists and public pressure that almost caused him to leave the university.[7]

"They've harassed the hell out of me and incited violence against me," said Khan, who explained that he is not the only student who has been targeted. Khan clashed with TPUSA, he says, when the organization attempted to get the university to reinstate a Native American sports mascot. "My guess is that [the student government] recognize that TPUSA is aggressively and intentionally creating a hostile campus environment for crass political reasons, and the students are over it."

While Turning Point has created a robust rhetorical controversy around "free speech," positioning themselves as the embattled political minority on socialist college campuses, their interventions on campuses cannot be reduced to a function of speech alone.

"This all has direct, palpable effects on people on their campuses—immigrant students, targeted faculty—and an indirect effect of chilling speech in the classroom," said Amanda Gailey, Associate Professor at the University of Nebraska, who was targeted by Turning Point in 2017 for her own gun control activism and support of a graduate student who had been singled out. "TPUSA uses a false front, appearing to be local college and high school kids, but they are really a kind of human shield for the powerful politicians and lobbyists collaborating with the group. They seek to radically transform American universities for the worse, funding racist and homophobic messaging while simultaneously chilling dissent from people who worry about their vulnerable jobs."

"This isn't a free speech issue because I am not advocating that we prohibit conservative student speech or assembly," concluded Gasponi. "I'm only advocating that this specific organization be barred from using campus resources because they are connected to violent white supremacist organizations, threaten and harass our students and faculty, and corrupt our student government."

The volatile campus struggles over terms like "free speech" give Turning Point the umbrella terms it needs to shade all of its pernicious aims, from campaigns against contingent faculty to the public shaming of coeds. And this cover has given them what they appear to want most: the ability to storm through campuses with impunity, positioning political resistance as a grand battle to unmake modern democracy.

While TPUSA has staked their reputation on the defense of "free speech," student activists are increasingly pointing out the organization's effect on campuses. There is political gain to be made in masking aggressive political mobilization with such rhetoric. The Texas State resolution, which is unbinding but still a tool of influence—an act of speech itself—is a call to organize in opposition to the coup Turning Point is launching on campuses throughout the country.

We're Being Played

Milkshakes aren't terrorism.

"Andy Ngô is an independent journalist in the Pacific Northwest. . . He was at an antifa rally over the weekend, minding his own business, covering the news—he's a journalist—when he was beaten almost to death by antifa. . . Andy, I'm glad you're capable of doing this interview. Tell us what happened?!"

Tucker Carlson offered the perfect platform for the far-right journalist and provocateur Andy Ngô to tell his story. Ngô is a slight and nebbish man, not known for a boisterous or loud presence. Slowly, he told Fox News viewers a harrowing story of being attacked by a vicious mob that was out for blood. He stuttered slightly and went at a snail's pace, exemplifying the disorientation typical of a traumatic brain injury. Carlson, for his part, repeatedly returned to the blunt force trauma that Ngô alleged he sustained.

Carlson was not the only person to seek out Ngô that week. His story began trending after CNN's Jake Tapper retweeted a video of the attack on Ngô posted by a reporter at *The Oregonian*. Tapper commented, "Antifa regularly attacks journalists; it's reprehensible."

Within a few hours, the videos of Ngô's altercation and the feverish first-person accounts he spoke into his cell phone camera became the top trending story on Twitter in the U.S. Soon #Antifa-Terrorists reached the most popular hashtag slot, cementing Ngô's story as yet another example of an embattled conservative journalist subjected to the increasingly volatile cruelty of the militant left. This came largely because of the tone of stories around the incident, framing what happened to Ngô as the most recent case of the common "terrorism" by antifascists, and Twitter activists used this rhetoric to make sure that any discussion of the incident inferred the terrorist nature of the movement. Narratives of far-left villainy, like Ngô's run-in, have become a staple of conservative click-bait. Burgeoning social media stars like Ngô feature as both their protagonists and propagators, building careers on the outrage they drum up in their followers while claiming to barter in neutral reporting and brave truth telling.

On the Ground Reporting

On Saturday, June 29, 2019 a large coalition of community and activist groups held a counterdemonstration to protest two complementary rallies organized that day by the Proud Boys and #HimToo, a not-quite-yet movement created by affiliates of far-right group Patriot Prayer. Both right-wing groups have held a number of unambiguously violent rallies around Portland over the past few years. Every summer since Trump was elected these organizations, which bill themselves as "nationalist conservatives," have publicly rallied and marched with no political platform beyond bigotries and opposition to the left. Participants suit up in body armor and helmets and rush counterdemonstrators, leading to brutal fights that have left a number of people hospitalized.[1]

The Proud Boys billed the June 29 event as the Battle for Portland 2, a reference to 2018's similar rally in which they collided with counterdemonstrators and initiated gang-style attacks that left their opponents with cranial fractures, staining concrete red with blood.[2] The antifascist coalition on June 29 consisted of more than a dozen organizations, including Pop Mob (short for Popular Mobilization), which focuses on "everyday antifascism" and organizes events that involve a broad base of community members who oppose hate.[3] For the late-June counterprotest, Pop Mob created a carnivalesque atmosphere themed around milkshakes—a riff on the recent protest meme popularized in Britain by antifascists who throw melted ice cream on fascists in street mobilizations. Basement tracks blasted from a PA system and people danced in booty shorts; it was hot, loud, and fun, drawing a contingent of hundreds who gathered before the main rally, partying and drinking milkshakes.[4]

Ngô was among the first to arrive at the antifascist demonstration, brandishing a GoPro on a pole and wearing goggles. His protective eyewear was suggestive: confrontation expected. In the weeks prior, Ngô had consistently beaten the drum on Twitter, repeating that he was nervous about how the day would play out. He was, admittedly, already a pariah in leftist spaces.

Ngô snaked his way through the crowd, pushing his GoPro in front of increasingly annoyed counterprotesters. The antifascist protesters planned to block the far-right from moving freely through the city; before their march even began, Ngô found himself in an altercation with some of the protesters, who threw milkshakes on him and hit him on the head. The Portland Police later Tweeted that there were allegations that the milkshakes had "quick dry cement" in them, despite there being zero evidence of this.

Ngô then created a mass media story by livestreaming the aftermath of his conflict on Twitter, saying that he had to go to the hospital for what was later ruled a brain bleed. He said police refused to help him and forced him to walk back through the crowd that had assaulted him, creating a harrowing portrait of a journalist under siege for simple reporting.

A New Kind of Conservative Celebrity

Ngô first gained minor notoriety after he was fired from his editorial position at the *Portland State Vanguard*, the newspaper for Portland State University where Ngô was a graduate student, for how he characterized the comments of a Muslim student at an interfaith event. Breitbart picked up the story and ran the headline "Muslim student claims that non-believers will be killed in Islamic countries," a point which the *Vanguard* felt mischaracterized the student's actual comments. Ngô was fired four days after the event, but that is really only where his career began.

He then went to the right-wing *National Review* and published a story, "Fired for Reporting the Truth," that argued it was the intolerant left that forced him to be fired from his position.[5] In this new right-wing magazine world, political correctness stands in the way of reality, and to be a true journalist you are going to have to exist as an embattled heretic. Breitbart continued to champion this story by making Ngô a poster-boy for conservatives persecuted at colleges, the perfect narrative for a right-wing blogosphere that wanted to portray university campuses as political thunderdomes.

Ngô went on to pen a number of Islamophobic op-eds and articles, including an article in the *Wall Street Journal* that suggested there were no go zones in London because of Muslim immigrants and that England is becoming an Islamic country.[6] More recently, Ngô has focused on trying to reveal reported hate crimes as hoaxes (particularly those committed against trans women) and exposing what he sees as the underreported violence of antifa. On an earlier appearance with Tucker Carlson, Ngô said that the left doesn't like him because he "goes after the grifters." Tucker agreed, saying "they hate the truth."

Preparing for a Reaction

Ngô presents himself simply as a neutral observer, the "true journalist," unburdened by pesky ideals. His detractors, meanwhile, question this portrayal, arguing that he is a political actor who engages in theatrics to draw a reaction.

On the spectrum of what gets to count as journalism, Ngô is hardly unique. Yet his recent antics have placed him front and center in a cottage industry on the far-right edges of political journalism, which insists that the mainstream media operates with near conspiratorial levels of bias against the right. All the while, supposedly silenced right-wing figures like Ngô have been interviewed on the biggest news networks; even neo-Nazi Richard Spencer has been invited on CNN as a commentator.

Owing to recent efforts by social media giants to snuff out the spread of hate speech and fake news, many conservative pundits have begun championing the idea that conservative voices are under attack. In May, the Trump administration opened an investigation into this possible bias, going as far as to put up a website where people could report their experiences of censorship. Pro-Trump commentators Diamond and Silk, video bloggers who are often trotted out by far-right politicians like Republican Congressman Steve King as an alternative image of the MAGA crowd because they are Black women, appeared at a House Judiciary Committee hearing in 2018 to talk about the censoring of conservative voices on Facebook, including their own (despite a lack of evidence to support such claims). Tucker Carlson owes his rise to prominence on Fox News to his lambasting of the liberal media. Following Ngô's pained account of his attack on Carlson's show, the host was swift to remind his audience (falsely) that CNN had defended the very same antifa that so brutally ambushed this poor journalist.

The same rhetoric has found purchase in campus organizing, where organizations like the nationalist Turning Point USA formed to support the campus conservatives allegedly under attack by the largely liberal-leftist faculty and student body. There is no safe space, they cry, for the silent minority, and since they represent truth and sanity, this constitutes a full-scale assault on civilization. The message has been further amplified by public facing members of the white nationalist adjacent "Alt Light." Figures like Alex Jones, Laura Loomer, Milo Yiannopoulos, Lauren Southern, among others have made professions of self-victimization. Crowdfunding sites like Patreon, a great resource for struggling independent journalists, also provide a financial infrastructure for those selling no more than unedited livestreams in which they "own the libs" and affirm the toxic hopes and fears of the far-right. Meanwhile, publications like the *Daily Caller*, *Quillette*, *Breitbart*, and *Heat Street* echo the same sentiments under the guise of serious journalism and intellectual argument.

InfoWars, which used to largely peddle conspiracy theories about nefarious Deep State actors, aliens, Bohemian Grove, genetic manipulation, 9/11 trutherism, and the like, shifted coverage during Trump's ascendancy. Instead of just exposing the hidden truths of the week, the InfoWarriors started crossing the street at Trump rallies to see the counterdemonstrators, forcing members of the public into unpredictable antagonistic conversations on camera. The number of views on YouTube soared, readership figures rose, and Super Male Vitality (a snake-oil supplement for men hawked on the InfoWars website) sold like gangbusters.

Today's right-wing voices use a shared lexicon to decry the left and its alleged collaborators in the State and corporate world, who threaten the rights and prosperity of "normal Americans." "From my cold dead hands," "enough with PC culture," "what about free speech?" In the media ecosystem of the far-right, a slanted reality is produced and reaffirmed: a world is projected in which demographic, political, and economic change threatens all that Americans hold dear. The subtext, as ever, is that "American" refers to white, heterotypical conservatives. And there are a thousand Internet hucksters screaming these all-American truths, forty-seven different ways on a 24-hour livestream cycle.

The far-right's consensus reality has little room for the facts that bash up against it. The fact, for example, that between 2009 and 2018, white supremacist and far-right extremists were responsible for 73 percent of extremist murders in the U.S. is not pertinent to the terror narratives Ngô and his fellow travelers want to tell and sell. According to the Anti-Defamation League, the far-right attacks are only increasing, with the number of fascist attacks hitting its highest peak in over two decades in 2018. Antifa, on the other hand, has been responsible for no deaths, and instead has been regularly credited with defending communities from far-right violence.[7] Recounting his experience protesting the intolerable 2017 United The Right rally in Charlottesville, scholar and activist Cornel West said, "we would have been crushed like cockroaches were it not for the anarchists and the antifascists."

Ngô's credentials are almost solely founded on his identity as a defender of truth against the militant leftists intent on returning us to the dark ages. He has few bylines besides op-eds and does little reporting other than streaming from social media, yet for his supporters he is a rallying point, a journalist beyond repute who is suffering for all of us in the face of anti-journalistic oppression. *Quillette* and right-wing blogger Michelle Malkin jumped to his defense and created a GoFundMe titled "Protect Andy Ngô," complete with a close-up shot of a tearful Ngô shortly after the attack. The fundraiser cleared almost $200,000—over four times an average reporter's salary. It will buy him much more than a new GoPro (the stated intent of the fundraiser), and yet the money has continued to flow in, not because Andy needs it, but because the people donating felt they needed to do something. They needed to do something about antifa, something about political correctness, something about the instability of their jobs, and about immigration and trans students in bathrooms and the left and their lives. The world is hard and change is unforgiving, and there is this guy, meek and desperate and indicative of the world that has harmed them, too. The donations trickled in ten and twenty dollars at a time, not for Ngô's recovery, but for the narrative he represents and advances. In the media ecosystem of the far-right, a slanted reality is produced and reaffirmed: a world is projected in which demographic, political, and economic change threatens all that Americans hold dear.

After the first GoFundMe campaign ended, Ngô created a follow-up fundraiser on PubliusLex where he is trying to raise $100,000 "to bring the violent members of antifa to justice." I'm sure he'll make double that.

The Story We Tell

Following Ngô's attack, journalists around the country came to his defense, ignoring nearly all context and consequences. Ostensibly left-liberal sources like *Vox* joined the indignant chorus, as did figures like Joe Biden. In all their righteous outrage, Ngô's mainstream defenders missed that this was not simply an incident of antifa-on-journalist violence, but a political conflict between a far-right agitator and his angry detractors. For certain journalists who have been hassled on the job, which is many of them in this increasingly hostile reporting environment, Ngô's narrative resonated. One after another, outlets pumped out think pieces about the danger to journalists evidenced in this incident, missing the salient fact that this was not an attack on journalists, it was a conflict with Andy Ngô.

It's no accident that other journalists walked away from the same event unscathed. Certain behaviors lead to conflicts, like shoving a camera in people's faces, or appearing friendly to one group of organizers, while hostile to another. This is Ngô's modus operandi. You don't have to justify what happened to him to understand why it did; it was not the result of reporting, but instead the consequence of a political and interpersonal conflict. What happened to Ngô reflects less on the world of embattled journalism than it does on the state of antagonistic right-wing content production. The easiest way to get such content is to provoke it, to ride existing social fissures into moments of conflict; nothing does that like shoving a camera in someone's face and shouting straw man questions. A predictably angered reaction confirms the hypothesis Ngô sets out to prove.

Ngô's work is targeted, not accidental, and results in real-world consequences for his selected antagonists. As he drummed up support after his assault on June 29, the far-right went into a violent rage, lashing out at the activists who had organized the milkshake protest, other journalists, and the city at large. Portland City Hall had to be shut down because of a bomb threat, leftist journalists received threatening messages online (myself included), and threats were sent to local activists promising death and dismemberment on camera. The false allegations of "quick drying cement" in the vegan milkshakes resulted in those organizers receiving death threats, while none of them had been personally implicated in any sort of violence themselves. Patriot Prayer supporters then organized a follow up rally in Ngô's name, promising to go to Portland mayor Ted Wheeler's house. Proud Boys and InfoWars celebrities promised to return to Portland on August 17 to violently confront "The antifa," or the city, or the mayor, or whomever they deem an enemy on the street that day.

Prior to the Portland incident, Ngô was already known for singling people out in a way that can focus right-wing resentment on an individual or a group like a laser. Following his Islamophobic stunt at the college paper, he clashed with Oregon CAIR (Council on American-Islamic Relations) over his statements associating the nationwide CAIR with suspected terrorism and hate crime hoaxes.

During a post–May Day rally hosted by Portland bar Cider Riot, members of Patriot Prayer showed up and began pepper-spraying and assaulting attendees and patrons. Witnesses at the bar reported that Ngô arrived just before Patriot Prayer leader Joey Gibson and his entourage, in perfect time to gather good conflict footage for his video stream.

Ngô barters in double standards; the political activities and commitments of his ideological opponents make them fair game for harassment and violent confrontation. Yet any confrontation with Ngô based on his own political allegiances and actions are deemed unjustified, if not monstrous. The journalists and academics Ngô labels as extremists are treated as worthy of intimidation, undeserving of the protections accorded real journalists and writers. When *Quillette* published a spurious study, based on no more than Twitter connections, claiming to name journalists (myself included) who were involved with antifa, Ngô helped amplify it. As a consequence, one neo-Nazi created a YouTube video featuring a number of the named journalists, with explicit calls for their deaths. Following the Cider Riot attacks, he revealed the name of a leftist woman who had her vertebrae cracked by a Patriot Prayer affiliate's baton. He appeared to downplay the violence she faced, stressing that she was involved in an unrelated protest in the previous year. She was not just a victim but a political actor. Maybe she had it coming.

For Ngô and his followers, it is the left that is a priori violent, spectacularized in media myth-making about antifa™. The reality is that antifascist protest, even when confrontational, is generally intended as an act of community defense against far-right violence and hate. When, as was the case in Portland, a notoriously violent, racist hate group returns to your hometown, threatening further violence, it is both reasonable and righteous to call for defensive and bold protest action. Yet, when a minor Twitter star reframes melted ice cream as a weapon, the real site of violence is obscured, further legitimizing the very real victimization of marginalized community members.

Cementing the Enemy

Antifa itself has become a punching bag in a way few could have predicted. It's not a particularly new social movement or protest practice; networks like Anti-Fascist Action and Anti-Racist Action long predated Trump's rise. In the late 1980s and early '90s, Anti-Fascist Action created mass mobilizations to break up the extreme right National Front and, later, the British National Party, around England, often engaging in mass conflicts with fascists in spectacles much larger than what we typically see in the U.S. Likewise, Anti-Racist Action went into areas where neo-Nazis were recruiting in the U.S., such as music venues, and physically removed them. Today's antifa iterations inherit parts of these well recognized strains of resistance. But as the GOP's base has moved to the right, increasingly intersecting with white nationalism, a wider swathe of people have been pulled into antifascist conflict. For the growing far-right media and political sphere, the idea of being a target of antifascist protest is intolerable.

Ngô and his cadre put public pressure on Donald Trump to make a statement about the Portland attack. When he finally did, the president pushed the exact buttons that the far-right hoped he would. "They better hope that the opposition to antifa decides not to mobilize," said Trump, "[antifa] don't go after our construction workers who love us. They don't go after the police. They live, like, in the basement of their mom's home. Their arms are this big [skinny]." The narrative has been cemented, that antifa is both dangerous and weak, a threat and an embarrassment. Antifascist motivations are wholly obscured in such a narrative, and far-right violence ever more legitimized. "They never go after Bikers for Trump," he said, neglecting the fact that antifa groups have been in conflict with that very demographic, the violent "independent Trumpist" base, the missing link between conservatism and white nationalism.

The facts remain: antifascists are not responsible for the kind of violence their opponents perpetrate. It's not even the same league, not even part of the same universe. Far-right organizations head into liberal towns so as to inspire violence, both their own and whatever they think they can stoke in their opposition by creating threatening situations in which antifascist organizers are forced to respond. This is the organizing strategy of the Proud Boys, it is journalistic strategy of figures like Ngô. Even if the two parties do not coordinate with one another, they are of the same spirit.

The far-right increasingly sets the tone for the rest of the U.S. media-sphere, in which their talking points become our fulcrums of debate, and Andy Ngô's oh-so-brutal attack by antifa was one such moment, designed, as it was, for mass social media sharing.

It would be wrong to suggest that Andy Ngô invented this model, but we've been played by this grift for years. Social media algorithms are all developed to serve and fuel an outrage model that systematically restructured our attention spans to respond to the kind of content that Alt Light personalities deliver. And in these boom/bust, rise/fall, grow/collapse cycles, why not make your point as egregious as possible? I mean, it certainly *seems* like antifa attacks all journalists and conservatives and America itself. Only a brave and important bearer of truth would point this out, and so you should probably donate. We have to keep fighting, do you know what would happen if we gave in? They would be at your door next.

* * *

As this volume is being put together, Andy Ngô has turned himself into a right-wing superstar. He has continued to sound the alarm of "antifa," publishing articles in the mainstream press over the preceding year alleging that different murders were committed by antifascists despite the lack of any real evidence pointing to this notion. As the Black Lives Matter protests erupted across the country after the police killing of George Floyd in Minneapolis, Minnesota, Ngô went into high gear calling this an "antifa" insurgence and blaming any form of aggressive protest either on antifascist organizers or using racially charged rhetoric to demonize largely Black demonstrators. For months Ngô strung together accusations of nefarious plotting, singling out reporters and activists, posting mug shots and personal information, and even alleging that different violent assailants were "antifa" without evidence.

In the midst of this cauldron of right-wing agitation, Donald Trump's allegations of "antifa terrorism," and the growth of white vigilantes trying to stop the protests, he filed a lawsuit against Rose City Antifa and several activists in the Portland area. The petition shows no evidence that any of the individuals named, or the organizations cited, had anything to do with his assault, and it is instead a list of identifiable activists who he is politically horrified by. All of this was done with calls to donate money to him, both for his journalism and his tort activism, and all of it preceding his summer book release. This volume, called *Unmasked: Inside Antifa's Radical Plan to Destroy Democracy*, promises to reveal the "truth" about antifa, complete with "a trove of documents obtained by the author, published for the first time ever." I was also pulled into this train of threats as Ngô used a video of me captured by the far-right organization Project Veritas of a book talk I gave to activists in 2017. He said that this was evidence I was a member of Rose City Antifa and that it was "radicalization training," despite the talk simply being about the history of the Alt Right and its roots in the German Conservative Revolution, the European New Right, and paleoconservatism. Dozens of reporters and writers were drawn into this, and the independent journalists who were documenting the police violence against protesters nightly were special targets of Ngô's constant barrage of accusations. As vigilante violence increased, and Proud Boys and other far-right groups staged attacks on Black Lives Matter protesters, Ngô continued the wave of fear-mongering. The belief that "antifa" were a new force of social disorder, that they were destabilizing society and engaged in frenetic violence was used as an excuse for escalations all across the country. The trumped up fears of antifa led to federal officer incursions all across the U.S., the heavy use of crowd control methods, including toxic CS gas attacks, and the growth a "vigilante identity" where armed combatants were committing to extra-judicial attacks on antiracist protesters. Dozens of attacks on protesters took place around the country, from a bomb attack and group beatings in Portland to over 104 car attacks on demonstrations between May and September of 2020 to the murder of activists by militia associate Kyle Rittenhouse in Wisconsin.[8] The culture of fear and victimhood, of which Ngô is the most recognizable agitator, has led to more violence than I could have imagined when I first wrote this article, and there are few signs that this violence is in decline. Just as Donald Trump builds vigilante consciousness as a way of bonding with his base and he cares little for the subsequent violence, as Ngô amasses thousands of dollars and Twitter followers he gives little attention to the violence and victimization his strategy inspires.

The incongruence of this portrayal of antifascists, the racist undertones of his treatment of Black Lives Matter, and the dangerous conspiracy theorizing running at the center of this rhetoric, has done little to dull Ngô's popularity. As a proxy for the far-right, he is the stand in for the fear and anxiety that conservative whites have about these social movements, and he validates those concerns with wild accusations and a link where you can donate.

The near uniform repudiation of Ngô has created a cultural alignment between reporters, academics, activists, attorneys, and other public personalities. The dialectic has grown, where his "strategy of tension" is also created a unified wave against him. As he continues his crusade against "antifa"—a word he uses for any political movement that scares him—he is likely building up the consciousness to finally undermine the callout-to-troll pipeline he has built over the past several years.

Wolf Age

No lone wolf truly acts alone.

The Walmart in El Paso was crowded on August 3, 2019 with back-to-school shoppers when a shooter opened fire and murdered twenty people, including a five-month-old infant. Just moments before, a twisted manifesto, titled "An Inconvenient Truth," was posted online.

"I am against race mixing because it destroys genetic diversity and creates identity problems," the manifesto posted on 8Chan reads. The "inconvenient truth" it refers to is the theory of "great replacement" taken from the title of the manifesto by the gunman who took forty-nine lives in a live streamed attack on a New Zealand mosque on March 15, 2019. The fear of demographic replacement, or "white genocide" comes from a conspiracy theory that suggests that white people are being pushed into non-existence by miscegenation, immigration, and low birth rates. In the words of the Walmart shooter, "Actually, the Hispanic community was not my target before I read The Great Replacement [...] In short, America is rotting from the inside out, and peaceful means to stop this seems nearly impossible."

El Paso came right on the heels of a mass shooting in Gilroy, California on July 28, 2019, where another white supremacist, infatuated with the social Darwinist book *Might is Right*, took an AK-47 to a crowd of festival goers, killing three people, including two children. Gilroy occurred right after Christchurch, New Zealand, which came right after the shootings at Chabad of Poway synagogue on April 27, 2019 and Tree of Life on October 27, 2018. Towns like Gilroy and El Paso, Charlottesville and Charleston, become forever impacted by these instances of cruel violence. Their names become ghosts, as if their identities have been swallowed and what remains is the visage of the worst thing they have ever seen.

Each shooting provokes the public's fascination with motivation. "We must stop the glorification of violence in our society. This includes the gruesome and grisly video games that are now commonplace," said Donald Trump in his public statement the Monday after the El Paso shooting, doing his hardest to avoid the real causes. In past years, motivations like bullying, mental illness, family problems, and even social collapse were thrown around.

This story is different. We know what is motivating the killings. The shooter wrote 2,300 words to explain himself.

And he was not the only one. This rapid succession of mass shootings is happening as hate crimes and global temperatures rise, inequality and precarity loom, and fascism returns to the political stage. There is an eschatology to current affairs under these conditions. People feel the sense of a looming apocalypse because the institutions that once protected them are falling apart. In this moment of crisis we can choose how to respond, with solidarity or with barbarism.

This is Guerilla War

This is the moment of lone-wolf violence where white supremacist anger has found a tactic. Even in eras of extreme racial terror, the perpetrators tried to espouse their crimes and lynchings with a logical jurisprudence, as if they were punishment for imagined crimes. Today, the shooters revel in their violent acts, as if the current state of the world is sufficient self-evidence that executions are necessary.

8Chan and forums like it have given a platform to this process. Radicalization through formal leadership, white nationalist publications, or organizations has limitations. Fascist media outlets can argue for mass violence, but they can be easily catalogued and marginalized, and social media sites usually take them down. 8Chan, on the other hand, has a smokescreen of millions of anonymous postings providing cover for racist propaganda. So someone can be hit with a barrage of messages encouraging them to turn to violence before the public is even aware of the conversation.

"Until law enforcement, and the media, treat these shooters as part of a terrorist movement no less organized, or deadly, than ISIS or Al Qaeda, the violence will continue," Robert Evans, a journalist with the collective Bellingcat, warns in "The El Paso Shooting and the Gamification of Terror." "There will be more killers, more gleeful celebration of body counts on 8Chan, and more bloody attempts to beat the last killer's 'high score.'" And the statistics of the total deaths in U.S. mass shootings since the 1990s indicates that he is right.

There is a discernible pattern to white nationalist violence that has played out since the early twentieth century. Slightly more moderate right-wing ideologues help push more explicit fascism into the mainstream. Once they do, the fascists ride a wave of success on hot-button issues, such as integration, northern school bussing, and immigration control. These issues give way to political platforms, which allow fascism a moment of greater organizational and ideological influence. Eventually, antifascists put the squeeze on them, their own incompetence gets the better of them, their slightly more moderate counterparts betray them, and they are cast out into the wilderness. This is the moment where the fringe of the fringe picks up arms and prepares for war.

"Too many people still think of these attacks as single events, rather than interconnected actions carried out by domestic terrorists. We spend too much ink dividing them into anti-immigrant, racist, anti-Muslim, or antisemitic attacks. True, they are these things. But they are also connected with one another through a broader white power ideology," writes Kathleen Belew, the author of *Bring the War Home: The White Power Movement and Paramilitary America*, in the *New York Times*. "Likewise, too many people think that such shootings are the goal of fringe activism. They aren't. They are planned to incite a much larger slaughter by 'awakening' other people to join the movement."

The Alt Right saw the most immediate success of any white nationalist movement in the past forty years, which is why the years of decline after 2017 hit them so hard. Their influence departs significantly from traditional white nationalist movements, like the Ku Klux Klan or Aryan Nations, because they manage to reach a mass audience through social networks rather than through bland meetings at an Elks Lodge. This has made their impact even more persistent, such that, although their formal organizations and media outlets have taken a huge hit, an invisible cadre of angry young white men are still taking the ideological bait.

Operation Werewolf

In the world of neo-fascist esoterica, you might hear the term "Wolf Age" bandied about. This is the period we are supposedly living in. Wolf Age comes from the Odinic way of saying "Kali Yuga," a term appropriated by fascists from the Vedic prophecies. Kali Yuga is the last of four ages and is the stage when humanity is at its lowest form, separated from enlightenment and social bonds. Racist "Traditionalist" philosophers like the ultra-fascist Julius Evola reinterpreted this as Nazi cosplay, seeing the Kali Yuga as the end time defined by degenerate identities, particularly non-white people, women, and secularized Jews. The Kali Yuga, or Wolf Age, has become a catch-all for the era of decline that members of the far-right think we are living in, an idea often built on paranoid delusions about the "traditional family" or "white survival."

The Wolf Age is named as such because it is when wolves emerge. Evola wrote that in the Kali Yuga, people have to become spiritual warriors and "men against time," living out their principles in total war against the system. Neoreactionaries, another form of pseudointellectual fascism popular in Silicon Valley and found in abundance on 8Chan, claim that these spiritual warriors need to recede from the Kali Yuga, build subsistence farms, and wait for the Golden Age to return.

Other men can't wait. Instead, they emerge as wolves, visioning themselves as soldiers fighting for their tribe. In a world where the fate of "your people" is on the line, little else can matter. White genocide is a fable told to gain recruits and illicit impulsivity. It determines the course of people's lives and adds to their despair.

This white panic has been years in the making but is only now beginning to reach a critical mass. In 2001, Pat Buchanan, a figure at the heart of the American conservative movement and a check-in station for people on their way to full-blown white nationalism, released *Death of the West*. The book posits that America is losing its identity due to "mass immigration," the de-emphasis on Christianity, and the move towards multiculturalism. It is no accident how nearly it replicates the title of Oswald Spengler's 1922 book *The Decline of the West*, a German conservative revolutionary book that set about a nationalist worldview in Europe and helped solidify this persistent gothic fantasy that the "West" is under assault and must be defended at all costs.

"We may deny the existence of ethnonationalism, detest it, condemn it. But this creator and destroyer of empires and nations is a force infinitely more powerful than globalism, for it engages the heart. Men will die for it. Religion, race, culture and tribe are the four horsemen of the coming apocalypse," Buchanan writes in his 2011 book *Suicide of a Superpower*. He places ethnic nationalism right where he wants it, as the essential driving force of geopolitics.

"We are trying to create a nation that has never before existed, of all the races, tribes, cultures and creeds of Earth, where all are equal. In this utopian drive for the perfect society of our dreams we are killing the real country we inherited—the best and greatest country on earth."

The identitarian movement, which is the European version of the Alt Right, has created a mass movement targeting migrants and refugees. The identitarians have reframed history as an ethnic struggle so as to subvert the way participants see themselves and their mission.

"We are returning to the archaic, that is, the eternal condition of mankind, which the brief parenthesis of 'modernity' made us forget, in other words, the rivalry of peoples, of ethnic and cultural blocs and of civilisations," claims Guillaume Faye, one of the perennial leaders of the European New Right, in his manifesto titled *Why We Fight*.

Buchanan has been joined by a whole range of authors and figures that exist in the grey area between the GOP and something else, sometimes called the Alt Light, sometimes national populists, and sometimes simply the people who take genocidal ideas and coat them in Americana.

The stories here, whether by Spengler, or Buchanan, or on 8Chan all send the same message: White people are finite. They have finite land, finite cultural space, finite populations. And finite time to do something about it. This is not a proposition that results in public policy or seasoned debate; it demands the kind of action that the shooters know the public would condemn but they imagine history would venerate. Sometimes you have to become a wolf to protect the flock.

That Liberal Media and Motivations

These shootings are always covered in the same way by media outlets: placing the individual front and center. The shooter is the center of the news stories, and the police, reporters, and community are charged with the task of getting to the heart of why they did it. In the better stories, the survivors are there too, but understanding personal motivation is still key: Who are they? What were they thinking? What drove them to it? Fascism is not about mental illness, but about ideas and anger. While the reporting will certainly talk about the influence of white nationalist movements, they still focus on how a shooter drove nine hours to El Paso to kill, and went into Walmart because he was lost and hungry.

In the wake of a violent attack, the news is at the mercy of law enforcement, who sets the tone for how a crime is dealt with. The social factors that lead to these events mean nothing in a courtroom and are often missing from the reporting.

In a letter to Franz Mehring, Friedrich Engels writes that "ideology is a process accomplished by the so-called thinker consciously, it is true, but with a false consciousness. The real motive forces impelling him remain unknown to him; otherwise it simply would not be an ideological process. Hence he imagines false or seeming motive forces."

We often understand lone wolf shootings as the act of a single individual, without seeing the structural and ideological forces taking place behind their backs. But we also implicitly understand that when a lone wolf killer is acting on white nationalist ideas, they are never truly alone. To explain that people often seek formal connections between the killer and white nationalist organizations, yet in an era where formalized organizations are becoming less central to political and social action, the effort could be in vain.

This does not mean, however, that these shootings are simply outbursts of the deranged. They are part and parcel of a white insurgency that has found its voice in an emerging fascism. There are people responsible for this beyond the shooters themselves. White supremacy is real and undergirds the rise of mass shootings. White nationalism has created an impetus for violence, teaching the how and the why by building an ideology, an apocalyptic scenario, and a method of action. One person pulled the trigger, but thousands took part in reconfiguring their worldview. It is therefore important to reject these singular narratives about the individual and see it in its larger context. The shooting is one moment in a guerrilla war that white nationalism has staged with all of us as combatants.

"If men define situations as real, they are real in their consequences," wrote William and Dorothy Thomas.[1] This era of lone-wolf killings is a sign of where we are at in the U.S. and what we can expect for the future. The Armageddon imagined by white nationalists is one of their own making, but we all have to live in it if they continue to try to make it real.

First as Tragedy, Then as Farce

Shortly after the attack, and when the casualty numbers were still being calculated, the Lt. Governor of Texas Dan Patrick released this warning to antifa: "Stay out of El Paso. Stay out of Texas [. . .] scratch Texas off your map and don't come in [. . .] it is not the time and place for them to come at any time [. . .] stay out of Texas." This comes directly after Texas Senator Ted Cruz introduced a resolution to declare antifa a "domestic terrorist organization." The spring of 2019 saw antifa panic reach new heights. While the body count for the white nationalists piles up, antifa is charged with minor scuffles at protests. The threat of white nationalist violence is, right now, at its absolute peak, yet we live in a world of inversion. Right-wing rhetoric has painted the left as the terrorists.

In a subsequent House Homeland Security Committee hearing, FBI's Assistant Director for Counterterrorism Michael McGarrity acknowledged that nearly 90 percent of terrorist plots under federal investigation came from the far-right, yet the agency makes no particular distinction between left-wing and right-wing violence, lumping anti-racist activists together with neo-Nazis.

"U.S. law enforcement doesn't do enough about violent racists because as an institution, it itself is violently racist and contains white supremacists in its ranks," says Natasha Lennard in *The Intercept*. "The new categories give the FBI further cover for the same bad practices."

When Trump came into office, one of the first moves he made—maybe out of spite for Obama—was to shut down the Countering Violent Extremism Program, which allocated $10 million a year to fund organizations fighting white nationalism, including a $400,000 annual grant to Life After Hate, an organization that tries to get people out of white nationalist organizations. The Department of Homeland Security's Office of Community Partnerships was also cut to a small fraction of what it was before, further tamping down the possible interventions by law enforcement that could actually stop white supremacist murders. The trumped up fears about antifa only continued into 2020 as the far-right and Trump tried to accuse the genuine uprising against police killings as "antifa," and stoke antagonistic beliefs that antifascists were a clear and present terrorism threat despite all evidence to the contrary.

Since the 1990s there has been a nationwide shift in priorities from the focus on the radical right to a cynical focus on targeting Muslim immigrants and left-wing agitators. The radical right is Trump's base and making enemies out of the left and people of color is better political theater come election time.

At the same time, the institutions that help incubate this violence remain unchecked because there is really no way to check them. 8Chan is a literal safe space to signal your rage, and it takes real world antagonism that comes from white nationalist propaganda and Trump's dog whistles to compress them into their purest form: a mass shooting.

"The El Paso shooter's manifesto was filled with dread for the future, including his own. These fears have been stoked by Trump, while 8chan has given them a specific expression in the form of a public massacre," counter-far-right researcher Spencer Sunshine told me. "These murders will continue regularly as long as Trump is in office and 8chan is online."

8Chan soon went offline because Cloudflare, which provided the security services that keeps websites like 8Chan online, cut the cord on the site. 8Chan was then dealing with service outages as cyber-attacks are common, which may limit its life. Now you can find it on back channel URLs, and its founder has roundly demanded for it to be taken down, and yet its role is still central in stoking the far-right. Now it is the primary place to find "Q-drops," messages from the supposed apocalyptic prophet of the Q-Anon movement that is driving the American right off a conspiracy cliff. Trump also suggested that more aggressive action should be taken against white supremacist terrorism, an unlikely statement if there ever was one. There is an inherent limitation to both as no one expects Trump to provide any meaningful solutions for stifling the growing white nationalist movement, and if 8Chan is shut down the admins can simply hop to another service, and another, and another. Liberal solutions lack the teeth to take out white nationalism at its roots because they fail to understand that this exists in every community and radicalization happens from a thousand sources at once.

The Death of the West

"As the earth thus becomes crowded with a corrupt population, whoever among any of the social classes shows himself to be the strongest will gain political power."

—Srimad Bhagavatam 12.2.7

As the pace and scope of fascist mass murders increase, the counter narrative about frightful antifascists surges alongside it. The reality of the violent threats we face is met with denial. The rhetoric that inspires violence has the power to grow in the years ahead. If "Send Her Back"—the frequent chant at Trump rallies that refers to Ilhan Omar—is now part of an acceptable political theater, what's next?

There is a certain reality to the Wolf Age prophecy: we are living in the "death of the west." The decline of the economic hegemony of Western countries is real. And so too falls white hegemony piece by piece. We are the generation of collapse where every falsehood about how the world works (economically, ecologically, politically) is turned on its head. What is not yet decided is whether the breaking apart of capitalist hegemony will be liberatory or despotic. Meanwhile the masses of our coworkers, our friends, and our neighbors are polarized in both directions, making even the most banal of places unsafe.

White supremacy is the autoimmune disease of the working class. It can overpower instincts and make a working-class person think they are fighting against competition and scarcity when really they are killing off their only defense: class struggle. As the crisis deepens, which it undoubtedly will, white supremacy will attempt to offer racist ideology as an answer to working class problems. This could lead to an insurgency that, with the toxic mix of national populism, conspiracy theories, economic implosion, and 8Chan, could be a recipe for explosive violence.

Crisis creates a break with the normal flow of politics and identity. Ideology redirects that break toward its prescribed narrative. This is why when a white worker looks at their bleak future, they are presented with a number of ideological ways forward. They could blame the bosses and the capitalist class who has created perpetual instability through deregulated global capitalism and find socialism as the solution. They could also look at the same precarious life and decide to punch down, to blame non-white workers. White supremacy drives this undying appeal to the basest instincts of the white masses, creating a machine running entirely on resentment and blame rather than the ability to see who is really causing our woes and why.

"The problem is that the desire to liberate and the desire to oppress are the same fucking desire," Kevin Van Meter, the author of *Guerrillas of Desire*, told me once late at night years ago. He was echoing Gilles Deleuze and Felix Guattari, who write in *Anti-Oedipus* that "the masses were not innocent dupes; at a certain point, under a certain set of conditions, they wanted fascism." That desire is inside us and can go a number of ways depending on the conditions we create.

Whether it is Donald Trump, Alex Jones, the churches we grew up in, our fathers, or our friends, a culture of violence has been teaching us that the only way to be truly free is to accept an ideology of tyranny. That lie has become so persistent that it doesn't take 2,300 words to understand why someone brought a rifle into a crowd. The given script was simply played out with brutal efficiency.

Within hours of the El Paso shooting another shooter opened fire in a popular nightlife spot in Dayton, Ohio, killing nine people. There is no reason to think this will stop.

The lines for this type of violence have been drawn, and every economic factor that inspires it has grown. In the face of this apocalypse we could easily embrace nihilism, a strategy of emotional survival, but that misses the real story. The conditions of crisis are also creating an insurgent counterculture that demands a different world. A generation who grew up with this crisis-driven inequality and injustice refuse it on a mass scale.

"I was just thinking about if I had a child and, you know, if I wasn't around, how I would want another man to react to seeing my child running around. So I just jumped fast and got as many kids as I could," said Glendon Oakley, a bystander who saw a huge crowd of kids in and outside of the mall where the El Paso shooting occurred, and decided to take action.

"I didn't even think. I just grabbed as many kids as I could and ran five stores down to the exit," he told *Task and Purpose*. "We got there and ran into a whole batch of police pointing their guns at us. I wasn't focused on myself, and I wasn't focused on my surroundings... I was just focused on those kids."

"I got all the people that I could, I even found a little girl that was missing from her parents, and I got her, too. I tried to get as many people as I could out," said Leslie, a Walmart employee who was saving kids, to a local news station.

While the fragmentation is growing, so is the passionate response of people in communities across the country who refuse to join white supremacist terror and commit instead to mutual aid. This is the choice offered to us in this moment of crisis. We have to make choices about which impulse to indulge.

While there is a tendency to see legislative reforms as the solutions to the problem, it is the committed struggle of people in communities that has the ability to seed something different. Community support, defense, solidarity, and organizing has the ability to not only confront the far-right, but also undo the conditions that lead to its growth in the first place. This doesn't mean that reforms are useless, but they are not the end. We are.

The metaphor of wolves and sheep has become popular in white nationalist corners of the Internet, using "alpha male" analogies for the zero sum game they imagine the world to be. In the period of the Kali Yuga, you are either one or the other. This dynamic of superior and inferior, they argue, will drive us into a restoration of the world's proper order. That is the world we live in because it is the world that white supremacist terrorists live in, but we don't have to leave it like that.

Instead we can commit to a vision of a different world entirely, one made more possible today because of the cracks in the current social system, and we can spread it. Just like Oakley, we have to move with our herding instinct to save as many lives as possible, even if that feels alien to the situation around us, and step forward to build institutions of safety, support, and interconnectedness. Without our action, the far-right will write a horror script for the future.

A History of Violence

For jury deliberation to finish in six hours there had to be consensus from the start. James Alex Fields had become the object of universal public hatred when he drove his Dodge Challenger into a crowd of antifascist protesters in Charlottesville, killing Heather Heyer. He was pronounced guilty on six counts, including first degree murder, earning him life in prison. In the nearly year and a half since Fields plowed his car down Fourth Street, he has remained almost catatonically silent in his cell, awaiting trial while every Alt Right personality screamed to every media outlet that would listen.

Antiracist protesters, including Heyer's mother, packed the courtroom every day. After the verdict was announced, local organizer Rosie Parker led a public chant of "you will not replace us," employing the white nationalist refrain made famous at Charlottesville, a reference to "white genocide" conspiracy theories about "white replacement." Other survivors of the attack, like Marcus Martin, who had his leg shattered when Fields's car sped into the demonstration, were there, using the trial as a moment of collective accountability for the city.

Fields had no one there. This was not surprising for a noncelebrity racist, a person who knows no one and who no one knows. While he remained silent, white nationalists used him as pundit fodder, nearly placing a cross on his back as he became the image of their victimization by liberal society. After trashing Heather Heyer in every conceivable way, from claiming her weight was responsible for her death to simply applauding murder, they focused on the claims of self-defense that Fields's attorneys proffered to the jury.

Their logic works like this: with protesters all around, and emotions high, Fields was frightened, had an explosive reaction, and slammed on the gas as a way of getting out of the situation. White nationalist websites like Red Ice Creations have gone to painstaking lengths to prove this, including sifting through available video footage frame-by-frame and offering conjecture about Fields's motives.

When the guilty verdict came down the Alt Right commentary continued, not so much out of empathy with Fields, but rather with concern about how it will affect them as a movement.

"There does not seem to be any reasonable evidence put forward that he engaged in murderous intent," said Alt Right founder Richard Spencer to the Associated Press. A bold statement for someone who neither witnessed the murder nor was present when the evidence was delivered in the courtroom. The reporter of the story later claimed she did not know who Spencer was.

Christopher Cantwell, who became famous for his frothing racism during a *Vice* documentary on Charlottesville, only later to be caught sobbing into his camera phone when he discovered he was facing charges, went into a rage on the white-nationalist social media website Gab.

"The show trial and CONviction of James Fields is merely a symbolic victory for you, which you'll forget in short order," said Cantwell. "Knowing that any of us could be next, it will drive us toward your complete and total destruction, as a matter of necessity for our very survival."

Across the white nationalist blog and podcast universe, there is a central narrative, that Fields was railroaded by "antifa" in the streets and the courtroom. No white nationalist will get a fair trial because of Fields's act, which was not coordinated, not representative of the movement, and not his fault.

"No One Wanted This to Happen…"

In the case of Fields's crash, the first point that the white nationalists who organized Unite the Right pivot to is that, of course, this was not sanctioned behavior. They wanted to hold a rally, hear a few speeches. It's as simple as that. Even if they were to take responsibility for the sprawling street fights that followed, the kind of blatant bloodthirst that Fields is accused of is totally counterproductive for their movement. While the white nationalist leadership will live and die by this talking point, Discord chat logs revealed by Unicorn Riot show that those involved in the actual planning of the event were ready and prepared for possibly lethal violence against counterprotesters.

As white nationalist leaders like Richard Spencer have maintained for decades, public acts of extreme violence, often taken in isolation and with little control by formal organizations, set the racialist movement back. And it did, in catastrophic ways, as was seen with the radical decline of the Alt Right following Charlottesville. They want a movement that can transform their militancy into mass struggle, with a focus on conversation, culture, and meeting their target demographics where they are at. Plowing a car into a crowd of people does a lot of things, but it rarely moves the unconverted.

The Alt Right then shifted to focus on Fields himself, who he was, and whether he really was representative of their growing ranks. Fields, for his part, played the outsider well. With few connections to movement leadership, or with friends or anyone else for that matter, his history was one of violent aggression against his mother and what teachers refer to as a fascination with the Third Reich. In place of focus on white supremacy, they draw attention to his alienation, painting him as another socially awkward triggerman lingering in the back of the classroom. It is the conditions of the modern world that dictate this behavior, rendering his violence essentially "apolitical." After all, ideas never have sway over such a deviant mind.

More than that, his actions may even have been justified, they imply. A common rhetorical tactic on the right has been to blame violence, from Proud Boy gang assaults to Patriot militia armed standoffs, on their leftist opposition. Responsibility rests with the protesters who surrounded Fields's car, or were even just near his car, which more or less indicts just about all protests that do anything other than yell at flag-waving neo-Nazis from yards away. In such comments, we glimpse how the Alt Right views itself: beset on all sides by tyranny, about to be destroyed unless someone chooses to act.

A Man against Time

This logic of blaming the opposition is not new to Richard Spencer or the Alt Right, but can be noted throughout the history of the white nationalist movement, always an insurgency that is, at least publicly, rejected by the surrounding communities. The image of the lone racist killer, more triggered by their "outsider" experience than the organized racialist movement, is an outlier, as they see it, far from the mainstream of their movement. Instead of blaming fascists you can blame any number of other social factors, from drug addiction to mental illness, all catalyzed by the unfair liberal hordes who refused to let him be himself.

On October 27, Robert Bowers headed into the L'Simcha synagogue in Pittsburgh ready to kill. He stated openly on Gab that he was motivated by perceived Jewish involvement in refugee resettlement. While this is a sober statement directly in line with the antisemitic conspiracies that are at the foundation of the white nationalist worldview, he was again disowned by the Alt Right media as a person out of step with their movement. And besides, they scoffed, the refugees the Jews are bringing in are even worse.

On June 17, 2015 when Dylann Roof opened fire in the Emanuel African Methodist Episcopal Church in Charleston, South Carolina, white nationalist leaders like James Edwards and Jared Taylor went to great lengths to point out both that he was out of his mind and that he was lucid enough to be reacting to the threat of non-white people in the U.S. Roof was clear in his manifesto that he was inspired by the "race realist" rantings and misleading race and crime statistics put forward by the Council of Conservative Citizens.

A fringe member of an already fringe white-nationalist movement commits an act of seemingly random mass violence, which, because it is non-programmatic and not a part of a larger movement project, is disowned by the white nationalist movement and described as completely out of character for their community. The problem is that no matter what their leadership says, no matter what their organizing priorities actually are, it is the most reliable form of action that the white nationalist movement produces.

There exists a reliable pattern inside of American white nationalism. Rising to visibility through hot-button issues, fascists will see a moment of skyrocketing influence and use it to latch onto a slightly more moderate right-wing movement so as to gain influence and recruit. During the Civil Rights Movement, explicit racialists and the Ku Klux Klan used the pro-segregationist movement and the White Citizens Councils to gain respectability with Jim Crow Southerners and to expand the Overton Window with regards to race. In the 1980s, it was paleoconservatism, a more "Old Right" version of Republicanism that rejected the internationalist and neoliberal Neoconservatism, that gave the extreme right access to the conservative base, particularly through figures like Pat Buchanan. More recently, it has been the Internet-celebrity cadre of Civic Nationalists, often referred to as the Alt Light, consisting of people like Jack Posobiec, Milo Yiannopoulos, Alex Jones, and Lauren Southern. Open fascism is generally seen as contemptible by most of the public when presented on its own. With a friendlier partner, however, fascists can slowly normalize their politics and grow their ranks.

Inevitably, the moderates reject the radicals, and the fascists lose their access to the mainstream. This process leads the movement to collapse much of its public-facing infrastructure, devolving into desperation as infighting reconfigures the once hopeful core. It is then that individuals, usually isolated both in their personal life and from positions of leadership and respect in the white nationalist movement, decide to take desperate action. The rhetoric of white dispossession is so extreme that recruits are driven to an evangelical frenzy, and when the movement loses its political viability there are few places for these ideologues to put their burning rage. When electoralism, mass movements, and above-ground action fails, there is always a gun. Now is the time for monsters.

They Want a Lone Gunman

While this model of fringe-actor violence is implicit to the white nationalist movement, it has also been explicitly advocated by parts of the movement. Coming off of a series of attempts to create a counterstate insurgency both in the Klan and paramilitary-styled white power groups, self-styled guerilla race-soldier Louis Beam penned a famous essay called "Leaderless Resistance" arguing that white racialists should take autonomous action against targets rather than join stable organizations easily infiltrated by federal agents. White Aryan Resistance founder Tom Metzger wrote "Laws of the Lone Wolf" arguing that racist soldiers can take to the streets, seeking out targets for direct action, focusing on a strategy of violent consciousness raising rather than coordinated movement building. And their ideas worked as "seemingly random" attacks ensued, from skinheads on street corners to shootings at Sikh temples and Jewish community centers. Metzger became persona non grata after his organization encouraged members of Portland skinhead gangs to murder someone with a baseball bat, and he went on to become a ghost commenting on the unfairness of the system. None of these crimes were part of an official strategy outlined in the documents of a chartered organization, because they didn't need to be. The white nationalist movement was more powerful, meaning more violent, when it was diffuse.

White nationalist organizations prepare people, sometimes members and sometimes their periphery, for violence, but will never take responsibility for it. By creating a narrative of persecution and survival, by depicting insurrection as the only viable option, and by nursing impulsive brutality, they intentionally foster an internal fire, the only logical consequence of which is violence. This is, in part, because of the unwillingness of their leadership to reckon with the actual consequences of their work. When Richard Spencer talks about "peaceful ethnic cleansing" and then stands in utter shock that his words inspire counter-demonstrations, that his neighbors in Virginia or Montana want him out, he refuses to see what is plain for the rest of us. This is also a result of their tribalism and ideology. They simply don't understand how their ideas lead to violence since they are simply so rational, their community so logical.

When a member of the white nationalist movement then puts thought into action, their fringe status is employed as defense. Fields may not have taken action if it was not for the crushing loneliness of his life, a void that allowed for his white identity to be activated by nationalists reaching out from a message board. That quest for identity has always been their strongest selling point, just as the most distraught have always been their most ardent actors. It is certainly easier to be the Last Rhodesian than a mere part of a lost generation unable to find a career or community.

Their disavowal of violence rests almost solely, then, on the fact that it is "unsanctioned," that it did not come down by command through the organizational ranks. The problem with this is, through the history of white supremacist terrorist organization, rarely did the violence of the membership result from official dictum. Much of the historic Klan violence throughout the South, particularly from the Civil Rights Movement on, was technically not a part of official Klan activity, but simply its members working together based on relationships and ideas forged in the Klan. In the pogroms that hit New York City and Boston in 1942–43, the Catholic teens involved were largely inspired by the Christian Front organized by Father Charles Coughlin, but they were self-organized, their action the logical result of what was argued for in private meetings and radio addresses. The Aryan Nations National Congress made it clear that their movement was peaceful, all while helping The Order to begin bank robberies and assassinations, mobilizing the Aryan Brotherhood in prisons, and training paramilitaries who would later take action against communities of color and law enforcement alike.

While these organizations will publicly commit to nonviolence, and sometimes even privately urge a different style of organizing, in their rhetoric, behavior, and personal affinity, they encourage this type of autonomous violence. This creates a model of extra-judicial violence, tied to the members but not the organization, allowing for a sort of plausible deniability.

There is nothing abnormal about James Alex Fields's decision to hit the gas and end the life of Heather Heyer. This is how it works. While Richard Spencer may think that Fields has been railroaded, Spencer himself is responsible for creating the conditions and molding the actions that took place since it was the logical conclusion of the Alt Right's rhetoric and vision. There is no aberration at play since spontaneous acts of extreme terror are an organic feature of their movements, no matter how peaceful their public face. With the increasing number of these moments of explosive ferocity, it should be apparent that the Alt Right is no less violent than earlier generations brandishing a swastika or a robe. Their violence lies in their ability to sway the fringe, to create conditions for attack, and to mobilize the public rather than just formal members, and with the Alt Right they were able to get rid of formal organizations (for the most part) in favor of a radicalized multitude. Without the barriers of organizations and optics, they can do anything, and now they are.

If it wasn't Fields then it would have been somebody else. Their movement has been punctuated by failed men seeking martyrdom each time their organizing work implodes. This is not a flaw in their system; their model works as intended. Fields sacrificed himself in an emotive explosion, spurred to action by the movement which will no longer provide him support, and Richard Spencer will use his name to gain donations for the next public rally. There is no end for this process: it has followed the peaks and valleys of the white nationalist movement since its infancy.

White nationalist violence has to be understood within the complicated social framework in which it exists, a framework intended to manipulate the fringes of the movement to take on the dirty work and carry out its underlying methodology. The fact that Fields may not have been a formal member of one of its coalition organizations, or even a part of a tangible friendship circle, does not take away from his membership in a movement. Instead, he is the perfect image of what their movement creates, the clearest example of who they are and what they do.

So Fields is guilty. They are all guilty.

Contested Space

Even the name Alsarath comes soaked in the blood of the lore.

"It's the last phase of the moon before the new moon, the last little sliver. The new moon is a good time to set new intentions and bring new energy into your life. Alsarath, then, is for letting go. Alsarath is a time of introspection and rejection," says Margaret Killjoy, half of the two-piece neofolk band Alsarath. Killjoy started the project with Jack Olg in 2019, after both had been tinkering in various doom and black metal projects and were looking to integrate some folk songs. Wouldn't it be cool to start an explicitly antifascist neofolk band?[1]

The novelty of such a question may be lost on some people, but it could stop others cold. Neofolk is a post-Industrial romantic genre that repurposes folk sounds with dark themes and styles borrowed from metal, goth, and other ephemeral genres, but it was a creation almost entirely of the boots-and-braces type. It is essentially a fascist music form intended to launder in fantastical ideas about white history while maintaining a plausible deniability about the artist's intentions. Since their earliest appearances, bands like Sol Invictus and Death in June have been some of the prime targets of antifascist organizers across the world.

An antifascist neofolk band may seem like a contradiction in terms, but Alsarath weren't the first ones to try this heterodox confliction. There is a growing legion of neofolk, dark folk, and similar genre'd bands that are identifying themselves as antifascist. Though this genre of music has been instrumental to the far-right, it has its own appeal and value to people on the opposite extreme: celebrating ancestral traditions, agrarian living, pagan religions, Indigenous folkways, opposition to empire, anti-patriarchy, utopian thinking, fantasy, spirit, and dreams. They are romantics in their own right, writing a totally new world into being while dressed in black and plucking electric mandolins.

"I'm drawn to black metal and neofolk precisely because they incorporate aesthetics based on those values. This wasn't a conscious choice, of course. I like the music that I like. But in retrospect, it seems obvious that these values attract me. As anarchists, we interact with those values too," wrote Killjoy in an essay much-cited in the antifascist neofolk scene.[2] The point here is clear: we have some stake in romantic art forms, those driven by memory and passion, and if we cede that ground to the fascists then they literally own the impulse. By taking it back or, more importantly, taking it over, we reclaim a part of ourselves that they hope to brand as theirs. What antifascist neofolk does then is say that the natural inclination towards this type of music—its aesthetics and imagery—does not tie you to the Right. Instead, that is a fascist manipulation of reality, and they do not get to define our musical tastes or our lives.

This is where the notion of contested spaces comes in. These are spaces, sometimes literal and oftentimes cultural, that can be filled by both the far-right and, well, everybody else. For many people who grew up in working-class communities, and rural spaces in particular, contested spaces are found regularly as the far-right digs in roots to recruit and build. There is often an impulse to cede that ground to the far-right, to say that the place may be definitively "owned" by white nationalists, in the way that some people write off rural America as hopelessly reactionary or decide that a genre of music must belong to them.

We saw this particularly as the fascist version of skinhead gangs expanded in the early 1980s into punk clubs and biker bars, but in reality there were antifascists on those same dance floors, and they were not willing to let their music, their neighborhood, their Ben Shermans and Doc Martens, or their watering hole be owned by this insurgent threat. So they fought it out. This often meant literally fighting, as the antiracist skinhead movement marked by Skinheads Against Racial Prejudice (SHARP) and the Baldies formed to kick Nazi punks out of neighborhoods and music venues where they recruited and threatened people.[3] It also meant taking back the cultural space: creating music that was openly antifascist, reviving politicized musical events and output, and connecting music and political work.

In the late 1970s, the Anti-Nazi League was created in Britain to stem the meteoric rise of the National Front and anti-immigrant violence. Organizers began collaborating with Rock Against Racism to pull together some of the largest antifascist demonstrations in history, ones that were built around giant concerts. Rock Against Racism was a successful model developed on contested spaces, where high profile racist behavior by artists like Eric Clapton and David Bowie, as well as the creeping neo-Nazi music scene, demanded an intervention. They made it possible (and profitable) to make open antiracism a key part of a band's identity, and in doing so push back on fascist entryism.[4]

The post-war fascist movement also had an intentional new strategy: metapolitics. This concept was incredibly important to fascist movements, which turned towards a deeply philosophical and aesthetically centered vision of fascist politics. Matthew N. Lyons defines metapolitics as activities that aim to "gradually transform political and intellectual culture as a precursor to transforming institutions and systems," rather than "organizing a mass movement to seize state power."[5] Cynthia Miller-Idriss traces this conception of metapolitics to the creation of far-right academic and intellectual institutions, saying it is "more than just ideology" because it "aims to seed the cultural changes and ideological foundation required for the public to accept the establishment of a white ethno-state."[6] Without ideological, educational, and cultural influence, the revolutionary aspirations would not be able to take hold since they would seem totally disconnected from people's potential range of political and social thinking.

Metapolitics as a concept is usually ascribed to Italian Marxist Antonio Gramsci, but that is a bit of a misnomer, and the way that metapolitics built the post-New Left fascist movement is unique. The far-right believed it had lost the cultural war for hearts and values, and so they had to play a long game with the culture to make their larger political vision even remotely possible.

There continued to be white nationalist organizations, ranging from the suit and ties to the shaved heads and swastika tattoos, but there was also a more strategic element that wanted to use cultural factors to influence the masses. For decades, the left had a strong place in art—particularly pop art like film and music—so the far-right wanted to jump into that realm as well. The goal was to build a meta-political consciousness in people so that politics had the capacity to affect change downstream. Instead of just arguing for political points, recruiting and "doing politics," they would try to change people's sense of self, their underlying values, and their emotional reality.

This builds on the work of fascist esotericist Julius Evola, who became increasingly important to fascist movements through his vision of a perennialist hierarchical world.[7] The intellectual fascist European New Right made this strategy explicit, supporting far-right philosophic work and reviving an "ethnopluralist" vision of ethnic separation, agrarianism, and a return to identitarian religious values. The rhetoric and model shifted to one more in line with the postcolonial values of the New Left, reframing the traditional turn towards empire (such as the defense of French Algeria) to that of anti-imperialism (which they say homogenized races and peoples). Instead of traditionalist racism, their language was couched in the language of socio-biology, and they used arcane arguments to detach their racism from the easily recognizable form. More than all of this, they would tell a story about who Europeans are, what defined them, and what they could be again (if we shuffle off this modern deception).[8]

This is the model that inspired Alt Right leader Richard Spencer to build his mini-empire, where he focused on creating an intellectual and artistic counterculture filled with fascist notions about race, gender, religion, and society, so that they could build up a milieu that was ready for radical social change.[9] The left's power was not in its institutions, which were proxies for physical control, but in their hegemony: they controlled our dreams. The Alt Right built its entire modus operandi on metapolitics, and figures like Daniel Friberg, an enigmatic figure at the heart of Alt Right media projects like Arktos, left the street-level fascist movement in an effort to focus entirely on this model of cultural hegemony, rather than fighting for just meager political victories.[10]

The best example of the Alt Right's metapolitics at work was neofolk, a music genre that was built on the Evolian vision of "men against time." Instead of proselytizing with didactic political songs, they would romanticize Europe's past, its paganism, its empires, its lost traditions, and create a yearning in its people. A culture began to spring up—of white youth attracted to a mythic sense of self, of racialized pagan revivals, and dramatic art forms. It spoke to them with the power that music often does, but neofolk was never upfront with its intentions—those were deeply laid in its DNA. "Europe—or rather a highly mythologized and idealized concept of Europe—is central to the ethos of apoliteic music," wrote scholar of the far-right Anton Shekhovtsov, using the word *apoliteic* to describe the absence of an overt political message where instead there are deeply philosophical ones. "For fascists, 'a secret Europe' is hidden in the interregnum, while the Europe of the 'deadly' liberal democratic order and of 'homogenizing' multicultural society triumphs. Those who feel devastated by the alleged loss of an old Europe of aristocratic hierarchy, organic ethnic-cultural community, sacrifice and heroism have nothing for it but to 'retreat into the forest' and find the answer to the current situation there."[11]

So neofolk romanticizes something that never truly existed, a nostalgic memory that was projected into our minds by the propagandistic force of white supremacy. The message of neofolk is then to mythologize Europe, to mourn the loss and to call for rebirth—the core elements Roger Griffin uses to define fascism. He calls fascism:

A genuinely revolutionary, trans-class form of anti-liberal, and in the last analysis, anti-conservative nationalism. As such it is an ideology deeply bound up with modernization and modernity, one which has assumed a considerable variety of external forms to adapt itself to the particular historical and national context in which it appears, and has drawn a wide range of cultural and intellectual currents, both left and right, anti-modern and pro-modern, to articulate itself as a body of ideas, slogans, and doctrine. In the inter-war period it manifested itself primarily in the form of an elite-led "armed party" which attempted, mostly unsuccessfully, to generate a populist mass movement through a liturgical style of politics and a programme of radical policies which promised to overcome a threat posed by international socialism, to end the degeneration affecting the nation under liberalism, and to bring about a radical renewal of its social, political and cultural life as part of what was widely imagined to be the new era being inaugurated in Western civilization. The core mobilizing myth of fascism which conditions its ideology, propaganda, style of politics and actions is the vision of the nation's imminent rebirth from decadence.[12]

And neofolk artists aren't the only ones using metapolitics to achieve their goals. Far-right comic books have been released in recent years, anime artists stump for nationalism, video game creators romanticize the Third Reich, and a pack of Nazi furries even let off a chlorine bomb at a midwestern convention. The reality is this concept of apoliteic is used by a multitude, across artistic and cultural spaces, in universities and bookstores, and it has a transformative effect that practical politics simply can't achieve on its own. We do not just live in a homogeneous shared culture, but an intersecting web of subcultures, many of which define identities even more completely than the country we live in or the church our family attended. As people construct their sense of self, what right and wrong means, how they circle together in "in-groups" and "out-groups," these spaces matter. And so these spaces are worth fighting over. As Nancy C. Love wrote, music works on the brain to trigger ecstatic responses, and politicized, particularly aggressive music acts to connect an emotional experience with political, ideological, or identity-based messaging. People internally act out scripts when listening to the music—imagine themselves as heroes in the frame presented by the music—and therefore the music can solidify influence in a way that pressing arguments or loaded prose never could. It happens in a person's body, they feel it in a transcendent way, and permitting that process to go on keeps one of the most persistent methods of radicalization intact and fiercely alive.[13]

This is why a certain intentionality has evolved as people begin to address the "fascist creep," as Alexander Reid Ross calls it, into the spaces they already inhabit.[14] When someone is inside of a subculture, or an organization with subcultural agency in particular, they have more power than they would have individually in the shifting ether of mass politics. So responses have ramifications, just as the battle over a union's internal election or a fight inside of the National Rifle Association creates ripple effects in towns across America. The emotive artistic process is one that antifascists have access to, if they choose, and so the onus doesn't have to be put on musicians to use their art as vessels for politicization. Instead, activists can propagate, support, and create space for music that has a countervision.

Soccer's United Front

In 2018, one of the most interesting stories to come out of professional sports was in the Terraces of Portland's professional soccer team, The Timbers. What most American sports do not share with their European counterparts is the culture of "football clubs," where "supporters" get together to root for their team. In Europe, this is what dominates football as a sport, as committed supporters (don't call them hooligans) join clubs to conduct a combination of performative fandom and community service. Most of their activity is apolitical; it is just a group getting together to wear swag and lead chants for their team, but not exclusively.

For years, there have been openly fascist clubs across Europe, Russia, and elsewhere, recruited in by the National Front looking for a white, working-class male base.[15] These Ultras (another term for militant supporter) have been involved in anti-immigrant, anti-Roma, and other brutal fascist activism, and violence is never far behind as a street gang culture has been cultivated along with the tribalism of team sports. Italian clubs, particularly Lazio, are notorious for this, as are Beitar from Jerusalem, Zenit in St. Petersburg, Russia, and others.[16] To counter this, there has been an even larger collection of explicitly antifascist, radical teams and supporters' clubs that are involved in political organizing, particularly in support of refugees who have been the target of fascist Ultras during resettlement of the past several years. These clubs include AS Livorno (Italy), Rayo Vallecano (Spain), and Olympique de Marseille (France), and dozens of others.[17] FC St. Pauli has become famous across the world, coming out of a squatter neighborhood in Hamburg, Germany, and tied directly to the movements that came to be known as antifa.[18]

Sports are the purest essence of a shared, working class culture, particularly when a strange sense of tribal loyalty is cultivated around the most arbitrary things: a team you like. The supporter club takes this dynamic through the stratosphere: common logos, shared chants, and even membership in an extraneous organization dedicated to fandom. This creates a contested space, both inside of the group and in the rest of the physical space (the terraces) that the club inhabits on game day.

The Timbers Army, the supporters club for the Timbers FC, had always leaned left, doing support work for refugees and with a commitment to antiracist politics they learned from explicitly politicized supporters' clubs like Gorilla FC—one of the four clubs tied to the Seattle Sounders. They took the Iron Front as one of their common logos: the downward three arrows prominent in the resistance to Nazi Germany that signify an opposition to fascism, to monarchism, and to authoritarian communism. Fascism had become a serious issue, as far-right activists had started to show up at games around the country (including the Proud Boys in New York City), and they wanted the terraces to continue to be a welcoming place for everyone. The logo would be brandished along with the dual-axes of the Timbers, and fans would put it on shirts, banners, scarves, and signage. As the surrounding culture heated up with hyperbolic fears of "antifa," Major League Soccer (MLS) decided to ban all "political imagery," and that included the Iron Front. That's when the Timbers Army declared war.

They began a series of tactical moves: boycotting chants, staging protest actions, and brandishing the symbol anyway. The league retaliated by kicking fans out of the stands, and disabused many from using their season tickets. Other supporters' clubs joined suit—everywhere from Atlanta to Chicago—and even the Timbers' key rivals in Seattle started wearing the logos, or joining in with the shared protests in the terraces. In a world known for its partisan loyalties, this was one issue they could all agree on.

The pressure mounted, and supporters threatened to pull their season tickets and stop the nightly performance where they gather in the same General Admission section of the terraces, light off smoke bombs, have a drumline, and chant together in a timed unison. It has become a staple of the aesthetics of each game. These supporters are what makes soccer, soccer. As the women's team, The Rose City Riveters, the players union, and the larger trust that propagates the supporters' clubs all stood in support of the Timbers Army, MLS was forced to the table to negotiate. The Timbers Army came together with a coalition of antiracist organizations to "educate" the league, and MLS eventually backed down and revoked the policy.

A Song of Blood and Fire

It was unusual to see the media just descend on a metal festival in Brooklyn like they did with Black Flags Over Brooklyn in February 2019, but this was a standout. In the dodgy world of extreme music, metal musicians often revel in the ambiguity that the use of shocking imagery has, but Black Flags was taking a different approach: this was explicitly antifascist, so Nazis could fuck right off.[19]

The two-day festival, which mixed black metal with grindcore and even hardcore, with bands like Racetraitor, was intended to have a particular effect. It bridged two ethoses, the "fuck you" of metal and the total refusal of bigotries in antifascism, a marriage that makes sense after the fact. The festival was the creation of anarchist music journalist Kim Kelly, who brought together years of music promotion, radical organizing, and heavy metal insider knowledge to put the festival together.

"I believe that it is important to create explicitly antifascist, anti-oppressive spaces within the metal scene, and while the thriving leftist metal Twitter is a wonderful development and a community in and of itself, we're not going to win this war by logging on," says Kelly, who got the idea after missing a show by antifascist black metal band Dawn Ray'd and decided to just make one herself.[20]

There is a symbiotic relationship between metal musicians and the people who hate them: they have been blamed for corrupting the youth, so they might as well offend in spades. From the "Satanic Panic" of the 1980s to the delinquency of the 1990s talk show youth, metal had a role in driving parental fever dreams, and its outsider status also made it the perfect vessel for the far-right. A version of metal steeped in authoritarian imagery, nativist re-purposing of European paganism, and the militant "anti-PC" vibe was a breeding ground for the far-right, so much so that black metal is at the center of some fascist movements across Europe. But do these fascist politics actually define the genre?[21]

"There are many bands in the past that have used nazism and white supremacy as a cheap and convenient shock tactic, it has an aesthetic which is easy to plunder for those of little imagination, and in recent decades it has been little more than abstract rebellion. When people see the effects of this around the world however, deportations, racism, homophobia, sexism, workers' rights being decimated, it all of a sudden doesn't seem that exciting," says Simon B, singer and violin player for Dawn Ray'd. "This also means that those who have long been antifascist are looking for music that reflects the times we live in, people want songs that are politically motivating I think, every decade has had its protest songs, and right now black metal is very current and en vogue."[22]

While bands are pushing back on the far-right in general, and fascist sympathies (particularly images and public statements) are becoming less accepted by their peers, some bands are taking things a step further. Dawn Ray'd has been joined by bands like Underdark, Gaylord, Ancst, Allfather, Neckbeard Deathcamp, Book of Sand, Redbait, Tarpan, and dozens of others that have made antifascist a key plank, not an afterthought.

"The medium of black metal is co-opted by fascists who use it to express anger towards things that aren't real," says Hassan Muhammad of the communist band Sarapast. "On the one side you might have them expressing anger towards Christianity; on the other you might have them expressing anger towards their incorrect perception of immigrants being a source of trouble in their respective countries... The music genre itself is very potent and powerful, and it can be used to express real anger, like the anger of Black people suffering under police brutality."[23]

This gets to the core of the genre; what makes it dangerous and what makes anger an actual weapon. The far-right imagines itself as threatening because of the pressure it places on liberal democracy, but all this does is make the implicit, explicit: it challenges nothing fundamental about society because the bigotry it stokes was always foundational to institutional structures. There is nothing dangerous there.

"[We have to stand up against fascism in the metal scene] for the same reason that one should stand up against it in any situation. No authoritarian ideology that makes us less free, censors our opinion, discriminates for absurd reasons, stands against minorities, other cultures, origins, skin color, sexual orientation, should be tolerated," says Vincente, the artist behind the Chilean one-person ambient black metal project The Ecologist.[24]

"Outsiders associate metal with the far-right because we haven't given them many easily accessible reasons not to, and some of the genre's most notorious origin stories (in the case of black metal, at the very least) are steeped in blood, murder, homophobia, and neo-Nazi violence," says Kelly, but this is only part of the story as the actual complexity of music gets erased by the reductionism so often applied from the exterior. "Antifascist metal is the most dangerous kind there is, because it holds the revolutionary potential to enact actual change, to challenge oppressive structures and systems of power, and to provide marginalized people with the support and space they need to become more involved with a scene that desperately needs their perspectives. What could be more dangerous than destroying the status quo? What's scarier than a peoples' revolution?"[25]

Neofolk was an even tougher sell as a genre that could be redeemed, which may lend currency to its importance. The genre came into being with bands like Death in June, Sol Invictus, Changes, and Fire + Ice, founding itself on a subtlety lacking in most street level fascist groups. Many of these people, such as Tony Wakeford and Ian Reid, were involved in actual neo-Nazi organizing, or, like Robert Taylor of Changes, were deeply rooted in racial Odinist organizations.[26]

Other bands were taking a different approach. They were highlighting the egalitarian aspects of ancestral traditions, or folk practices that fought against the "great enclosure," or the war raged by witches against patriarchy. These were romantic visions that built an emotional reality out of myth, but they had profoundly different motivations and starting points. Bands like Sangre de Muerdago focused on regional folk music that was attacked by fascist movements.[27] Newer projects like Nøkken and The Grim built a minimalist style merged with occult pagan mystery magic.[28] These are disparate projects, often with little explicit politics except that they wanted nothing to do with the fascist creep and were going to do something to stop its encroachment.

"Sadly, in the neofolk scene there's a bunch of examples of overt racism and white supremacism. We believe that bands like us have to create a scene where everyone is welcomed and united by music," said the Spanish neofolk band Vael in a collective interview.[29] Confronting racism and white supremacy was an uphill battle that bands had to fight, but projects like Autumn Brigade, April of Her Prime, Emerson Dracon, Byssus, Twilight Fauna, and others were up for it. Some were coming from explicitly Nordic pagan folk, and following the lead of bands like Wardruna in explicitly taking back the Northern Traditions from racists. And other projects, like Amanda Aalto, Hindarfjäll, and Wåhlin, spoke up even when their project was far from modern political identities and clashes.

"You cannot support a band that has Miguel Serrano quotes in its lyrics or wears National Socialist iconography just 'to make controversy,'" says Emerson Dracon, a martial industrial (a militant sounding variant of neofolk) artist in Argentina. "We have to fight against that. Smash fascism. We have to form a new kind of audience, give support to those alternative communication and media channels, and spread revolutionary content in all the ways we can. You cannot tolerate segregation, classism, or racism once. We have to bury that shit once and for all."[30]

Projects started to form around the concept of an explicitly antifascist neofolk, with the music website *A Blaze Ansuz* acting as a central hub. Here bands were profiled, music playlists were created, and the idea of an antifascist neofolk started to be normalized, which both angered and pressured the otherwise complicit neofolk music scene.[31] Bands like Alsarath and Ashera started from this milieu, understanding themselves as antifascist neofolk—the genre now had a proper name. This set a new standard in the music scene, and now that some bands were identifying themselves as antifascist, it opened the door for others.

"In the search for individuality and creative exploration, a lot of the artists who are adjacent to fascist beliefs do absolutely nothing to create anything truly worthwhile, they simply replicate themselves ad nauseam," says Jay Nada of the dark folk magic project DAES, a part of the Left/Folk collective that helps bring antiracist neofolk bands together.

There is no room for fascist parasites in a free world. There needs to exist an alternative space, unambiguous and unafraid of pushing against the fascist art grift. This cultivates a greater breadth of creation and development, a greater exploration and questioning of our world and the human condition. Fascist entryists are clever, with their plausible deniability, their apolitical disguises, and they work effectively against people looking for an alternative to mainstream art/culture. Those of us who are aware, and know better, must continue to push back against the fascist insect. In fact, we should do so joyously. We cannot let our various shades of interest and personality be subsumed by the forces of stagnation and false authority. To the losers who just want to put their eternal fathers in charge.[32]

This scene is building slowly, creating record compilations and fundraisers and helping to spread antifascism as a viable alternative to the mainline neofolk scene.[33] There is friction in this work, but it is useful in building both a vibrant artistic space that is inclusive, and in siphoning power away from the nationalists. They no longer hold a hegemony over an entire art form.

"Since the beginning folk was the music of the oppressed against their oppressor and it's really difficult for us to understand how possibly neofolk became the voice of false rebellion and elitist thinking. So we think that antifascism is the way to take neofolk back to its own origin and meaning and to use it again against the oppressor," says Evor Ameisie of the Italian anarchist neofolk project BloccoNero.[34]

Both neofolk and black metal became contested ground, in part, because of the perception of that whiteness is overwhelmingly the demographic, which is itself changing. The white culture that romanticized Europe has been replaced with the reclamation of Indigenous folkways and musical styles from around the world and its musicians stray from the narrow expectations that these scenes previously held. Women and gender non-conforming people are leading metal bands and building a new scene that aims to shatter old barriers and replace them with a cosmopolitan vision. This music really is for everyone.

Northern Traditions

The most direct of these cultural clashes is in the world of heathenry: the Nordic pagan traditions that have become so soaked in white nationalist appropriation that most people assume the symbology is simply interchangeable. There are a multitude of reasons for this, but the primary one is that the nineteenth-century Romantic nationalist movements homed in on pagan spirituality as an alternative to what they thought were the degenerative effects of industrial capitalism and the loss of "traditional" feudal social relationships. In doing so, the heathen religion, with its warrior ethos, was picked up specifically by those looking for a volkisch spiritual identity. This evolved through the years, with people plucking out early works by Carl Jung to suggest that the Germanic gods were implicit only to people of Northern European heritage, a sort of spiritual archetype only for the folk. A "folkish" form of heathenry expanded, and organizations like the Odinic Rite in Britain or the United States's Asatru Folk Assembly and Asatru Alliance propagated this model. Across the world, heathenry was a part of the fascist cultural metapolitics, either explicitly or symbolically (as was the case with the European New Right).[35]

Like the skinhead aesthetic, heathenry is one of the most thoroughly contested terrains—it is so defining in fascist circles that it is easy to say that it is "theirs" to begin with. The problem is that spiritual traditions speak to people unconsciously, and there is nothing implicitly true about their interpretation of heathenry. Instead, its lore and traditions tell a story of a resistance to oppression, dogmatic identity, and imperial conquest, all of which bely the actual persistence of the fascist narrative. They have convinced even their detractors that heathenry is theirs even though this assertion doesn't line up with the facts.

This is why a few groups of heathens have created a counterculture that pushes back on every folkish notion with an eye toward hegemony. "The biggest thing that drew me to starting Heathens United Against Racism was regularly seeing what was going on in the heathen community. Particularly in the rest of the broad pagan community, which I hadn't had a lot of experience with up until that point, was treating us with a lot of suspicion...We had to consistently prove that we weren't a bunch of violent skinheads, and the fact that there were groups who were doing that kind of thing reinforced that image," says Ryan Smith, explaining the formation of the antifascist heathen collective Heathens United Against Racism (HUAR).[36] The aim was simple: to fight back against the fascist heathens, and to do it as heathens. The goal was both political and practical: to exercise their interpretation of their religion as a war faith against tyranny, and to create a vibrant space for that religion to even exist. HUAR grew, as a distinct group of heathens were radicalized inside movements like Occupy Wall Street, and began asking big questions about how to confront something they knew was a problem in heathenry. They could use the same tools people were utilizing to take down dictators and confront corporate power.

> It started out trying to be more of a mass based organization, but that proved to be challenging considering the nature of how diffuse and scattered the heathen community and pagans in general tended to be. For example, a particularly active pagan community might be a few hundred people in an area the size of San Francisco. So instead, it was a lot of recruitment, raising awareness, education, and a lot of our agitation and educational work was done online because that was the easiest way to actually reach the biggest number of people possible and the pagan community really comes together online. If the Protestant Reformation was the product of the printing press, then paganism is a product of the Internet and the digital revolution.[37]

The approach to confronting white nationalism inside of heathenry is targeted and intentional, an effort to live out the principles that drew members to the spiritual tradition by confronting an enemy who tries to claim the same space. "I think it's important and strategic for heathens, and the variant related groups that work under the Norse Paganism umbrella, to push back against fascist appropriation because even though the fascists are the minority among us, they tend to be the loudest and most destructive," says Sophie Martinez, a Latinx heathen active with HUAR.[38]

> The most useful strategies I've seen involve folks who cultivate community to use some forward thinking. Creating policies (and remembering to update them) for your events, groups, etc. that involve inclusive policies. But it's not enough to simply have

inclusive policies anymore—especially in today's political climate where bigotry and fascism are both louder than they were just a few years ago—you need to create policies and enforceable protocols to address people causing harm from your spaces. If you cannot create healthy policies, and if you cannot enforce healthy policies, you may need to seek out members of your community willing to do that work for the spaces you create (whether they are in person or virtual). At the end of the day, communities not doing that kind of work will be abandoned and forgotten. Another good approach is to reach out to folks who have been actively fighting white supremacy and other forms of bigotry in pagan communities for a while. We are everywhere, and some of us are open to giving advice on how to protect your communities, or advice on how to determine if certain behavior is problematic. Some of us can also tell if a particular individual or group should be avoided based on language used on websites or profiles. It is important to understand that the descent into fascist ideology can be subtle, and groups that have been doing this for years have perfected the art of wrapping up bigotry in a bright shiny bow. Once you understand what to look for, things become easier (and slightly more terrifying).[39]

Other groups, including the Svinfylking, Heathens Against Hate, Heathens for Racial and Cultural Diversity, and Heathens for Social Justice, have also moved to push out the racists, and to do so hegemonically so that they don't have a way back into any pagan community. There has been pushback though, and major heathen organizations like The Troth refused to decisively act against racist heathenry, causing denunciations, splits, and a massive backlash. This led to a number of projects that created waves throughout the pagan world. Declaration 127, was one of these. In September 2016, citing a piece of the runic Havamal poems about committing oneself against dishonest demagogues, 180 pagan groups denounced the fascist Asatru Folk Assembly (AFA). The mantle was taken up across the globe, and as HUAR spread the message inside and outside of the pagan world, the folkish corner of heathenry was pushed further and further to the fringes. Now new groups have formed with a similar antifascist model, such as the Havamal Witches, who are dedicated to confronting sexism in the religious space. The AFA and other fascist heathen groups have been pushed entirely out of pagan circles and are now firmly associated with the Alt Right.[40]

When HUAR began, folkishness was commonly accepted in heathen circles (almost like it was a denomination—you could disagree with it but it was included in the canon) and today every organization associated with the folkish tendency is a complete pariah to the pagan community. Organizations like the Asatru Folk Assembly have now been universally recognized as a hate group that engages closely with the Alt Right and whose leadership is involved with the "identitarian" movement fighting refugee resettlement in Europe.[41]

Anarchist heathen collectives, like A Circle Ansuz, carved out their own unique theological interpretation while also connecting to a "red and black" approach to politics and antifascism.[42] There is an antifascist dimension in heathenry now, and it is assumed that this symbology or spiritual inclination is no longer seen with universal suspicion. Similarly, Wiccans have also worked to kick out the transphobic "Dianic" groups that had become common; Celtic spirituality is becoming fiercely anti-nationalist; and revivalist movements around the world are being pressed to take sides. There are fascist pagan movements that are a prescient threat, but they now have opposition in every corner, which has undermined their claim to the religion, the natural interpretation they think they hold, and it has carved out a path for paganism in an entirely different direction.

"Paganism and Heathenry are vectors fascists use to enter radical spaces, but it would be facile to conceive of them as natural fascist breeding grounds. Revivals of historic customs and practices have a long history, including the nineteenth century Romantics, so conceiving of such tendencies as fundamentally reactionary would only alienate people and cede cultural ground to the far-right," says Alexander Reid Ross.[43] To allow fascists to define entire cultural spaces would give them a permanent foothold and massive gains and influence.

Fight Club

The far-right is not defined solely by its extremist politics but also by its instruction. In recent years a phenomenon sometimes tied to post-fascism has emerged, in which the radical right disabuses themselves of distinctive politics in place of simply outsider behavior. While the politics of such groups like the Proud Boys sound like standard Republican fare, their instrumental use of violence, both as a binding agent and as a form of political expression, pushes them into a collection of groups broadly called far-right.[44] Because of the right-ward shift in mainstream politics—influenced heavily by the influx of radical right national populism—there is often little to distinguish a conservative politician from a militia or Alt Right gang member when it comes to very specific politics. Instead, radicalism is expressed in their reliance on violence as a political methodology and what David Neiwert refers to as an "eliminationist" rhetoric about political opponents.[45] The Proud Boys, patriot militia organizations like the III%ers, and the broader "independent Trumpist" phenomenon are founded on violence and aggression.[46] The political operation of Trump, which became the apocalyptic operating condition of the entire GOP, manufactures these sorts of "Vigilante Identities" as a way of creating enthusiastic support for whatever they come up with. These are the new "last men of history," standing against a wave of supposed degeneracy.[47]

This aggression and violence has created a crisis in the left and among marginalized communities trying to stay safe, and speaks to the cultural role that the political right has played in a lot of different communities. They have totally captured rural gun culture, and are increasingly making their presence known inside of gyms, mixed martial art (MMA) circles, and in the larger fitness and health worlds. Groups like the Wolves of Vinland are defining the gym as their own spiritual center, casting out anyone that does not fit into their narrow vision of bodily autonomy, and as the Overton Window shifts there are more and more of these subcultures that willingly accept this dynamic.[48]

Organizations like Redneck Revolt (now defunct), the John Brown Gun Club (now autonomous from Redneck Revolt), and the

Socialist Rifle Association sought to create an alternative to the racist conspiracy mongering of militias and the National Rifle Association, hoping to speak both to rural experiences, gun hobbying, and the very real need for self-defense. Trigger Warning Queer and Trans Gun Club did the same thing but with an LGBTQ+ focus, noting the excessive interpersonal violence queer folks face.

The Huey P. Newton Gun Club, among others, brought together BIPOC members to train with firearms in a model inspired by earlier projects like the Black Panther Party for Self-Defense. Their three-point program says:

1. We want immediate end to police brutality and the murder of black and brown [people].

2. We want to cease black on black violence and self-hatred.

3. We want to arm every black men [sic] and woman throughout the United States, which has been the greatest fear of the establishment.[49]

The organization mixes a strict code of ethics with a survivalist program built around practical skills and community resilience. They were an active force during the protests in the wake of George Floyd's killing in May 2020, and echoed the tradition and history of community self-defense and reliance that their group builds on. The Not Fucking Around Coalition (NFAC) is another recent gun club to surface. They provided security for Rayshard Brooks's sister and did protest patrols after Ahmad Arbery was killed by white vigilantes in February 2020. Their connection to antifascist movements is obvious as they brought upwards of one thousand fully armed people to Stone Mountain, Georgia, on July 4, 2020, to counter the presence of the far-right and demand the removal of the biggest confederate monument in the country: the vestige of confederate generals blasted into the side of the mountain.[50]

"Our initial goal was to have a formation of our militia in Stone Mountain to send a message that as long as you're abolishing all these statues across the country, what about this one?" said Grand-master Jay, the founder of NFAC. "We are a Black militia. We aren't protesters, we aren't demonstrators. We don't come to sing, we don't come to chant. That's not what we do."[51]

Stone Mountain was the site of the founding of the Second Gen-eration of the Ku Klux Klan, and a popular site for white suprema-cists and neo-Confederates, despite the town being 80 percent Black. This was a profound utility in creating a counterforce that over-whelmed the space and disallowed reactionary militias, the white defenders of the South, to have access and intimidate the residents.[52] Questions were raised afterwards about NFAC and ties to antisemitic and conspiracy politics, but despite their complicated and conflicted presence, they are still an example of these gun clubs attempting to create a counterforce to the dominant white gun culture that is tied to far-right attacks and vigilante mobilizations.[53]

While they are often billed as organizations for community self-defense and empowerment, gun clubs function in a multitude of ways. They shift the gun culture merely by their presence, develop-ing a space where people can participate despite identity (or where often-excluded identities are the center), and they help spread skills more broadly. In this, they capture the attraction that many militia organizations have, while building up a strong sense of community, a defensive skill set, and a mutual aid model. These groups often have a similar function to mutual aid groups, such as those politicized projects that emerged during the beginning of the COVID-19 pan-demic or during the summer wildfires, which transferred experience in activist projects over to a transformative mutual aid model.[54] Guns are not the seed of a liberated society, but there is a long history of empowering communities with survival skills, including firearms, as a way of building autonomy, safety, and relationships. The utility of these organizations as antifascist groups is obvious and has been clear since the creation of projects like the North Carolina NAACP chapter that became a joint NRA chapter under Robert F. Williams's leadership, in an effort to fight against Klan terror. The need for these community sustaining projects, from resource-based mutual aid to community self-defense, will only increase as the effects of climate change increase natural disasters, climate refugees are met with nativist anger, and economic deprivation creates more dramatic market crashes.

What Alexander Reid Ross labels the "fascist creep" takes place in the radical fringes as politics and social values are being deconstructed, reconfigured, and reassembled.[55] The strength of radical politics is to get at the fundamentals and try something new, as well as acknowledge vulnerabilities.

Gyms have been a difficult place for creating a vibrant antifascist community because of the costly overhead and the hegemony that major chains hold over the industry. However, there are standouts that refuse to cede physical training only to far-right actors who build a consciousness on marginalizing different body types and perpetuating ableism. In Portland, Oregon, the Bleeding Hearts Kettlebell Club has worked to put community first in a radical space built around health and fitness rather than shallow ideas of bodily "normalcy." Kettlebells are unique in that they are often used by people struggling with injuries or body differences that put them at odds with orthodox weight training methods, so there is an implicit politicization to the central focus on the kettlebell. Run by women and gender non-conforming people, their space is reclaiming the idea that strength, health, and physical striving are not narrowly defined by the mainstream fitness community.

Mixed Martial Arts may be one of the most contested spaces because of the hyper-masculine culture and influx of fascist fighters into gyms around the country. Organizations like the Rise Above Movement, the Hammerskins, and other white nationalist groups have made training in MMA one of their central features, which they use in the now common, protracted street battles against antifascists around the country.[56] This has made the idea of antifascist gyms all the more necessary, so that confidence and safety skills can be built for people who may be the target of Alt Right gangs.

"An antifascist, anti-sexist, and anti-racist martial arts gym will provide needed self-defense training for those most at risk of not only far-right violence on the street, but also patriarchal violence in the home. Physical training is a crucial and often neglected component of anarchist practice. We believe that fostering material resistance starts with the most intimate of material forces—our bodies," says the founder of the antifascist community gym Haymaker in Chicago.[57]

The far-right's use of fight clubs has several tactical advantages, which lead to easy recruitment because "they combine an entertainment culture that valorizes violence and hypermasculinity with a natural set of physical spaces and places where ideological messages can be intensified," writes Cynthia Miller-Idrriss.[58] The Reconquista Club in Kiev, Ukraine, is an especially concerning example of this since it was created by the neo-Nazi Azov Battalion, which has attracted American white supremacists from groups like Atomwaffen, and was named after a fifteenth-century pogrom.[59] In Europe and Russia, the clubs counter-balancing the massive influx of the far-right into the world of fighting have become critical, and many of them operate inside of squatted buildings and offer classes for free. RKS Gwiazda Gym (Moving Sport Club - Star) in Warsaw; the Female, Lesbian, Intersexed, Non-binary, or Trans (FLINT) network in Germany; and feminist gyms like Sidekick and Roter Stern Jena, aim to make self-defense a key strategy against abusers and against the encroaching violence of fascist gangs and vigilantes. Along with the fighting prowess gained, these spaces promote some of the things sorely missed when these clubs are ceded entirely to reactionaries: healthy exercise, body confidence and autonomy, and the strong sense of community that comes through shared practice.[60]

"We live in a horrible world in some regards, especially as a woman. The amount of street violence that you get, especially on the left if you're on demonstrations ... sometimes things can turn pretty nasty. You want to be able to defend yourself," says Ella Gilbert of Solstar, a left-wing, antifascist gym in London. "I think there's a distinction to be made between active violence and self-defense. And if somebody is attacking me, I'm not going to stand there and take it." Rather than celebrating violence, the organization is built around channeling people's energies and aggressions into a positive setting, focusing on protection rather than assault, and maintaining a set of strict principles.[61]

Antifascism Becomes Ubiquitous

While antifascist cultural work can be a form of activism, such as a person using their presence in a subculture as a way of fighting back against fascists in the same space, it isn't a new tactic. "Militant antifascists routinely organize cultural and social events that allow the movement to interact with supporters and the broad society," writes Stanislav Vysotsky in his book *American Antifa*, looking at the dynamic way that antifascist groups have historically created a cultural space with everything from movie showings to concerts to arts events. "Within subcultural spaces, the predominance of antifascist culture serves to dissuade fascists from organizing or taking action because it marginalizes them in relation to dominant tendencies in the subculture."[62] The battle over ideas and identity play out in these subcultures that act as "contested spaces," where antifascists play a role in pushing them out of a space where they could use the arts for recruitment, but also in the battle over ideologies and social identities. Antifascism is about the access to space—physical and temporal—and eliminating access is a break in the chain of racist radicalization.

Fascists are not allowed to organize in these spaces, they are not allowed to have their own subcultures, they are not allowed to take over arts, sports, or any cultural institutions. Within this world there are people battling against fascist comic book artists and reframing the industry. The same thing is taking place in the video game world, inside of the academy, across sports leagues and churches and union halls. The reality is that people are meeting fascism where they are because fascism is not just a top down political structure but also a mass movement of working people turned against their own interests in a desperate bid to hold onto privilege. A real movement against fascism hits it from all sides: in the streets, in public meetings, and in music venues and corner bars. The far-right has poised its attention on our sense of joy and identity, so those ephemeral concepts are hardened into points of struggle.

The intentional focus on culture involves other practical elements as well. These sorts of community spaces create infrastructure; they literally become places where people meet each other, build relationships not just out of sheer political utility, and can raise money and transpose people from casual interest to committed organizing. In Germany, antifascist music labels and clothing companies like Fire and Flame and True Rebel Streetwear have become a place where style and political literature mingle, where a cultural identity seeps into a political one. This invites new people to antifascism by easing them into a political consciousness that is inlaid with their artistic sensibilities.

This model has been the foundation of newer antifascist organizations, like Pop Mob (short for "Popular Mobilization") in Portland, Oregon. Built on the idea that mass participation is required to push back on insurgent far-right groups, Pop Mob build carnival-like protest spaces that exist alongside more militant antifascist groups. Starting in 2018, they held mass events with speakers, music, and fancy costumes, and they focus on creating a welcoming atmosphere so that more and more people will want to join this coalition effort. They call this "everyday antifascism."

"What we are really trying to do is destigmatize what it means to be antifascist... I wanted to change the conversation and narrative about what it means to be an antifascist and it looks a lot of different ways... It can be your grandmother, it can be someone in the [black] bloc, it can be a school teacher," says co-founder Effie Baum.[63]

The above examples normalize antifascism by increasing its presence and its ability to ingratiate itself culturally. By transposing an organizing principle (no platform; the total refusal of fascism) into a social one, everyday antifascism becomes present in every aspect of life. Plainly put, this model ends the idea that fascism is something to be debated, it is instead something to be totally extricated. Outside of the world of conscious politics, where "live and let live" approaches allow white nationalism to perpetuate, a cultural antifascist sensibility starts to erode any of the "apolitical" ground that nationalism uses to cordon itself off from challenge. The space that fascism could occupy grows as the crisis that helps to inspire it expands, as conflict rages and white nationalism tries to more firmly establish itself as a dominant social force in a fragmenting global culture. We are experiencing a profound shift in our time—a reaction to global financial and climate collapse—and the cracks in the edifice mean that so much is possible: a potential world of horrors or one of new beginnings.

Antifascism is an issue of space. The contested space is shared by opposing parties, and while there is a lot of cultural space (and demographics) that are part of this battle, all space is really contested space. The neighborhoods; the gym; the school; the conversation; the mental, emotional, and spiritual space. And if you want to win, then fascists can have none of them.

How Racists Dream

Metapolitics and Fascist Publishing

For John Morgan, an American expat living in Budapest, controlling the form the world takes comes down to shaping how white people dream.

It is hard to imagine that Morgan, a quiet, nebbish man with curly hair and a meek smile, is at the center of an international fascist renaissance, but this is the reality of fringe politics in the social media age. When it comes to building a propaganda infrastructure capable of radicalizing a generation, it is just as likely to come from a bookish copy editor as it is from a charismatic march leader. Morgan was the creative force behind much of Arktos Media and, later, Counter-Currents, publishers known for creating the intellectual foundation for a new fascism.

Morgan's history in publishing reveals an important but neglected side of the story of U.S. white nationalism: the focus on building a "metapolitic" rather than the direct mobilization that many expect from "white power" authors of the 1980s and 90s. Metapolitics refers to the ways of thinking that are "pre-political," the emotional center that feeds political motions. It engages with the paths of identity, morality, values, nostalgia, relationships, and the whole matrix of how people see the world. This explicit turn to metapolitics occurred when nationalist intellectuals, drawing on the ideas of Italian Marxist Antonio Gramsci, began seeing that a new kind of social struggle was necessary after the fascists lost World War II. To win public support they couldn't just make their arguments, they had to change the way the public thought before they even heard the arguments. If they could reshape the values of their people through art and literature then they would speak in the only language that mattered, and victory would simply be a matter of the long game.

Today, crushing economic uncertainty and climate collapse has reignited big questions about how we should organize our world. In response to a failing status quo, a far-right influenced by esoteric philosophers of tradition and reactionary white supremacist "identitarians" has begun to challenge the left for the monopoly on dissent through metapolitics as much as through direct politics. The emergence of national populist parties around Europe and anti-immigrant extremism codified in political discourse are symptoms of this instability. "Alternative Right" emerged in 2010 from this metapolitical stew when then-nobody Richard Spencer saw an undercurrent emerging. In the fringes of the American right, where he lurked, paleoconservatives, racial pagans, white nationalists, European New Rightists, and Traditionalists were establishing the intellectual foundation for an aboveground fascist movement. He coalesced this crew around his new website AlternativeRight.com where they worked to renew racialist thinking and pseudoscience, nationalism, and Aryan mysticism.

Part of why the mainstream media, government agencies, and NGOs missed the massive white nationalist insurgency that peaked in Charlottesville and with the election of Donald Trump is that they were looking for a dinosaur. While the old school racist organizations like neo-Nazis and the KKK still certainly exist, in frightening and violent numbers, they were not the growth sector. Instead, it was a kernel of ideas that had been crystalizing, feeding on white angst and identity, and waiting to be carried into the real world. It has been the role of fascist publishers to do this work. These publishers are a central part of the fountain of discontent and racialism that feeds far-right movements and has radicalized a population, shifting the political discourse away from liberalism and headfirst into caustic nationalist war. We see the trolling, the racial slurs, the hate crimes, but we don't see the dreams that white nationalism is built on, and that is where it begins.

This space is where Arktos Media and Counter-Currents worked, becoming the literary wing of the Alt Right, publishing books of European far-right philosophy, nationalist fiction, and esoteric manifestos. If the Alt Right was going to focus on building metapolitics, Counter-Currents and Arktos were going to be their literary foundation, and this was John Morgan's mission.

Arktos Media's New Traditionalism

The spike in white nationalist visibility, the formation of the Alt Right, and the linkage with the European "identitarian" movement, all has Arktos Media at its center.

"It always leads back to Arktos. I really do believe that they have been incredibly influential," says Carol Schaeffer, whose pioneering reporting unlocked how Arktos connects the often disparate global fascist movement. "You really couldn't have an 'identitarian' movement, which is really at the heart of dozens of groups, without the books and without the library and without the resources that Arktos has provided."

While the project was co-founded by Jacob Senholt, its journey is really that of former Arktos editor John Morgan. As he would tell it, Morgan found his path to the right in his university libraries while an undergrad. Looking to explain his angst, he first came upon the German "Conservative Revolution," which led him to the European New Right, a canon of French philosophers led by Alain de Benoist that reinvigorated the far-right in the 1960s. Benoist came out of the nationalist movement to maintain French Algeria but after the May 1968 uprising, anti-colonialist revolts across the world, and the rise of the New Left, he changed his tone. He used postcolonial rhetoric to argue for "ethnopluralism," a sort of nationalism for all peoples, and argued for semi-autonomous regions based on ethnic, religious, and cultural identity. His form of nationalism was more diffuse, laced with neo-paganism, and used anti-capitalist, anti-imperialist, and, especially, anti-American arguments that obscured his racial intentions.

"I would actually buy back issues of *Telos* in order to read Alain de Benoist," Spencer told me in 2017, when discussing how the European New Right was the spark for him that led to the creation of AlternativeRight.com. "Even when I wasn't fully knowledgeable of the French New Right, I could just tell I had much more in common with the French New Right than American Conservatism." Traditionalism, paganism, anti-Christianity, universalism, and globalism, all created a philosophical collage that was added to the hodge-podge that became the Alt Right.

One of the threads the European New Right picked up on was Traditionalism, namely of Julius Evola and René Guénon. Traditionalism saw that all religious traditions descended from one single divine source, but only when they kept their "chain of initiation" and hierarchical "exoteric" practice. Evola took the notion a step further and went in an explicitly racial and imperial direction, arguing that we are currently living in the "Kali Yuga," a "dark age" predicted in the Vedic scriptures. Evola believed that we were currently being ruled by the passions of the lower castes, workers, women, people of color, and pernicious secularized Jews, and that we had to return to a mythic Golden Age of imperial rule by a priestly caste.

Evola and Benoist made the largest impression on Morgan, but since their work was sparsely translated into English, he set about meeting compatriots online. The crowd he met eventually formed the publisher Integral Tradition Publishing in 2006. The print-on-demand revolution gave them the resources to do this since they could publish translations of books that would not sell a huge number, and so they could print them as needed rather than investing heavily in a volume that might only sell a few hundred copies over many years.

Morgan moved to India in 2009 to focus on Integral Traditions full time while living at a Hare Krishna ashram with another staff member, and eventually connected with far-right white Krishna leader Bhakti Vikasa Swami, who is generally maligned in the Hare

Krishna movement for his violently regressive gender ideas. In late 2009 they shifted directions when they met enigmatic far-right Swede Daniel Friberg, who had made a name for himself across nationalist movements in Scandinavia, all the while popping in and out of jail for offenses like possession of automatic weapons.

"It's hard to ignore the fact that Friberg kind of seems to be always at the root of a lot of different projects. He has been extremely prolific as an extreme right person," says Schaeffer. "He's not a core theorist and thinker. He acts much more as a connector and organizer, and somebody who is really working to legitimize the movement while still remaining core to its true values, which is hate."

Friberg, who financed the operation, started his career with boots and braces in the white power scene and was in and out of prison between 1995 and 2010. He quickly moved away from skinhead subcultures to a series of organizations including the far-right Sweden Democrats, the Swedish Resistance Movement, and the Nordic League, which he founded. In 2004 Friberg finally found the European New Right, and a lightbulb went off. He tried his hand at a number of explicitly metapolitical projects that could engage in a sort of cultural battle, including the website Metapedia, which is a white nationalist alternative to Wikipedia known for vulgar racism and extreme antisemitic conspiracy theories (such as claims that homosexuality is a form of Jewish Sexual Bolshevism). In 2009 he joined together with a Norwegian far-right politician and two others to form a media company, which would absorb Integral Traditions and the rest of the inventory of the Nordic League.

This would be Arktos Media, which focused largely on the same books as Integral Traditions Publishing, such as translated works of Evola and the European New Right. The Arktos catalog is still dominated by three authors: Julius Evola, Alain de Benoist, and European New Right author Guillaume Faye, known primarily for his aggressive Islamophobia.

Over the years they branched out to books of other types of racial esotericism, conspiracy theories, deep ecology, and white nationalism, and have been helped by the increased popularity of figures like the Eurasianist Aleksandr Dugin and Markus Willinger.

"We don't have any specific agenda at Arktos. We are not trying to promote a particular ideology or political system or whatever," said Morgan in an interview with the THA Talks podcast:

I just call it "alternatives to modernity." What I mean by that is . . . all societies and all government systems, in spite of some remaining cultural differences, all basically subscribe to the same basic suppositions about politics. Even philosophically, to a certain extent. So our idea at Arktos was that we wanted to present books that challenged that. And say well, just because it has become the globalized way of doing things in recent years that does not necessarily mean that it's the best way. . . I admit that there were aspects of fascism and national socialism that were interesting.

Arktos intended to be what Morgan defines as the "True Right," a transhistorical notion that is supposed to rescue the current right-wing from its foundations in liberalism. The "True Right" believes in hierarchical autonomy, the idea that identities are fixed, and human beings are unequal along these identity lines of race, class, caste, gender, and so on. This is what has helped him create a big tent of ideas, generating support from racial ecologists to neo-confederates to national-anarchists.

This led to some strange books, including those of Finnish ecologist Pentti Linkola. Arktos published Linkola's 2009 book *Can Life Prevail?*, where Linkola argues that rapid population reduction needs to be put into place, which could be result in a mass genocide of billions. Linkola prefers authoritarian dictators and strict national boundaries, all in the name of a neo-Malthusian vision of the environment that justifies some of the most atrocious forms of human killing. An excerpt from the book was, strangely, featured in the left-wing magazine *AdBusters* around the time that the magazine began promoting the idea of Occupy Wall Street, giving Arktos a boost from an unlikely source. This is central to Arktos's mission: taking ideas from the left like anti-capitalism and ecology, but for decisively right-wing reasons, like racial nationalism. They even sold books by primitivist writer and Deep Green Resistance founder Derrick Jensen, who argues for a mass return to hunter-gatherer lifestyles through armed struggle (Jensen did an interview with Counter-Currents in 2019). Arktos has also been known to publish a range of books on Hinduism, including generally well-regarded authors (such as Sri Sri Ravi Shankar), which they seem to be able to do by virtue of their obscurity.

Arktos's largest boost came with the arrival of the Alt Right. While the Alt Right had essentially been around since 2009, it really launched into the stratosphere in 2015 when a number of popular bloggers and podcasters like *The Right Stuff* joined the movement and started trending hashtags like "Cuckservative" in its name. Then Donald Trump came along, and they hit a moment of perfect synergy: their ideas had become palatable.

Arktos's own connections grew over the years, and despite claiming to be uninterested in "activism," they certainly built relationships. As Schaeffer reported, Arktos worked directly with members of the Hindu-nationalist Bharatiya Janata Party, drawing on the long history of white supremacist use of Vedic scriptures and fascination with Hindutva. When they moved operations to Hungary, they worked with the antisemitic fascist party Jobbik. They have maintained connections across Europe's national populist sphere, from the Front National to Golden Dawn, using their subcultural pedigree to make friends.

"If we're talking about a 'global' far-right, we need to look at organizations like Arktos, which is working hard to expand the reach of fringe far-right thinkers internationally," says Tess Owen, who reported on Arktos for *Vice*. She points out that it is the internationalism that made Arktos so significant, including publishing authors from nineteen countries and publishing some of their titles in up to eleven languages.

Morgan and Arktos moved to Budapest, Hungary in 2014, looking to get back to the Europe they so desperately longed for. They began pushing books popular with the Alt Right, including books by Friberg himself. This positioned Arktos Media as the intellectual center of the Alt Right since they had published a huge offering of intellectual work that would give the Alt Right the appearance of depth. In 2018, as the Alt Right was fading from the limelight, Arktos released *A Fair*

Hearing: The Alt-Right in the Words of Its Members and Leaders, an anthology featuring people like Richard Spencer, American Renaissance founder Jared Taylor, and academic antisemite Kevin MacDonald. Arktos saw that the "identitarian movement" in Europe, which was largely the popularized social movement inspired by the European New Right, was analogous to the Alt Right in the U.S., and so they began publishing their work heavily as well. As they grew, literature, audiobooks, and neofolk music were included in their sales catalog, including bands associated with far-right occultism and European nationalism like Rukkanor, Sol Invictus, and Blood Axis.

Arktos has also ventured into weird, fringe science and secret government conspiracies, a murky world where their outrageousness passes without much attention. This is what led them to be associated with the Flat Earth International Conference in 2017, which was also covered by fellow Alt Right media operation Red Ice Creations.

Arktos, then, dove head first into the few avenues of intellectualism that fascism already had and has used that canon to build up an obscurantist library of the weird, pushing the limits on what kind of work they can publish so as to define their twenty-first century fascism as more than genocide mongering. But it was another behemoth of far-right publishing, Counter-Currents, that has emphasized the aesthetic dimension as essential to shaping the soul of the movement.

Books against Time

When Arktos moved to Hungary in 2014 the relationship between Morgan and Friberg began to disintegrate, with Morgan alleging financial mismanagement and substance abuse on the part of Friberg. Morgan had felt mistreated as Friberg lived a lavish lifestyle, allegedly frequenting popular clubs and sleeping till noon while Morgan languished away on Arktos for sub-minimum wage (by American standards). As reported by Tess Owen, in 2013 Friberg was appointed to the board of Wiking Minerals, whose owner had been shelling out money to fascist and anti-Islamic movements around Europe. In

2015 he became the CEO, a post that seems odd because, as Schaeffer has pointed out, while he has claimed to hold an MBA from Gothenburg University, there is no record of this. Friberg oversaw the Alt Right website Right On, which Morgan worked on regularly, including a frequent podcast, but Morgan was still financially struggling and seeing little respect from across the professional desk. Morgan eventually contacted an Arktos shareholder about the potential embezzlement and after Friberg found out he fired Morgan who, despite holding a couple shares, was just an employee. Without much of a work history, and very little money since he got far below American pay rates, he was in his forties with nowhere to go. That's when he talked to Greg Johnson from Counter-Currents. He joined Counter-Currents in August 2016 and started his exit of Arktos.

Counter-Currents, founded in 2010, was the brainchild of movement philosopher Greg Johnson. In a white nationalist movement known for its working class and rural base, Johnson stands out with his erudite name dropping, tailored suits, and PhD. While Johnson had a brief career in academia, he was inspired to change career paths when he was first introduced to white nationalism in 2000. Once he believed his race was in an existential battle to survive, nothing else really seemed to matter.

After a controversial two-and-a-half-year run editing the white nationalist journal *The Occidental Quarterly*, Johnson had bad blood with the publisher and needed a new gig. What resulted was Counter-Currents, a book publishing house founded on June 11, 2010 by Johnson and his comrade Mike Polignano, which focused on what Johnson was coining the "North American New Right."

"[The goal was] to create a metapolitical publishing house of a 'North American New Right,'" said Johnson. "A model for what we do, and what we want to do, is Verso (formerly New Left Books). They put out some high-quality work that has a definite political [and] metapolitical agenda to it...We want to create a forum, a kind of exciting intellectual movement where people who have something to contribute to creating a New Right intellectual synthesis and a New Rightist counter-hegemony can try their ideas out, develop them, hone them, and then propagate them out to the world."

His New Right was similar to both the Alternative Right and the European New Right, supporting much of what historically was known as fascism while rejecting some of the organizational "excesses" of the interwar fascist parties. Johnson says that this difference is in "approach rather than doctrine," and works toward the "transformation of culture to create a consensus supporting the ethnonationalism for all nations."

Each book published by Counter-Currents is chosen based on the publisher's belief in the quality of its content and its ability to build a base, rather than on whether it can sell a heap of copies. Johnson reports that each book will sell about one thousand copies in its lifetime, though some of its smaller, more literary fare sell far fewer.

"One of the factors that we have to keep in mind is that practically everything we publish we put out for free on the Internet beforehand," says Johnson. Their actual book sales are for novelty or because the customer wants to support Counter-Currents financially, not because they can't find the material. "People like free stuff. The growth audience for us consists of Millennials and they grew up with free stuff on the Internet, and we live in an increasingly post-book-oriented age."

This is why Johnson saw massive growth of web traffic in 2016 for their thousands of articles, but their book sales remained fairly static. Since June 2010, when the website became active, they saw steady month-to-month growth through November 2017, when they had 206,887 unique visitors, when Alt Right interest was peaking. This trend reversed itself as a result of "deplatforming" and public backlash against the Alt Right, and they saw a fairly steady decline to 131,856 unique visitors in March of 2019.

Johnson's mission started, in a lot of ways, by following the lead of the eccentric Nazi, Savitri Devi. Known for her outlandish claims, like that Hitler was an avatar of the Vedic god Vishnu, Devi mixed esoteric Hitler worship and Hinduism in a strange synthesis that continues to have ripples across the right. Johnson started by publishing her archive before putting her books back into print, including her opus *The Lightning and the Sun*. Johnson dove headfirst into this esoteric sphere, publishing, for example, two books by Collin Cleary, best known for dense books on heathen theology based on a concept some writers have labeled as "metagenetics." Inspired by a tract by Carl Jung analyzing the rise of Hitler, metagenetics is used by "folkish heathens" who see the Nordic pantheon of mythic gods emanating from the subconscious of people of Northern European descent. Gods are Jungian archetypes that represent the spiritual and psychic nature of the Germanic peoples, and therefore the neo-heathen religion, as practiced today, is an attempt to reclaim that racial consciousness.

While Johnson himself does not believe these things in a literal sense, he views them as useful mythological metaphors for what he has determined are the human qualities of tribalism and proper social organization.

While Counter-Currents uses obscure literary and philosophical titles to obscure its motivations, Johnson is rather candid about his white nationalism. Some of his best sellers are collections of his articles, which he compiles into volumes with titles like *Truth, Justice, and a Nice White Country* or the more recent, *The White Nationalist Manifesto*. His blog is filled with regular contributions on race and IQ and "Jewish power," and he provides interviews with neo-Nazis like Northwest Front and Combat 18 organizer Harold Covington.

What makes Counter-Currents unique compared to other neo-fascist publishers is that it sought to reclaim the literary and artistic space from the left. It built a stable of its own fiction authors, a key figure of which it found in former English professor Andy Nowicki. Best known as a reactionary Catholic and contributor to the original AlternativeRight.com, Nowicki chose to publish with Counter-Currents despite claiming he was not a white nationalist. Nowicki was the co-host of Richard Spencer's first podcast, *Vanguard Radio*, and became the editor of AlternativeRight.com with Colin Liddell when Spencer took over the National Policy Institute. Nowicki and Liddell had a famous falling out with Spencer in the beginning of 2013 when Spencer, tired of what Nowicki and Liddell had published on a website known as his creation, shut down AlternativeRight.com without much fanfare.

Nowicki's most famous book on the Counter-Currents line-up was *The Columbine Pilgrim*, a story that follows its main character,

Tony Meander, as he contemplates the meaning of mass shootings and eventually lands on suicide. While Nowicki was no literary luminary, he was one of their own, and his work became popular in the early Alt Right as an example of their literary prowess.

Johnson is best known for rescuing artists and authors who have been marginalized for their racism. Formalist poet Leo Yankevich was recruited largely because he was a vocal racist and antisemite, even though it rarely appears in his work. Seattle's iconoclastic porcelain sculptor Charles Krafft entered the Counter-Currents fold after an article in *The Stranger* revealed he was a Holocaust denier, someone who doubts that the Holocaust occurred according to historical consensus. Krafft's work largely includes things like creating sculptures of guns and Hitler out of the same floral porcelain that you might find in formal china in the 1960s, ironic Americana at its best. Authors like H. L. Mencken and H. P. Lovecraft have been the subject of Counter-Current books and articles because they were proud elitists and racialists, and Johnson went as far as to name an award for literary achievements after Lovecraft. Kerry Bolton, known for his huge repertoire of apologist books about Russian nationalism and fawning treatments of fascist authors like Francis Parker Yockey and Oswald Spengler, did a volume called *Artists of the Right* for Counter-Currents highlighting the work of modernist writers sympathetic with fascism like D. H. Lawrence, Gabriele D'Annunzio, Filippo Marinetti, W. B. Yeats, Knut Hamsun, Ezra Pound, and Wyndham Lewis. Counter-Currents is filled with books and articles of film criticism that tries to reclaim different movies as their own, including *The Matrix*, *Eyes Wide Shut*, *Fight Club*, and various comic book fare, continuing to build the right-wing literary canon.

While each of these books does its own work to disseminate right-wing ideas, it also has the effect of reframing existing art so that the far-right seems more permanent and present. In this context, fascists are not fringe, they are a part of our literary and artistic history, and that perception helps their presence to appear more palatable and normalized. When Counter-Currents is able to show off well-known artists like Charles Krafft it creates a bridge to an art community.

To Johnson, this publishing work is essential to the white nationalist project. His view, since the start of the Alt Right's public presence, has been that there is a lot of work still to be done on the metapolitical front, and the Alt Right simply is not in a place yet where they can get in the streets and fight the left, which is why he rejects their activism.

This analysis may have been brilliant foresight because, as the Alt Right increasingly becomes persona non grata, Counter-Currents has been largely shielded. Johnson has organized conferences, like the Northwest Forum in Seattle, where he now lives, which has been confronted by antifascists, but not close to the extent that organizations like Identity Evropa or the Traditionalist Workers Party have faced. Still, Johnson has not come under the radar entirely and was run out of San Francisco after Bay Area Antifa published his information. More recently, his work (and photo) was exposed by a Hope Not Hate investigation that infiltrated Alt Right circles with a clever backstory and a hidden camera.

Surfing the Kali Yuga

The space carved out by Arktos Media and Counter-Currents is larger than the books they sell, because, in a sense, that is secondary. The books, while influential in their circles, are important for a different reason. They add the appearance of philosophic depth, the sense that if there are volumes upon volumes expounding a wealth of ideas, these racists and their supporters can't be simply braindead skinheads.

It also provides the claim, or cover, that their work is simply that of ideas. For Morgan, his claim is that critical inquiry leads him to his conclusions and that it is the inquiry itself, that move to rethink modernity (however he defines it) that is leading the charge. This is the "free speech" defense couched in flowery jargon, essentially suggesting the opposition is simply trying to rob them of their right to think things. This neglects the fact that, from its very start, this was political organizing, from its inception to its conferences to its front facing media. The metapolitics they are building, based on the theories presented by the European New Right, are intended to be a covert way to convert the underlying culture of the West. This is a political mission, one that seeks results from its investment, even if that investment is in arcane books about Indo-Aryan languages. The "free speech" argument here tries to depoliticize the political, not from its effects but from its public branding, providing it both the cache of intellectualism and the plausible deniability. If you oppose them in their quest to save us from the dark age of the Kali Yuga, it's you that are the agent of repression, they are just asking questions. In a political world John Morgan knows a political act—from posting flyers to casting a ballot to writing a poem to detonating a bomb—and the power of telling white people they were right all along. He has bet his career on it.

"What makes Arktos so dangerous is that their titles are widely available: they've managed to skirt corporate bans on hate content by shrouding their ideology in pseudo-academic language," says Owen. "Far-right publishing companies like Arktos have sought to give white nationalism a veneer of pseudo-intellectual legitimacy by dressing up old, ugly, racist ideas in euphemisms. For example, their authors don't talk about whiteness, they talk about 'European identity.' This is part of a calculated strategy: Move out of the fringes, and into the political mainstream."

This is intentional not only to bring in new people, but for them to solidify their ranks. Every great movement has figureheads, thought leaders, people that can show the way, and those are the foundations that take an impulse and make it a multi-generational social movement. This requires a canon, literature that can act as an ideological foundation (whether they are read or not).

"To have an intelligentsia you have to have things like Arktos and Counter-Currents," says Spencer Sunshine, a researcher of the far-right who specializes in understanding the syncretic aspects of these movements that often defy conventional understanding. "A group that has the pretense of sophistication, like Identity Evropa, is aided greatly by Arktos and Counter-Currents ... intellectuals can stick around and influence the movements for years."

The books have been influential in the quietest of ways, purchased online and read without watching eyes. This has been profound for the growth of the Alt Right and can help to solidify a fascist ideology in a person who may have only had a passive fascination with far-right blogs or YouTube videos. This work has historically been profound, with Julius Evola in particular motivating the fascist terrorism in Italy in the "Years of Lead" in the 1970s or today in the Eurasianist Russian nationalist movement led by Aleksandr Dugin. Even Steve Bannon revealed the influence of Evola on his thinking, a move that shows that his ideas are more than troll deep.

Their metapolitics are a direct challenge to the left in as much as they try to undermine its vision at the source rather than only battling over political outcomes, like resulting immigration or affirmative action policy. Instead they want to take over how white people dream, to colonize imagination, and replace it with a new sense of right and wrong. But the left can build a metapolitic of its own, living in the world of vision and inspiration, and ensure that the mass of people susceptible to nationalism have a counter-narrative, one that sees their liberation bound up with those of the marginalized communities that fascists hope to trample on. This can mean returning to the world of art and ideas, not decoupling practical organizing from the creation of ideas. A metapolitics of the right works when equality and democracy lose legitimacy, a hegemony whose loss would mean the end of the post-enlightenment project. Much of the failures of the social democratic left to live up to its promises, from loss of the New Deal and New Left in the eighties and nineties to the turn towards neoliberal economics, has created a feeling that the left lacks a utopian impulse to change the world. That is a metapolitical framework that fascism is taking up with intentionality and vision, yet it is one the left molded and built and can be reclaimed.

"For the left to have a metapolitic the left has to have a vision and I don't know that it has a vision," says Spencer.

For the Alt Right, Counter-Currents and Arktos, particularly Evola and the European New Right, has helped to move people along their ideological path and introduce them to styles of European nationalism that helped coalesce them into a conscious mass movement. This has all been in the service of building an American "identitarian movement," and the Alt Right has done well to refashion the strategies of Generation Identity and other identitarian direct action projects that are growing across Europe. This is the model of fascist movements in the twenty-first century: less electorally focused, instead developing multitudinous mass movements that play on the same impulses that the left does, and using cultural, social, and artistic means as a point of struggle. In a way, the conditions of the Internet and the fragmentation of political organization that the left has seen over the last twenty years has now been taken up by the far-right, and now an asymmetrical cultural war is taking place in rapidly changing European and North American cities. In this world, publishers mean as much as a Grand Dragon of the KKK does and unveiling them should be imbued with an equal level of immediacy.

Friberg, Johnson, and Morgan have been successful in their primary goal: to introduce a metapolitic that can corrosively break down Western liberalism. While they are minor in comparison with major publishers and academic institutions, their efforts have the potential to take an influential spot in the world of dissident radical works. Around issues of white identity, these publishers are a large reason the Alt Right were able to create an intellectual framework and claims of legitimacy. For any movement to succeed it has to build up a body of ideas that can take followers beyond immediate impulses and can give their desires profound conviction, and that requires a layer of intellectual work that is simply vacant from much of the street level white nationalism. This is why an academic caste exists in these circles, to continue to reinforce the sense that the mass fascist movement is really onto something.

To understand these publishers, these people, is to understand how white nationalism functions. There are underlying logics here, ones that are attempting to feed bigotry with motive, and without plotting the relationships and output a counterforce is impossible.

The organizations that made up the ground game of the Alt Right, like Identity Evropa, have viewed themselves like a vanguardist cadre, and this literary canon has become a way that members are able to develop and solidify their ideas.

"Many [Identity Evropa members] are learning these truths on the Internet and in the safety of their own home," says Nathan Damigo, the founder of Identity Evropa discussing what role these books and websites play in the radicalization process.

The Alt Right started to decline in 2017 in a perfect storm of ineptitude and organized antifascist pressure, which peaked after the violence of the Unite the Right rally in Charlottesville. Both Morgan and Johnson sat that one out, saying it was a bad idea, but no one wanted to listen to two bookish academics inside of the increasingly volatile white nationalist movement. Now the Alt Right has seen significant "deplatforming," the refusal of social media and web platforms to host them. This has come as activists have pressured Twitter, Facebook, Patreon, web hosting services, and public venues to disallow white nationalists, and they are listening. This has been incredibly effective for left organizers who are striking a blow at the foundations and has destabilized organizations in a way only possible when the thought creators are singled out.

This was actually not a new issue for the publishers. Johnson generally did not sell Counter-Currents titles on their website, but instead used the Amazon Affiliate program to get a portion of the sales of the books when people purchased the titles from a link from the Counter-Currents website. Amazon shut down the Counter-Currents Affiliate account years ago. Now Amazon, which is a massive seller for both Counter-Currents and Arktos, is shuttering white nationalist titles one by one, and as of this writing few titles from either publisher remains. They are quickly trying to establish alternative sales platforms, including selling the e-pub formats like Mobi on Selfy, but without the Amazon behemoth in their corner it will be really difficult for them to survive.

This may end up being fine for Johnson and Morgan, who seem content to live in a world of ideas and eke out a living by peddling vanity projects to a dedicated following. For Friberg and the rest of the movement, this is not enough, and the books will remain a pathway toward revolution. These books are simply a seed, it is what the far-right does with them that matters.

Introduction to Armageddon

A piece of my family is from the diaspora, scattered and barely known. Moshiach is appropriately the messianism that will wipe away the past and build something new, something yet to come and in which we will wait with bated breath. Eschatology has become a common language during this climate collapse to explain the doom that foretells the future. The term *Armageddon* comes from the ancient Israeli city of Meggido, the city where Revelation determined the final battle between God and Satan would play out (it's unclear which side the Christians thought the Jews would be on). That final conflict defines the word, since Meggido was the supposed center of a sequence of wars against Ancient Egypt. But that also puts it in line with the messianic Hebrew tradition that blends the prophetic and the political. The final battle was like the final messiah, one that would free us from the tyranny of the oppressor and of the flesh.

We often read end times prophecies with the certitude of American mega-churches, but in Megiddo, there is an inherent uncertainty. Gnostic readings of the scripture threw doubt on the prescribed victory, and even if God was set to be victorious, there is still a fight to be had as the world dies. There is a choice here, between heaven and hell, or perhaps socialism and barbarism, but the promise is not just of salvation, but of bitter feud. If there was anything that the Pentecostals got right, it was that the Bible promised blood by the buckets.

We are now living through a mass extinction event. The world is shooting past the two degrees Celsius marker that signified a total breakdown of ecological and climate patterns, meaning we have tipped into uncharted waters. Unquenchable drought, crop failure, and famines are becoming more frequent and the rain forests are burning. In Iceland, a country literally named from the ice that dominates its surface, they have held a funeral for the lost glacier. The icecaps are next, and an estimated one million species with it. According to the National Center for Climate Restoration, in a study that dominated news cycles before it was forgotten entirely, this means that by 2050 we could see total societal destruction. Nations and economies will crumble, populations will see mass casualties, the promises of liberal democracy will look like a house of cards.[1]

Total War

We must look at the obvious. This is not something that will only happen if we don't act, even if we mobilize every resource we have to fight it (though we still should). It is happening right now. We are living through it. And it is going to hurt.

"What is love? Love is not idealization. Any true lover knows that if you truly love a woman or a man, you do not idealize them ... You see perfection in imperfection itself, and that is how we should learn to love the world," Slavoj Žižek said once, while covered in trash.[2] He was calling for us to become even more alienated from the natural world, to refuse to romanticize it and instead see it as mechanically as possible. Only through this melancholy could we see the reality of where we are.

There is a certain reality we now have to live with, an ugly one that we have created, and that cannot be minimized through fantastic stories about how we can avert disaster. This reality is not a permission for pessimism, but instead requires great motivation. In this moment we cannot stop the inevitable, but rather we must live through the crisis with a commitment to coming out on the other side in a new world. One that starts now, one that sustains us through the pain, and one that carries us through better than when we began. In this new reality of current collapse, it is no longer about just fixing things, but about survival.

The apocalypse as a term is often misunderstood as the end of the world, but instead it is the end of our world, the one we have today. We are experiencing an apocalyptic event by any measure, but that means the end of the structures and systems that define everything from our governments to our commodities to our social relationships. They will not exist as we know them in the future, they lack the permanence we ascribed to them. Global capitalism, carbon fuel sources, infinite growth, destructive forms of mass production, and liberal democracies were all built on quicksand. When we discovered what we had done we were already sinking.

To create a real fight we have to become post-apocalyptic, to think about how we build something new that protects people now and can give us the tools to find that sustainability. We have to fight because we have no choice, and we can't do that simply by trying to protect what we have had. Instead, we must think about what we will need in the future, because we are there.

Part of this painful relationship with reality is to look soberly at what the collapse has done to us. The shocks of social instability are happening more dramatically and more frequently, forcing tough choices on masses of people around the world. As crisis becomes the new normal, splits will form in the working class, with privileged groups fighting to maintain their menial comforts and kick their own reckoning with a changing world down the road. The Global South has been feeling the results of climate change for years now, and as new phrases like "water wars" enter our lexicon, Western countries display their arrogance in their inability to connect the dots. Fascism often forms as moments of crisis creates breaks in a consensus group, whereby privilege becomes sacred.

The Death Rattle of All Nations

Climate change will be seen most presciently in the manufacture of "the refugee" as an infinite category; dislocation will become a mass experience. This reveals the ongoing reality of colonialism, whereby global capitalism forces migration by extracting the resources of useful soils, stable weather patterns, top soil, and cool air from the Global South. As migration grows internationally, the nationalism of Western nations will continue to define their cultures of dissent, particularly when that demographic change begins to tip political hegemonies and is viewed against the precarity of the new economy.

Roger Eatwell and Matthew Goodwin define "national populism" as the anti-elitism that forms in these moments of change, not necessarily triggered by bad economies but instead by the perception of economic decline and the displacement of social privileges. Here the "native" identities and cultures bite back, they are given priority against what they see as the decadence of globalist cosmopolitanism. Feelings of instability are correlated in the public's mind with the influx of new identities, because the crisis is not of a lack of resources, but of their own identity. We can tie this directly to the seemingly unstoppable rise of the Alternative for Deutschland in Germany, the Front National (now "National Rally") in France, to Brexit and Casa-Pound and the Freedom Party of Austria (FPO) and Trump's GOP. Most people on the left have been unable to determine exactly how national populism works, particularly seeing its evolution as a response to the cultural revolutions of the 1960s rather than just as a recent fascist insurgency.

Eatwell and Goodwin define national populism using the "four Ds": distrust of political elites, the fear of the destruction of their culture, the perceived deprivation of adequate material support like jobs or homes, and the dealignment of the people with their conventional institutions for political consciousness, like established political parties.[3]

National populism is also a war against soft power, the ability to shift the centers of social control from the place of culture, argument, and propaganda. Instead it fetishizes the return of hard power, the swift hand that determines political reality not by influence but by determined force. The left is viewed as a failure for not living up to its promises, though it was never an actual left that we had but instead a meddling neoliberal democracy. That sense of failure stokes the need for a completely new type of vision, one that continues to be revolutionary but refuses to accept the kind of left anticapitalism that crisis may have inspired before. Both the left and the right are driven by what fascist studies scholar Robert Paxton calls the "mobilizing passions," the energies that draw people to profound social discontent and the desire to remake the world. The right is starting to surge as the blueprint for these passions because the left has appeared unable to actualize a solution. That has led to national populism and the pathway to fascist insurgencies as a global response to the movement of peoples.

We are seeing a massive demographic shift in Western countries, one whereby the far-right populist reaction is one of entrenched white supremacy and ethnic identity, rather than purely economic anxiety. Instability across the global South, which can only increase at this point, has triggered mass migration to the North, and now these populations are reconciling their state of ethnic identity as the demographic composition becomes less monolithically white. Eric Kaufman labeled this "White/Shift," the point at which previously dominant white societies go through a period of transition, a point which they think leads populations who are not monolithically white to identify with the earlier white cultural standards through mass assimilation.[4] The question is not how long this will take to happen (it happened before as the WASP majority became the minority and was replaced by a more contemporary "white" American that encompassed everyone from Catholics to Italians to Slavic peoples), but if it will happen at all. Instead, it could be a state of true cosmopolitanism, whereby the cultural hegemony of history is unseated by a new culture marked by intersecting and emerging cultures living together. The point here is not *if* the world is changing (we have no choice in the matter), but how whites will react to those changes, and this is already happening. Across Europe this has been most starkly observed with the militant Islamophobia that motivates the anti-refugee movements of PEGIDA, the English Defence League, and UKIP, not to mention the more militant white nationalist of Bloc Identitaire. Immigration is a result of this crisis, and the nations (who are responsible) will change because of it, a natural progression as the planet changes and human populations logically respond to it.

While people naturally respond to crisis with mutual aid, years of racial tribalism and nationalism has twisted our natural instinct and when placed into the context of "immigration" that programming can override the community's caring instincts. We can expect instability to become endemic. We have been living on borrowed time, the constant ascent of capital and the promise of prosperous perpetuity, but that is a privileged narrative that is both ahistorical and not universally experienced. As the temperatures rise we will see the cataclysmic expansion of pandemics, either from things like the flourishing of mosquitos expanding once-regional illnesses, or more Lovecraftian fears, like what is hiding under polar ice.

Conflict and violence will rage as resources become scarce. There is an old platitude that the summer temperatures brings out the rage in people, and that will certainly be true of nations and ruling classes as they resort to blatant imperialism in the face of catastrophe. It will be as if a seven headed serpent arose from the Mediterranean, false promises will be awarded with integrity, and the gruesome will be made flesh. At least it certainly could be.

How the Gods Die

The other half of my family comes from Nordic stock. In the Norse pantheon, the story of the Aesir and the Vanir, we have an end times narrative called Ragnarok, the death of the Gods. It is hard to compare Ragnarok to the Biblical end, since heathenry simply does not see time in matched terms (it has trouble reckoning with the future, it usually looks to the past), but the Gods are seen as family relatives of the parishioners who share in pursuits in equal measure. This means, while they are honored, they are hardly worshipped in the same way, since they engage in the same journeys we all do.

For Carl Jung, the Gods were manifestations of early experiences lodged into the collective unconscious, and many in pagan circles today would agree that the Gods, while possibly real figures with their own agencies, are also understandings of the natural world, its cycles, its ups and downs, and its emotional resonance. Animism shows us that the Gods are in all things, particularly the natural world, and the honorance of them would be to observe reality as it is and build lives in accordance with it.

The Anthropocene, which is the era when the earth is affected and permanently altered by human beings, would then be the unseating of the Gods, to place them as reactive to human societies who bore into them and change their cosmology. At Ragnarok, the weather is tossed into a catapulting mess of flood and storm, overwhelming the worlds in water.

Ragnarok is Old Norse for "Fate of the Gods," a fate that was, essentially, to be murdered in graphic detail. The demon wolf Fenrir leads a tear across the earth, firebrimming, consuming everything like a rabid virus. The sky then cracks open and fire-giants emerge from Muspelheim, led by Surt, lighting the way with a blazing sword. The fire crosses the Bifrost and takes the rainbow bridge to Asgard, and Heimdall announces their arrival as the bridge crumbles and breaks. The Gods choose to enter battle, the choice was already made for them, and the worlds around start to stretch and crack at the seams with no way out. Odin attacks Fenrir, who swallows the old man before he is killed by Vidar. The wolf Garm and Tyr die in mutual resignation, as does Freyr and Surt, Thor, and Jormungand, Gods dying simultaneously.

Ragnarok is not about capture, victory, or defeat, it is about losing everything until there is nothing. Nothingness without end (Ein-not in Hebrew). The world is plunged into the sea and the void expands and consumes all things. Now there is nothing, what there was before, and existence—not just humans but of everything divine—was a dream.

We do not play into the story of the Gods, because they are encompassing all things, but Fenrir could be here inside us as a dormant virus. When we have destroyed their state of being, undermined the natural functioning of the earth, we could be the ones holding the smoking gun of Ragnarok. The end has always been a war, us against the earth, us against each other.

Our Apocalypse Commune

Instead of aversion thinking, and especially denial, we can hone survival and transgression. The question should be how to live through this crisis and come out the other side stronger, with functioning societies, and with a vision of how to rethink instability as a vulnerability we can exploit to rebuild something ecstatic instead of the dying world we have now. Survival and the continuance of struggle are offensive, rather than defensive, positions, and can be defined by principles that draw us to the kind of fight we want.

Organizing is the key, not just because of what we want to stop, but because of what we want to become. In December of 2015 I was holed up in a house in North Portland, Oregon trying to blockade the police from an early morning eviction. We had been anticipating this (foreclosures happen fast, but the resulting eviction plays out over years), as the family had been fighting a foreclosure eviction with community organizations, it had been near silence before word came in that a marshal was coming. A mass of about a hundred people were able to form a plan and come together to stop the Sheriff's execution of orders, not because we had long-term contingencies in place, but because the people who were near the space had trained and done this work for years. A deep well of experience was activated by circumstance.

We have to build those skills, the ability to coordinate with people to solve tasks on our own, otherwise we will fall to pieces when the walls around us crumble. We exist inside and outside of a State that performs a mass of functions and with which we coordinate our own actions. In its absence we are forced to live up to utopian promises, to look at a society's needs and accommodate, to live through direct action, and, hopefully, to transform those skills from responsive measures into foundational principles of a new type of social organization. This requires various systems of social reproduction to pass skills down and by engaging in "survival pending revolution," a phrase that comes from the Black Panthers who created projects like the Free Breakfast program and community health and dental clinics to meet people's needs. Without organizing in revolt to the current conditions, we will be unable to embed the tools needed to thrive through the crisis and build our new foundations.

Us, When We're Together

We cannot survive the collapse alone. All across rural America there are "preppers" who are planning to live out the apocalypse by hoarding food and fighting their neighbors. This type of solipsism is a death sentence, since we need a collective to meet the complex needs that even individual people have, not to mention whole communities. Skills, relationships, and gifts all come from group coordination, which means building community bonds now so that meaningful connections exist when they are needed later for survival.

"While the wilderness survival skills certainly can't hurt, it will be empathy, generosity, and courage that we need to survive," says Chris Begley, an anthropologist and director of The Exploration Foundation (and wilderness survival instructor) who studies how and why civilizations collapse. As much as he enjoys teaching students how to start fires and build shelters, he knows that this is not the foundation of survival and that there is no scenario when living out rugged individualist post-apocalyptic fantasies make sense. "Kindness and fairness will be more valuable than any survival skill. Then as now, social and leadership skills will be valued. We will have to work together. We will have to grow food, educate ourselves, and give people a reason to persevere. The needs will be enormous, and we cannot run away from that. Humans evolved attributes such as generosity, altruism, and cooperation because we need them to survive. Armed with those skills, we will turn towards the problem, not away from it. We will face the need, and we will have to solve it together. That is the only option. That's what survival looks like."[5]

We are best when we live out the principles of a new society as a form of survival today. Rejecting the alienation of industrial capitalism and the false communitarianism of tribalism are steps towards the type of relationships that can endure. These can, and should, be founded on sincere bonds, federated on a wide scale for coordination, yet do not need to be modeled on radical political movements as we know them today. These political projects are founded on earlier models of how politics is done and, in almost all instances, fail to replicate the kind of relationships that people will hinge their future on. The bond itself is the political act, to reject isolationist pessimism and commit to the commune, and through that struggle to hash out a vision for a better type of world. There is no shortcut path to utopian revolutionary societies, and there is no amount of "points of unity" that will ensure your community will remain exactly as you hoped it would be. Instead you are going to have to make it with what you have.

Individualism, the sanctity of the traditional family, the boundaries between peoples and identity, are arcane relics, bargains of survival in a world with expired rules.

Abolish All Borders

The equator is about to become unlivable. Temperatures are spiking, the land becoming barren, drought, disease, pestilence, and violence will creep across the hyper-exploited regions of the Global South. "The earth isn't dying, it is being killed. And the people killing it have names and addresses," folk singer Utah Philips famously said. A lineage of colonialism, industrial capitalism, and globalization ripped up the lands of South America, Asia, and Africa and then attacked it from the air with carbon emissions. This is making these areas increasingly uninhabitable, which forces a mass train of migration. This is triggering the privileged masses of the Global North to reify their historic roles by enforcing borders through the reclamation of national identities. They expanded across the world through Manifest Destiny, and once they had their fill they closed the door behind them.

The free movement of people is the only option for survival, borders are a falsehood created only as protectionism for hyper-exploitation. The crisis we are in, of destroyed land and subsequently displaced people, is the manufacture of a mass refugee class, and the violence that the Western states will respond with is border genocide. This is a defining feature of Armageddon, where dominant classes will fight against a growing lumpenproletariat wave looking to take back the Global North's ill-gotten gains.

There is only one choice here, to side with the one globalized mass class and reject the false narratives of national sovereignty. The function of this is bifurcated. On the one hand this is the only logical conclusion to the forced migration of people, which happens as our own participation in mass consumption has triggered the migration in the first place. But on the other hand, this creates an opportunity for global solidarity across identity lines to develop. This will help forge the tools necessary to take on the offenders who created the crisis in the first place, who will try to use this chaos to further consolidate wealth. Revolutions of the multitude, particularly in late capitalist or post-capitalist class relations, comes from the ability to realize shared conditions and to commit to militancy. To be truly internationalist.

"The multitude is the real productive force of our social world, whereas Empire is a mere apparatus of capture that lives only off the vitality of the multitude—as Marx would say, a vampire regime of accumulated dead labor that survives only by sucking off the blood of the living," wrote Michael Hardt and Antonio Negri way back in 1999, before the return of classical imperialism hollowed out our sense of internationalism.[6]

The new state of migration helps to break down national boundaries between workers, and the shared precarity of the new economy and climate created a common experience. When communities are forged in a new cosmopolitan reality, they are stronger and hold a greater capacity to act in unison. This doesn't ignore the existing hierarchies internal to the mass classes, but it creates new conditions whereby those contradictions can be addressed head on.

The instability that we are transitioning to can be one of fortified borders or no borders, and it is the destruction of all national boundaries that leads to the eventual destruction of all nations, of all private properties, and the social constructs that the rich use to further exploit the rest of us. If we want to flourish on the other side of this Armageddon, then we have to choose to do it as one international federated community. To commit to the commune, all of us together, is the strength, the inverse of the tribal.

All Tools on the Table

Historically, the riot has more precedence than the strike. The use of a strike, most commonly in labor disputes mediated by a union, is the withholding of labor, though it can be the withholding of other types of participation. The riot instead is a form of mass rebellion where guerilla action is taken in accordance with the particularities that the community or individual bring to the table. For much of history the riot held sway, only to be unseated by the strike within the last two hundred years.[7]

This descends from the shift in both economic and political roles. Before the era of waged labor, particularly in the peasant years preceding capitalism's full realization, a person had difficulty making a strike an effective option. A strike requires an institutional role, such as a worker, whose participation in a system is required for that system to function. When a person withholds their participation along with others who shared that institutional role, they grind the process to a halt and their power is made obvious. Before the era of waged labor this model was more difficult, and a direct strike against structures of power that was not specific to a dictated role was more expedient. Before the era of mass politics, when politics was determined by aristocratic decree, most people lacked identities as political actors. A mass movement of politics was inconceivable since governmental activities were done by dictate (with legitimacy loaned from the pulpit), so there was little option as an internal stakeholder.

It took a shift into mass participation, the elimination of the commons, and the exploitation of Enlightenment values of individualism for the strike to be possible. Marx and Engels created the construction of the worker as the vulnerable point of the dialectic: capital created the worker for exploitation, but that unique position could be capital's undoing.

As automation, the "gig economy," and economic decline ravage communities that once relied on unionized factories, public employment, and a reliable social safety net for stability, the ranks of the lumpenproletariat enlarge. Historically Marxists loathed the lumpenproletariat. Clara Zetkin suggested the "venal lumpens" were ripe for terrorism, a popular notion in Marxist circles that masses unable to sustain themselves through wage labor were personally bankrupt and strategically useless since they lacked the ability to strike. The unemployed, houseless, nomads, Indigenous communities existing outside of the economy, subsistence farmers, bohemians, and a range of conflicting and intersecting identities could be labeled as "lumpen"—those who don't have a role to reject. Mao focused on the rural peasantry, also without a regular position as wage laborers, but the role they found was as soldiers in protracted guerilla war. You didn't need to strategically organize workers to strike, shut down the economy, and start taking elements of the economy over if you could just take an armed cell into the mountains and descend on the cities ready for violence. This was a riot, not a strike.

What we are heading into is a destabilized economy where many, many people will be unable to hold positions of wage labor. Unemployment will grow alongside automation and further globalized shifts in capital, but those who are employed will increasingly be "self-employed," a moniker that used to convey a professional skilled caste and now increasingly signals student debt without steady income. People will piece together their finances in the best of cases, by renting out bedrooms, taking short-term assignments, and changing positions (and professions) rapidly.

This does not negate the strike as an essential strategy, but it certainly cannot be the only one. And neither can the riot, as we lack the ability to simply tear down what we abhor since it is happening in waves as the planet crumbles. A new diversity of tactics will emerge, blending strategies, reimagining them. The General Strike can make an appearance either as multi-workplace actions (multiple industries in conjunction) or issue based (climate strike). Non-traditional strike actions will emerge (Uber, Lyft), or coordinated actions from people receiving services (Wages for Housework, Poor People's Movement). And mass action, occupation, and counter-power will emerge as a way of grouping struggles. This means everything is on the table, nothing can be ignored, the riot, the strike, everything in between, and also the strategies unknown that will emerge from material circumstances yet to be revealed.

"Not so very long ago, however, such self-governing peoples were the majority of humankind. Today, they are seen from the valley kingdoms as 'our living ancestors,' 'what we were like before we discovered wet-rice cultivation, Buddhism and civilization.' On the contrary, I argue that hill peoples are best understood as runaway, fugitive, maroon communities who have, over the course of two millennia, been fleeing the oppressions of state-making projects in the valleys—slavery, conscription, taxes, corvée labor, epidemics, and warfare," said James C. Scott in *The Art of Not Being Governed*. The people who not only live outside of the structures of the State, but in direct opposition to it, live the life that shows us what is possible and, maybe, preferred. It was once that we would have to reject the world to allow for such a thing, but now the world will actually reject us. When instability is forced on the mass institutions of the State, we will have no choice but to turn to alternatives, to create structures that repudiate the previous institutions of control that, in this new era, lack the illusion of permanence.

This condition is and was the state of many people, those not fully even allowed into the current state of the system. George Orwell wrote of the proletariat in *1984*, a social class whose subjugation allowed them to not be burdened with the repression that came from citizenry: they were allowed to revel in sex, pleasure, and love. This more accurately represents the lumpenproletariat, a class that is disallowed full employment, and is manifested in ways as numerous as society. The riot still has salience, it still speaks through those people denied full participation, who exist in a perpetual state of anarchy, both the danger of disallowal and the freedom of a counter-society.

"Black exclusion from the social contract is existence within a heavily surveilled and heavily regulated state of subjection. We are carriers of the coveted blue passport still trapped in the zone of citizen non-being. We are simultaneously subjugated and teased with promises of liberation via individualized neoliberal self-betterment and swallowing of a long-soured American Dream whilst choking back dissonances and forcibly reconciling irreconcilable double consciousnesses," write Zoé Samudzi and William C. Anderson in the "Anarchism of Blackness," about the forced state of anarchy since Black communities have been disallowed into the American social framework, and forced to go it alone. "Black America has been reminded again and again that we are seen as a monolithic group of feeble-minded children to be chastised by the state for our own disenfranchisement and community disadvantage. If there is nothing to be offered that addresses the reparations Black America is owed on several fronts, then we should seek to secure these things ourselves through action." This state of outsiderness to the system (fundamentally different from the view from inside a workplace), requires its own set of tools, and they will increasingly have to be picked up as more and more people are simply disallowed from any sort of participation. This will, in essence, create an even more concrete series of advantages, since mere survival will require more or less formal structures of mutual aid and solidarity, and those structures can carry people into the next stage of our world.

The Utopian Impulse

The modern Western left is obsessed with material circumstances. (It's true, I literally just said that phrase.) But this misses a key reality about how and why people take action, and ideas and ideology hold incredible sway. The mobilizing passions of discontent and instability can lead us in a lot of directions, they create the energy to act, but what does that action mean? Is it in the direction of liberation, or does it turn back on itself through inversion? Power can shoot in a number of directions, and so ideas can determine its course. We don't need to shy away from them.

Ideologies help cement commitments to movements, while conditions propel them forward and prime people for action, so they should be seen in symbiosis. Likewise, we have to prefigure to a certain degree who we want to become. This is not just a case of Darwinian evolution; in the Anthropocene we determine our world, and we can determine our fate. To think that this is entirely the product of material conditions or the machinations of ambivalent Gods is useless; instead we can direct how we want those conditions to grow.

We either commit to the new world or we don't, and that requires acting in earnest, experimenting, visioning, and even a certain amount of idealism. We can reclaim the romantic, return ourselves to passionate living and dreaming. This crisis can be a revolution, and so we can live revolutionary lives, with art, community, and spirit at the center. We do not have to return to the status quo on the conclusion of merely surviving, and we can do that by making decisions about what we will strive for. We cannot determine the whole of our future, but we can choose what we run towards.

When the Lights Go Out

What's in your emergency box? Flashlights, canned food, jugs of water? I added prescription cat food, spare antibiotics, and chocolate. How much ammo do you have? These are great for an earthquake but they are poor for the impending collapse. Things will not collapse at once, they will simply get longer, louder, more difficult, more painful. There is no explosion, and definitely not a whimper, just decline and anger and violence. The end will be defined not by a single apocalyptic event, but a global war of conflict over resources, portrayed as national sovereignty and other fantasies, and the dissolution of structures we once believed eternal.

In a sense, this unravelling started years ago, creating a "refugee crisis" for decades (though this is only a crisis because the West clings to borders). We have also been fighting it, consciously and unconsciously, for just as long, committing to creativity and solidarity to survive. And so we continue this war, and know that there is no easy ending. Instead there is just the other side of it, what we can build out of it, and whether or not what we do now is able to overtake the weakening composure of the State's ramparts.

Our side of Armageddon is when we fight to remain a community and to sustain our vision of the world. We didn't choose the circumstances that are coming to bear on us, but we can choose how we are going to use this situation.

***

The concept of apocalypse has become incredibly fragmented for Americans terrorized by millennialism. The word is supposed to generally suggest the end of the world, whatever that means, but nothing is ever really over. One of the most popular genres of science fiction is "post-apocalyptic"—after an apocalypse has happened, meaning the apocalypse wasn't really the end. Instead it was simply cataclysmic (usually our world become desolate, dangerous, and acutely warmer than it was before), and provided a radical shift that brought an end to most (if not all) institutions of social life. This is quite a bit different than the stark apocalypse of the Bible, and a genre marked by its indulgence of fantastical cruelties (I'll meet you at the Thunderdome), but it is, in essence, hopeful. If there is an "after the apocalypse" then that means we, at least some of us, actually survive. The apocalypse is the violation, and what comes after is a determinate about how we pick up the pieces and try and (re)build. This narrative is often colored with warlords, disease, and S&M gear, but it doesn't have to be (we'll probably keep the S&M gear).

But we aren't just talking about this weight, this apocalypse, we are talking about the battle at its beginning. This is the point where the armies amass on sacred land and have to battle for what kind of world we are going to be left with after the fall. This Armageddon started long before we were born, in the infancy of industrial capitalism and its antecedents, but it was ignored and treated as a subtext. The eschatological version of this we are rushing towards forces this struggle to the forefront, because no survival is possible without it.

This is, of course, nightmarish, a tribulation that was not the fault of everyday people (anyone that blames working people for environmental collapse is a collaborator), but we will still be forced to go through it.

While Ragnarok ties up every loose end by destroying everything, there is always a counter-narrative. Some readings say that an incredible green world will actually come back from the same ocean. Vidar, Vali, Baldur, Hodr, Modi, and Magni actually survived, and they want to lead an entirely new world forward. Two people were hidden in the Wood of Hoddminir and will repopulate the earth, and the secret daughter of the sun will rise and conquer the sky.

Or none of it could happen. The world could die, we could be impotent to stop it, and we would have to deal with the fact that the "arc of history" only bends where we bend it, and nothing is inevitable. Nothingness without end.

The question is not if this is going to take place (the horrors of Armageddon becoming hyperreal) but if we can actually make it to the other side. But I have a certain faith here. We can build a new society, ingratiate the Old (and New) Gods, and find our way out of the forest. We have all the tools to do this already. We can just choose.

Blackface is the Story of White Identity

One Monday night in college a friend called to tell me that he was holding a Martin Luther King Jr. Day party. The centerpiece of this was people drinking 40s of Olde English, eating fried chicken, and playing N.W.A. He wasn't from a fraternity, but a corduroyed hipster from a local indie pop band. This wasn't the South; it was Eugene, Oregon. It wasn't the 1980s, it was 2006.

The series of controversies in Virginia politics in early 2019, bookended by Gov. Ralph Northam and Attorney General Mark Herring both admitting to appearing in racist costumes during college in 1981, inspired a slew of articles about change. This suggests that Blackface, one of the most dehumanizing caricatures of Black people imaginable, was perhaps just a tasteless joke in its time. Today our pasts are more easily accessible than ever, so the pundits are correct that a reckoning is taking place that they were completely unprepared for.

While anyone applying for competitive jobs online scrubs their social media accounts, it doesn't take long to find artifacts that people would rather keep buried. I was in college when Facebook skyrocketed, and because it placed no limit on photo uploads you often see massive albums for individual parties, captured at all angles. Search for any holiday or theme party and you'll find a slew of racist caricatures, from pale-painted Geisha costumes to wide-brimmed sombreros to full headdresses on white lacrosse players. It took me ten minutes to find a white student slathered in brown paint.

There will be a lot to account for as time passes, especially for those of us whose youth is easily accessible on social media backlogs. But how does this reality apply to something as blatant as a rich white student painting his face and posing next to a Halloween Klansman?

Blackface comes out of an American tradition of mocking slaves in theater across the country starting in the 1830s; through Reconstruction and into Jim Crow it continued as a brutal spectacle. The function was to exaggerate supposedly African features, apply significant stereotypes about intelligence and sexuality, and turn them into the basest of activities. Whites know themselves in apartheid by their shared revulsion at races they have ascribed "otherness" to, and Blackface allows them to purposefully rob Black people of all human dignity and to find joy in that cruelty. It has its own metapolitical function: while Blackface makes few political claims outright, it helps reinforce the lingering racial supremacy in the heart of Americana, encouraging the impulse that Black people have to be controlled, forced into subservience, and made victims of violence for society's good.

While the claim that "times have changed" persists as a defense, it was widely known as offensive by the time they slathered up their faces, and that's why they did it. These were intentionally offensive costumes, funny to them because they were transgressive, and, in doing so, they were able to appeal to something that was hidden yet never eradicated. They signaled to each other in the same way that the most extreme racist jokes, told in whispers in parties of insiders, still create explosive laughter. They may have walked the public lines of "racial progress," but in private they enjoy succumbing to racist narratives.

I was born in 1984 and throughout the 1990s and into the 2000s it was common to hear racist jokes told in public venues, not because we were monoracial communities, but because white kids assumed there were no consequences for those jokes. In perfect episodes of white blindness, the racist joke was an attempt to say that society was essentially post-racial, and therefore the "sensitivities" of anti-racism were puritanical and unnecessary. The racist joke then serves as a safety valve for the tension: white people can absolve themselves of responsibility by claiming that white supremacy has been sufficiently unseated.

The reality is not that these rich, white politicians have a Black-face problem, but that white supremacy makes itself known in shocking ways that were just as prevalent today as they were then. Heightened technology, cell phone cameras, social media, and the like have made this easily confrontable, yet most journalism seems lost in its ability to recognize it. The Blackface is one we have all known, from Greek Row to YouTube comedians, and therefore it elicits so much fear.

On Halloween of 2013 I was resigned to a quiet night at home—my partner was stuck at work—so I loaded up on candy. We lived in a busy suburb of Portland, Oregon, and since I was still reeling from some recent family tragedies, I'd been looking forward to some of the normalcy that comes from trick-or-treaters. Towards the end of my night a young couple came with their son who was dressed in a nice three-piece suit, a small lapel pin I had trouble making out in the dark, and a face that was almost blinding in its jet-black shade. I stood there stunned since, in the moment, I was having trouble putting together exactly what his costume was. His proud mom started humming "Hail to the Chief."

It wasn't until the Black-faced caricature of Barack Obama left my driveway that I got what his parents had dressed him up to be. There wasn't a hint of guilt in their eyes, and they either didn't know or didn't care about what they'd set their son up for.

The Virginia scandals will fade from the news cycle, but only because they'll be replaced by another similar story. And another. Because this is the story not just of white supremacy in America, but also of white people in general. It takes much more than personal accountability and retribution to uproot something fundamental to U.S. society. And that only starts when we know that culpability is all around us.

Because of Their Violence

White nationalism is implicitly violent; it cannot exist without it. The proposition is, on its own merits, steeped in the most expansive and profound sorts of violence. Even liberal American society, which cannot claim itself as an egalitarian community without revolutionary change, has to acknowledge the deep violence that led to its founding and that motivates every meager attempt at social progress. White nationalism sees the violence of the past, from slavery to colonialism to Jim Crow, as compromising measures: that violence is normal to racial relations, never extraordinary. This is the "spoils to the victor" mentality crossed with belief in the inferiority of the other that allows the genocide of Indigenous people and the ongoing racial revenge against Africa-descended people as a logical and normal response by whites, an ideology that has violence at its center. The return to violence for them is the return to normality it is how a people comes to know itself. So it is no surprise when that violence moves from implicit to explicit, from the structural violence of Western society to the targeted violence of white nationalist insurgents.

In 1979, the Maoist Communist Workers Party (originally named the Workers Viewpoint Organization—WVO) staged a rally in Greensboro, North Carolina, where they were organizing with a largely Black community of textile workers.[1] Their "Death to the

Klan" slogan expressed a certain militancy after decades of Klan terrorism. Through the 1950s and 1960s, the Third Era resurrected Ku Klux Klan enacted a paramilitary-style war against integration in the South, including lynchings, bombings, and assassinations. Black organizations had struggled to meet the call by creating antifascist self-defense organizations, such as Robert Williams joint NAACP/NRA chapter in North Carolina who fought back against Klan violence by arming the residents.[2] By the time the 1970s rolled around the Klan had ceased to be a centralized organization and had instead started to fragment, and David Duke had tried to turn it into a "respectable" white nationalist institution similar to contemporary Alt Right organizations like Richard Spencer's National Policy Institute.

The Klan had started to resurface in North Carolina in 1979, holding "educational" events and attacking a Southern Christian Leadership Conference protest of the incarceration of a Black defendant who was innocent and had a developmental disability. There the Klan opened fire, and a protester even fired back in self-defense, yet it was the Black antiracist demonstrator who faced the criminal charges. All of this was in advance of a Garden Grove showing of Birth of a Nation, the racist 1915 film that lionized the Klan and was the inspiration to the birth of the Second Generation of Klan activity in the 1920s. Organizers tried to stop the permit from being issued, but the city only challenged the protesters right to counter-demonstrate rather than the Klan's ability to stage their show. Many organizers with the Communist Workers Party had been focused on unionizing industrial shops in the area that had historically been a struggle (just as most of the South had been) with major strikes at Cannon Mills tracing as far back as 1921. "In 1979, the repression of organizing drives continued, while Klan activity increased," described Sally Avery Bermanzohn, an activist with the CWP. "The KKK drives a wedge between black and white workers ... it is very dangerous to deal with groups like the Klan that are so prone to violence. Building black-white unity is essential for a union drive, and dealing with the KKK makes it much harder for people to see eye to eye. Dividing workers along racial lines is a tried-and-true tactic companies use to keep out unions."[3] The fight against the violence of the Klan was implicit to their unionization campaign: their vision of success on the shop floor necessitated pushing back on the Klan, who wanted to organize the white workers. That day in Garden Grove they drove back the Klan successfully, which inspired the group to continue their anti-Klan organizing and organize a "Death to the Klan" march and conference for November 3. "When I saw the Klans with the guns I got nervous, really nervous," said Willena. "But when they backed up into that community center, all my nervousness left. IT was payback time! I was pushing back at those scums for all the wounds and hurts from my past. It felt good; it was a jubilation to me."[4]

In Greensboro, several Klan organizers from the North Carolina Knights of the KKK and the National Socialist Party of America had united to form the United Racist Front. When they went out to meet the CWP on November 3, they were joined by informant Ed Dawson, who was acting as a leader in the movement.[5] Dawson had worked with the police for the previous eight years after he was enraged that the Klan did not come in his defense during a criminal proceeding. Dawson had seen that Klan and Nazi leaders were starting to work together, driving a frenzy of support to "confront communists" in Greensboro and that they were acquiring machine guns to do so. He warned the police, who did nothing. The guns themselves were instigated by Bernard Butkovich, an Alcohol, Tobacco, and Firearms agent who had gone undercover with the American Nazi Party and pushed them towards fight and gun training. The police, for their part, delayed issuing the march permit to the CWP, handed out the march route to a random white questioner at the station, and demanded that the activists not bring weapons if they were to be permitted.

In front of news crews, the white supremacist faction opened fire on protesters, killing five activists rallied with the CWP and one of their own. As documents were later revealed, law enforcement had early knowledge of what was going to take place, a part of their ongoing efforts to infiltrate radical organizations.[6] The Greensboro Police Department did not put officers near the start of the march, despite understanding that the white supremacists would bring weapons. The nearest officers were blocks away and even abandoned their positions right before the march itself began.[7]

The Greensboro Massacre has taken a certain place in the history of Klan violence only because, to a large degree, it was the last public show of Klan paramilitary firepower in any coherent fashion and the State's culpability was apparent even to outsiders. The violence was so significant, the police failure so complete, that a Truth and Reconciliation Committee was formed to establish consensus that the slaughter was allowed to happen.[8] This was not the beginning or the end of white supremacist violence, more like a flashpoint that pressed it into our collective memory, and in the 1980s the Aryan Nations-affiliated organization The Order left a trail of blood, robberies, and assassinations across the country, offering an image of the revolutionary potential of their ideologies. Their ideas increased in virulence as well. Christian Identity took a vulgar reading of the Bible stating that European whites were the "lost tribes of Israel," Jews were in league with the Devil, and people of color lacked the humanity, and souls, of whites. A series of millennialist cults formed around the country, helping to spark the beginning of the militia movement with Posse Comitatus and acting as the theological core for the most radical white power organizations bent on overthrowing the government (which they called the Zionist Occupation Government, or ZOG). This led to some of the most militant acts of violence into the 1990s, from bombing campaigns to assassinations. In the urban corner, neo-Nazi skinhead gangs formed as a way of channeling youth anger toward impulsive acts of violence, and white supremacist organizations like White Aryan Resistance helped to push them into increasingly shocking acts of violence. Kathleen Belew shows that this period was marked by a turn away from white supremacist rear-guard violence, that of maintaining the status quo, to the increasingly revolutionary aspiration of the white power movement that came in the wake of the Civil Rights successes and the large number of veterans coming home from Vietnam. The movement, always violent to its core, increased the prominence of violence in its self-conception.[9]

When the Alt Right first made itself known in 2015 (it had been lingering around for years before that), people immediately signaled, rightly, that they were ideologically the same as their North Carolina comrades, only with well pressed suits, books of pseudo-philosophy, and an upper-middle-class arrogance. This method was, however, not new by any means. When David Duke took over the largest KKK contingent in the 1970s, he largely dropped the buffoonish robes and argued wedge issues like immigration and affirmative action. He gained support by railing against bussing in urban Northern cities like Boston, finding a way of just slightly coding his language to give whites permission to vent racial anxiety.[10] He later left the Klan to form the National Association for the Advancement of White People and, throughout the 1980s, built up a base of support and talking points that would lead to his catastrophic political runs in the late 1980s and early 1990s. About the time David Duke was making waves, Jared Taylor, a former *PC Magazine* editor with a degree from Yale, started American Renaissance, a "race realist" publication and series of conferences dedicated to reinvigorating academic-sounding arguments for the racial inferiority of non-whites and the perennial need for "a self-consciously European, Majority-white nation."[11] He brought together figures like *Forbes*-editor-turned-anti-immigrant-extremist Peter Brimelow and Kevin MacDonald, whose work has defined 21st Century antisemitism by suggesting Judaism was a "group evolutionary strategy" to out compete non-Jews for resources.[12]

This was, again, not new. Figures like Francis Parker Yockey had taken German Idealist and Conservative Revolutionary philosophy and melded it with elements of the left to attempt a smart, and sober-appearing take on white nationalism. Organizations like the Pioneer Fund, a fascist and eugenic foundation that funded "race science" research used in books like the *Bell Curve*, had existed since the 1930s, using establishment money to push the academy to validate their most atrocious ideas. The Council of Conservative Citizens, a neo-Confederate group founded in the 1980s as a way of engaging the original membership lists from the pro-Segregationist White Citizens Councils of the 1960s, began holding conferences with scores of public officials, including Mike Huckabee and Trent Lott.[13] At the same time, they were arguing that miscegenation was "against God's chosen order" and publicly venerated slavery and the antebellum South. In France, fascist academics like Alain de Benoist built the

European New Right by reappropriating post-colonialist, New Left, and environmentalist rhetoric to launder in fascist philosophy, all in the name of de-stigmatizing the "identitarianism" he thought was at the core of a nationalist revival.[14]

All of these organizations were more suit and tie than robe and hood, and the Alt Right was merely the latest incarnation of these, built for an audience of meme-lovers and those steeped in paleoconservative, Third Positionist, and European New Right tracts. The argument that the Alt Right tries make is that their presence is about ideas, not violence, and so the left's response is hyperbolic at best: it is preparing to respond to violence when all they have are unpopular opinions. The same was said for its organizational ancestors, all clamoring just to have their voices heard in this unjust system of "political correctness."

The problem, however, is that their violence is implicit for only so long before it can no longer be contained by its leadership. The Council of Conservative Citizens, long known for its ties to explicit white nationalist street groups with KKK and neo-Nazi affiliations, was cited as the inspiration for Dylann Roof's massacre at the Charleston church in 2016. The CofCC was birthed from the earlier pro-segregationist White Citizens Councils, which, after losing most of their fights over integration romanticized Rhodesia and South African whites who they believed were facing demographic eradication, an earlier version of the "White Genocide" conspiracy theory that motivated Roof and other shooters.[15] David Duke's era of the KKK has been accused of dozens of acts of violence, and its membership went on to form projects like White Aryan Resistance, which was sued into oblivion after its associates murdered an Ethiopian immigrant in Portland, Oregon in the late 1980s.[16] American Renaissance, as a central hub for the white nationalist movement in the U.S., has seen scores of the most violent edges of the racialist movement come through its doors (the behavior of those at the edges is more extreme than that of members at the center of the movement), including members of Aryan Nations who were looking for a home after they lost their compound when several members attacked a Black family passing by. It takes little to see the violence that is underneath the surface with their public facing organizations, all it requires is to look at its members, what they do, and what they want.[17]

By the time the Greensboro Massacre had taken place, Duke was deep into the refashioning of the KKK and they had tried to rebrand themselves as a "white advocacy" organization. This was at the same time as the white power movement was radicalizing towards race war; both tendencies working side by side, intermingling since the goals were largely the same.

The Alt Right itself has also been mired in violence since its earliest incarnations, though it was hard to pick up on in public discourse because of its diffuse and confused nature. Attacks have been inspired by the Alt Right, such as the March 2017 killing of a homeless man in New York by James Jackson. Jackson had been reportedly radicalized online by the Alt Right, including interacting with material from Richard Spencer, the founder of the movement. Jeremy Christian took out the anger he honed at Patriot Prayer events (an Alt Right-supporting-organization), murdering two people in an Islamophobic frenzy on a Portland train.[18] The "incel" movement, which means involuntarily celibate, came from the fringes of the anti-feminist web culture and motivated mass shooter Eliot Rogers and the car attack by Toronto's Alek Minassian. Brendan Tarrant was so compelled by the online presence of the Alt Right that, after penning a manifesto that contained the movement's key arguments, he strapped on a GoPro and livestreamed his murder of fifty-one people.[19] There are more as the news comes in, attacks linked to the Manosphere or those in the Atomwaffen Division, the Nazi Satanist inspired militant racialist organization, as well as an ever increasing list of Proud Boy assaults and desperate Q-Anon related lethal plots.

What the Alt Right leadership, like Spencer, will tell you is that these are a violent fringe of their organization and that they would never condone that violence. That is true in some cases, not in others, but it is beside the point. Throughout the multiple generations of the KKK, tracing back to its rear-guard action defending the lost Confederacy in the 1860s through the Second Era Klan's massive growth in the 1920s to its days with the violent United Klans of

America, the vigilante violence usually followed a pattern beyond that of the official functions of those organizations. While the Klan was clearly responsible for its murders, they were rarely "Klan sanctioned" in the most official sense, in the same way that Jim Crow relied on extra-judicial violence to enforce the softer codes issued by the State. The violent rhetoric, the revolutionary aims, and the apocalyptic tone has a way of sanctifying violence, and those "seemingly random" acts of violence are a sheer necessity for those organizations.[20] If they were to admit who and what they are, the public reaction would force the State to cave and target them, and, in times past, they certainly did. After a series of bombings, one that killed four young girls in Birmingham, Alabama, the FBI began to focus on Klan violence in the South. As Matthew N. Lyons has pointed out, this was not out of altruism but of its contest to the State: "Although FBI officials shared the Klan's racist ideology, they saw the Klan as a threat because it carried out organized violence without authorization from the state. They also looked down on most Klansman as poor, rural, and ignorant (a stereotype shared by many liberals then and now). By contrast, the FBI had no problem with the equally racist but more genteel Citizens Council. The bureau also did nothing to disrupt either local police brutality or the informal (non-KKK) vigilante networks that enforced white supremacy in many rural areas of the South."[21]

That happened only after the violence went from its implicit nature, where members were quietly encouraged to engage in violence in their personal capacity to the explicit violence of commands from a pulpit. Historically, there was more of a reliance on white vigilantes to carry out extra-judicial violence as a form of social control, and it was only as the militarization of the police increased in the 1980s (and the formation of the openly and revolutionary anti-government white power movement) that it shifted.[22] As the early Morris Dees lawsuit that stripped the United Klans of America of their $7 million in resources in 1987 shows, their rhetoric and intention was clear from the start.[23] The violence that these organizations rely on are always stoked with subtlety, rarely carried out as public praxis unless they want to completely destroy their aboveground wing and head into the world of pure armed struggle. This makes their violence more persistent, more ever present, always ready to spill over and take lives.

Since 2017, one event has haunted our collective memory, standing amidst the constant violence as the one we constantly point to as the moment the world seemed to change. Is the "Unite the Right" rally in Charlottesville in 2017 our generation's Greensboro Massacre? While there are some parallels, including the steady decline of the Alt Right as the communities they are trying to embed themselves in are able to see their agenda with clarity, it does not seem to match the brutality. There was a decision to publicly attack the CWP with military force, and that came from the central organizers and not just the fringe. While Charlottesville was the high-water mark in the public face of the Alt Right as a (aspirational) mass movement, that says nothing about its *potential* for violence.

What does it take for white nationalist movements to move from public facing community organizing to open acts of terrorism, or propaganda of the deed? History shows that it is failure and desperation, the inability to achieve their organizing goals in a conventional means and to, instead, turn to acts of spontaneous cruelty. The Order, Timothy McVeigh's 1995 attack on the Oklahoma Federal Building, and a series of skinhead shootings over the past twenty years have shown this: a feeling of helplessness is the best indicator that intentional acts of mass killing are a possibility.

The story of the Greensboro Massacre is significant not just for the intense chaos and police complicity, but for the complete acquittal that the triggermen were granted afterward. The city went to great lengths to hide its own complicity in what happened, to blot out the image of the union activists murdered by a confederation of white nationalists, and to deflect accountability. Even when the Truth and Reconciliation Committee began its investigation in 2004 it was limited in scope since it had no subpoena power, many people were scared to testify, and retired police were advised not to speak.[24] "The Commission finds strong evidence that members of the police department allowed their negative feelings toward Communists in general, and outspoken black activist and WVO leader Nelson Johnson in particular, to color the perception of the threat posed by these groups," the Commission said in their report.[25] The trials themselves were a manifestation of the racism implicit in the law enforcement structure that robbed the community of accountability and reinforced the free ability of the Klan to engage in violence.

> We find one of the most unsettling legacies of the shootings is the disconnect between what seems to be a common sense assessment of wrongdoing and the verdicts in the two criminal trials. When people see the shootings with their own eyes in the video footage, then know that the trials led to acquittals, it undermines their confidence in the legal system... the majority of us believe that the system is not just randomly imperfect; rather, it tends to be disproportionately imperfect against people of color and poor people.[26]

After the Greensboro Massacre, many of the white nationalists involved went on to become celebrities in the movement, seemingly untouchable. Harold Covington went on to help form the violent neo-Nazi gang in the UK called Combat 18, which often provided security for the British National Party, as well as creating the Northwest Imperative to call for like-minded people to move to the Pacific Northwest.[27] Frazier Glenn Miller, another co-planner of the attack and longtime white nationalist organizer, gave up on his larger work of building towards an ethnostate without Jews and decided to complete his mission by shooting a fourteen-year-old boy and his grandparent who were leaving a Jewish community center in Oakland, Kansas.[28] His years of work for his cause had seen nothing change in his favor and so, like so many before him, he loaded a gun and decided to take some people out on his trip into oblivion.

This desperation has become methodology since the 1980s as an eventual police crackdown and the left's counter-organizing has allowed little success for the revolutionary aims of the white nationalist movement.[29] Former KKK and Aryan Nations organizer Louis Beam outlined this most clearly in his paper "Leaderless Resistance," which favored autonomous violent attacks over formalized organizations since this negated the threat of infiltration and internal dissension.[30] This idea has been taken up by organizations around the world, and "Lone Wolf" violence has had a persistent effect in giving purpose to the fringes of a movement where they feel ineffectual. All the justification for spontaneous acts of ultraviolence are built in, whether individually or with a few radicals on a mission.

The event in Charlottesville was an attempt for the white nationalist movement to stand on its own away from the more moderate elements who betrayed their core ideas, and Spencer believed that an above-ground fascist movement could have currency. If dressed just right (khakis and polos), spoken perfect ("a question of Jewish power," "what is identity?"), then they could sway a set of those new to Trump's base. But the reality is that this was always a pipe dream because white nationalism is an unstable molecule, built for combustion, with hurt and cruelty as its connective tissue.

When activists in Charlottesville first heard of the event they knew what it would be, even if they could not convince those around them to take it seriously. There had been a sequence of increasingly hostile threats from the far-right, all coalescing around the wedge issue of Confederate monuments. "We expected there to be more deaths . . . we thought there were going to be gun fights. We thought they were going to shoot people. No, we knew it was going to be big. And what was difficult was trying to get the townspeople and the so called leaders to believe it," said Jalane Schiller, an activist with Black Lives Matter Charlottesville. "We knew that this was going to be bad . . . most reporters aren't paying attention . . . they thought we were just being alarmist."[31] Instead of taking the threat of the white nationalists seriously, they began monitoring the antifascists when they were holding trainings, organizing medics, and creating a support infrastructure for the day of.

As the day began, the violence was swift and immediate. The most iconic image from Unite the Right came from the night before, when hundreds held tiki torches, marched through the University of Virginia chanting "Blood and Soil," and attacked protesters holding vigil. The next day a thousand white supremacists were met by a thousand counter-demonstrators, clashes became endemic as Nazis hoisting shields in a phalanx charged antiracists. The Alt Right had their permits canceled and were pushed back, and a joy set in assuming they had been defeated, at least for the day.

"They had been ordered to disperse, everyone thought they were heading out, we thought we had won, there was a sense of relief and a sense of joy. It wasn't long after that that the incident [happened] at 4th and Water," said Don Gathers, a pastor who had been helping to organize the day's counterprotest.[32] This was where Fields charged his car into the crowd, throwing people into the air as his car created the inertia to start a chain reaction. Gatherers had been watching in horror as the day had progressed but were optimistic with the retreat of the fascists, and then saw a nightmare unfold and the jubilation collapse.

> We were constantly getting phone calls all throughout the day, and there was this heaviness that was hanging over the city the entire day. A huge cloud of despair. So when we go that last fateful call, we immediately jumped up where we were . . . and went tearing down Water street and we actually got there before the first responders did. That whole scene was just a complete nightmare. An utter nightmare. I told people it literally looked like a bomb had dropped on that immediate intersection. The buildings were still standing, but there were bodies on every corner. Bodies were disfigured, broken bones, there was blood, it looked like a scene in a war movie. . . I found myself standing right over Heather while folks worked on her . . . they were doing all that they could, but it's just an eerie feeling because it was almost as though I watched her soul leave her body. I saw her life leave her. It was as though you saw the life lift out of her as they were trying and doing all that.[33]

There was never a reason to believe that violence was inevitable, unless the rhetoric coming from the Alt Right was taken at face value. The clothes, the quaffed hair, the soundbites, all meant to obfuscate violence, and huge segments of the media sphere took them at their word. The voices demanding that people take insurgent fascism seriously were decried as alarmist, both on the right and the left, and then an army of a thousand armed Nazis stormed a Southern town.

"It was kind of terrifying actually when I saw it, because what I had been warning about had come to reality," says Christian Picciolini about the number of white nationalists that came to Charlottesville ready to fight. "I think it was a milestone. I think it was this big introduction to this movement, this new version of the movement. I think it showed people that it's not just your average tattooed skinhead and klansman. It's your daughter. It's your neighbor. And certainly the level of violence, I think even the imagery of it. The torches and the polos and khakis, it was a surprise to most people. I don't think it was a surprise to people who's been researching it, to activists or anything like that... I think the president waffling, the 'both sides' thing, it scared the shit out of a lot of people. This is real."[34]

The violence of white nationalism builds up until it finds a moment when it can spike through, often when their movement fails to meet above ground political goals. This could explain what ticked off James Alex Fields on this afternoon, seeing that antifascists were not just going to let them take their victories and claim a town as their own. What kind of violence happens on their trip to the bottom? The potential for violence in this "suit and tie" movement is there, their desperation assured, and the violence of their ideology is implicit. This could mean that more is on the way, but its leaderless nature means that the violence the Alt Right is fomenting could come from almost any direction. The killing of Heather Heyer was exactly one year from the Khalid Jabara murder in Tulsa, Oklahoma, in an Islamophobic hate crime. It was nine days after Patrick Crusius, influenced by apocalyptic white genocide conspiracy theories, entered an El Paso Wal-Mart and killed twenty-three people. It was eight years after Wade Michael Page opened fire on a Sikh temple, killing six people in what was at the time considered shocking and now feels mundane to many. It was 441 days before eleven were killed at the Tree of Life synagogue, 580 days before 51 were killed in Christchurch, 1,107 days before two Black Lives Matter protesters were gunned down in Kenosha.

"How many Black and brown people have been murdered? How many car attacks have there been?" says Susan Bro, Heather Heyer's mother, thinking about the continued violence since her daughter's killing. Between the end of May and the beginning of September in 2020, there had been more than 100 car attacks on antiracist protesters. "I realize we can't all live in outrage...but you can at least live in some level of activism. Some level of justice," says Bro.[35]

To comprehend the reality of white nationalist violence, both historic and impending, is to understand the central function of white identity: violence on the "Other." The character change between the Alt Right and the neo-Nazis is one of minor philosophic shifts and branding, but the underlying cause and the overarching message retain a key component of revolutionary upheaval, of the mythic battle for "survival of their race," and the desire for power. Richard Spencer, for his part, has shifted his rhetoric from one of simply the preservation of "identity" to the need to take and exercise power in a dominating way. This is not "real politic," but an acknowledgment that much of the language of identity that has filtered over from the European identitarian movement is disingenuous: what he wants from his ethnostate is a Great White Empire. And why shouldn't he say it? Their idealist vision is one that refuses to quit, that will take down opponents as it needs to, and its only reason to refuse violence is the optics. As the crisis continues to swell, as economic instability and climate chaos increases conflict, their capacity expands with infinite inertia. The triggers will only multiply, the conditions become only more conducive. This is not Trump's America, it is the U.S. from here on out.

For the antifascist left, this needs to be a reality check for what they face. The presence of white nationalism is not just ideological, or a political proposition, but it is the implicit encasement of violence, attack looking for a victim. The surprising growth of the Alt Right has had one less predicted effect, that their violent rhetoric and vulgar racialism would so thoroughly infect the conservative communities they tried to cozy up to. Their violence has extended to the MAGA-Belt, the Independent Trumpists whose anger has become explosive.

In 2020, as the Coronavirus raged, anti-mask protests denied its reality, and Trump ramped up racist fears as a campaign strategy, Derek Chauvin leaned on George Floyd's neck for eight minutes before he finally slipped out of consciousness and into the unknown. A complete insurgency, unseen for half a century, came in its wake, and so did the whitelash. The Proud Boys, which had been a dominant force on the far-right since the Alt Right's decline post-Charlottesville, came back into the fray, as did white vigilantes around the country. The Proud Boys, Patriot Prayer, and other far-right groups had become a constant presence in cities like Portland, Oregon by this point, engaging in targeted attack and street battles since Trump's election. While they often use the mutated rhetoric of self-defense, or describe themselves as conservative fraternities, their binding force is violence. The ideology itself has slipped a bit, of less importance that committing to the attack of opponents, where violence itself has become explicitly central. At the same time, open white nationalism itself has moved further right as the "bowl patrol" celebrates Dylann Roof and Atomwaffen and The Base prepare for mass murder as an accelerationist path to collapse. From the GOP to the "Patriot" subculture to the Nazis frothing for action, violence is passed along as a fashion for identity, a key to the whole question of who we are. The Proud Boy leadership continue to play dumbfounded by accusations of violence as President Enrique Tarrio claims that violence is forbidden, disavows the violence of members, and pretends that Proud Boys accused of violence were never actually members of the organization. As the GOP stokes a "vigilante identity" across the country it only sends messages of approval to groups like the Proud Boys that their violence is part of a greater plan to restore America, and the violence only spreads like a cultural pandemic.[36] While it is often the edges of these organizations that engage in the most egregious of the violence since its leadership has too much to lose, there is a straight line between the inner circle and the assaults and murders.

The Greensboro Massacre happened just over forty years ago, and yet it feels like the ghost of an earlier time. It was only this year that the city of Greensboro, NC, issued an apology to the victims for their negligence, and one of the survivors, Reverend Nelson Johnson, received it.[37] It got little news coverage, it was an old story that has been largely lost, but what really robbed it in the news cycle was that it was too familiar. We know white nationalist violence now, we live with it every day.

The fringe of the white nationalist movement is an essential part of it, and it is where the move towards "IRL" violence takes place. White nationalist organization will (almost) never "condone" the murders in the practical, instructive sense, but they don't have to, their message has been heard loud and clear. Their ideas have violence at the core, their behavior is poised and prepared for violence, the violence is the logical outcome of everything they have built. Richard Spencer has argued that his mission is for a "peaceful ethnic cleaning," but this is a contradiction in terms. This creates a perpetual dilemma for the communities they target, both in active points of confrontation and in daily life. The potential only grows without resistance to stifle it, but conscious community defense and bonds is the only thing that can weather the storm. We have to wrestle with the reality that their violence is genocidal and persistent and will never evaporate on its own.

"You're a marked man, your name is on the lips of every Klansman in the state. Your days are numbered and the best thing is for you to cooperate with me," a police officer told Nelson Johnson, one of the survivors of the Greensboro attack, as he sat in the hospital, terrified about who of his friends were going to die.

The reality is that they were marked from the moment they spoke up and stood up to the Klan. And they did it anyway. In the days that followed they organized a funeral procession, they carried their dead, a panic enclosing the entire city. "The main thing that consumed me that week was to project the image of being fearless. The Klan, cops, and FBI had killed our people. We were standing for right; we would not give ground. We would bury our people. We succeeded in doing that—and scared the death out of everybody," said Nelson Johnson.[38]

The events led to the creation of the Anti-Klan Network that year, which formed as a broad-based coalition to confront insurgent racist violence that intersected with the ongoing struggle for civil rights.

They announced a February 2, 1980 march in Greensboro, which brought out a massive show of eight thousand people to stand against white supremacy.[39] The events also inspired more militant organizations like the John Brown Anti-Klan Committee, an abolitionist antifascist organization that pushed a confrontational agenda and an anti-imperialist program of "Third World liberation" over its thirteen year life.[40] This was the antecedent for a massive wave of organizations, from Anti-Racist Action to the Southern Poverty Law Center, creating an infrastructure that lead all the way to antifa and the mass wave of antifascist organizations that confronted the rise of Donald Trump. The tragedy had to be mourned, we feel it together as just one example buried in the timeline of assaults and bombings and public executions, and yet the resistance reconfigured only larger than before. Antifascism is only responsive as a social movement, it has to exist in proximity to the far-right's threat, which is implicit to their promise of violence. The organizers in the Workers Viewpoint Organization were correct, the Klan was a threat to working people, it was never more visible when they blocked off the street and emptied rifles into the crowd. Inside these tragedies is the reason to keep going, to build back stronger than before, because the violence has never dissipated on its own.

"They are targeting [antifascist activists] because we're effective. We shouldn't be afraid to be effective. To do our jobs. To tell the truth," says Christian Picciolini. "We shouldn't live our lives in fear because of it. The most important tool we have is to be able to expose what's happening."

It was the violence of the encroaching Trump era that turned antifascism into a mass movement, the threats of the Proud Boys that hardened organizations, the terrorist killings in Synagogues and Mosques that created a wall of persistent refusal. What white nationalists think will push back their opposition, their capacity for violence, is what fills the streets. The culture of apocalyptic violence carries with it an endemic hurt, one that will paint an entire generation with fear and mourning, and also the seeds of a new type of social identity, one that understands this feeling of loss in the collective retribution that is faced by those responsible. The dialectic of their violence is in the waves of antifascists that it incurs, the kernel of a new plurality defined compassion, mutual aid, and the willingness to disrupt the systems that never served us. In an era of mass shootings and global pandemics we have been disfigured by an inescapable trauma, but it is also pushing us back into a community of care and defense. In a society where we rarely create the space to mourn, the growing mass actions against violence have taken the role of a public reckoning, transmuting that hurt back into a shield wall. We don't avoid the streets because of their violence, we overwhelm them because of it. We multiply, reproduce, change our spaces and our relationships and ourselves because of it. We escalate our expectations, for safety and ecstatic living, because we know the antithesis. We come out because we are afraid, and this is the only way to the other side.

Living Your Life in a State of War

In the past, revolutionary movements have been undone by a combination of ideology, propaganda, and expropriation. Turkey, however, has dispensed with such liberal forms of coercion in recent years. Maybe it is the Trump effect (and the Alternative for Germany effect, and the Freedom Party of Austria effect, and so on) that gives Turkey's president, Recep Tayyip Erdoğan, the freedom to cut the bullshit and simply brutalize the autonomous region of northeastern Syria. They have dropped the pretense of consented governance and replaced it with the most modern of genocidal tools: white phosphorous.[1]

After Trump decided to pull U.S. troops out of the Syrian conflict, Turkey did as we expected they would. Using proxy forces in the form of Jihadi rebels, as well as constant air raids, Turkey escalated its decades-long war on the Kurdistan Region. What has been established in Rojava since the State receded during the Syrian Civil War in 2012–13 is no less than the early blossoms of a revolutionary society. The principle of *democratic confederalism* is in effect. It is an idea introduced by Kurdistan Workers' Party (PKK) leader Abdullah Öcalan, who synthesized a new approach to politics inspired, in part, by American anarchist Murray Bookchin, along with the community councils that have long been a part of Kurdish culture. What we see here is a society in transition: one that is trying to move away

from entrenched patriarchy, through the intentional enfranchise-
ment of women; away from neoliberal capitalism, through the empowerment of cooperatives and communal resource development;
and toward a society run through direct democratic structures. All of
these efforts remain in flux; they are, as with any revolution in process, still finding themselves.

The significance of this cannot be ignored: we are watching
an anarchist vision (of some sort) take place in the real world. The
importance of this moment is also evinced by the increasingly authoritarian political actions of Turkey. The revolutionary changes occurred in the three autonomous cantons of northeastern Syria, but
they are now being compressed on all sides as Turkey commits war
crimes to destabilize the region. The Kurds have been forced back
into an alliance with Assad, and Russia and the United States continue to engage in an international blunder. A revolutionary society
may have become just a revolutionary moment instead—one that
could remain temporally fixed since this experiment could come to a
brutal end amid carpet bombings.

"It is not only the invasion, of course, which has already claimed
[the] lives of hundreds of civilians and displaced more than three
million. It is the world of nation-states involved in the so-called
Astana process," says Andrej Grubačić, a sociologist and organizer
originally from the Balkans, who has been active in Rojava solidarity,
including as a university professor in the region: "Turkish invasion,
paradoxically enough, is creating the possibility for completion of an
old Assadist dream, one of the so-called Arab belt, a project that was
initiated in the 1960s. This project of demographic engineering, of
breaking the Kurdish majority, was never complete, but I am afraid
that it now might become a reality. Between wars and processes of
turkification and arabization, of breaking the democratic autonomy,
confederalism of Rojava is in danger of becoming 'statified.'"[2]

A host of autonomous structures have emerged in Rojava, including experiments in transformative justice, women's empowerment,
communal economic democracies; thus it is an entire future of alternatives to state-ordered living that is jeopardized by the military
attacks. The choices they have are now to collaborate with enemies

or face extermination, which could decidedly end their autonomy, and return Kurdistan to the status of contested quasi-States. And that is one of the best-case scenarios.

So, the question that many on the international left are asking, particularly in the United States, is: Did we miss it? Is this a story, like the Spanish Revolution, about which anarchists will remain captivated? Is Rojava merely a brief window into a future foreclosed? Is it a reminder of what could be, but is not yet possible, or is it something we are living through in real time?

Revolutionary politics lives inside us, stoked through the intoxicating effect of massive, emancipatory ideas. These fantasies, visions of what could be possible, sustain social movements. This spark seems small—it lives largely in our imagination—but we are nevertheless seduced by its power to see something much larger (a small key opens a large door).[5] However, for most of us it is only in the briefest of moments that those ideas are put into action: the prefiguration of a new world that we see in a social movement or community space. They never expand to a whole society. The idea itself has to be enough—the idea that it could be real if the stars aligned (or if we were simply capable enough). Only a few times have these ideas been realized at a society-wide level, and Rojava has been one of the largest. Three million people in a country-sized land zone, establishing decentralized direct democracy in almost every area of social life, with the buy-in of almost the entire community. While it has often been described as a leftist fever dream, even the most cynical have had a reappraisal.

The story of the Kurdish geographic region (and people) is one of starts and stops, persistence in the aftermath of seeming total loss. The Kurdish ethnic group is dispersed across a number of countries, including Turkey, Syria, and Iraq, and it has been fighting for an established territory of its own for over a hundred years. Snapshots of Kurdish autonomy have collided with nationalisms of neighbors, who have reacted with ferocious repression and ethnic cleansing.

In 1984, the PKK underwent a shift from what began, in the 1970s, as largely a student movement to a Marxist-Leninist paramilitary organization that fought with the Turkish state in a protracted guerilla war, operating from the relative safety of the mountains.[4] The goal was national liberation through a socialist Kurdistan. After the PKK's leader, Abdullah Öcalan, was captured in 1999 and imprisoned in solitary confinement in a remote island facility, he began to shift the ideological orientation of the movement in a more libertarian direction. Öcalan's writings, which ultimately changed the entire outlook of the PKK, advocate for democratic confederalism, an egalitarian social system that rejects a State in favor of direct democratic community control and a rethinking of all of the dominating institutions of the society that came before. These include regional councils that would prioritize the participation of women, the collectivization of resources (while rejecting coercive acquisition), a focus on transformative justice, and the use of Bookchin's idea of social ecology as a means to repair the environmental destruction of the region wrought by resource extraction. Thus, all aspects of society are up for reinterpretation, from the role of women to relationships with the natural world. This is a revolutionary situation: an entirely new type of civilization is forming, in spite of crushing chaos surrounding it.

Internationale

An argument favored by pedantic parts of the left believes that Rojava, with its brief moments of tacit support from the United States, lacks the character of a true revolution. The Western left is accused of projecting its fantasies, seeing what it wants to see in Rojava, and trekking to its cantons to play revolution. This argument doesn't hold up because Rojava has been an international project from the beginning. Öcalan had reached out to Murray Bookchin for counsel before the latter's death, and Öcalan built relationships with his daughter, Debbie Bookchin, as well as the Institute for Social Ecology, of which Bookchin was a founder. This has helped to create an ideological interplay between the cantons and the worldwide movement toward bottom-up democracy, whether or not it calls itself anarchism. This movement includes projects like Symbiosis, which includes the Libertarian Socialist Caucus of the Democratic Socialists of America (which is larger than any other anarchist organization in the U.S.), Cooperation Jackson from Mississippi, and the Asamblea de los Pueblos Indígenas del Istmo en Defensa de la Tierra y el Territorio (APOODTT), with members of the Binniza Indigenous community of Gui'Xhi' Ro, who have kicked the Mexican state out of their village.

People from around the world have been invited to Rojava, not just to bear witness (though that was encouraged), but to participate in autonomous projects that are a part of its democratic structure. One of these is the Internationalist Commune of Rojava, which began in 2017 in association with the Rojava Youth Movement (YCR) and built itself around the principle "Learn, support, organize." Momentum from their international invitation has resulted in a number of campaigns, such as an educational academy and "Make Rojava Green Again," a project that has brought widespread interest, due to its use of the principles of Bookchin's social ecology as an answer to colonialist resource harvesting.

"Rojava is not a museum where the revolution can be examined and measured. Rojava is not a monument of past battles. Rojava is a living and developing organism. And those who approach it as revolutionaries become part of it," says the Commune to prospective recruits.[5] Volunteers are required to commit to at least six months of work, often sleep on floors, and must learn the local Kurmancî dialect. The Commune is not interested in tourism; they want committed participation. The Commune has earned itself an official place in the confederal structure of Rojava, which is to say that it is a very real part of the revolutionary society rather than just a collection of politicized transplants.

A different side of the international element was the support provided by volunteers to the militant effort fought by both the People's Protection Units (YPG) and the Women's Protection Units (YPJ) against the Daesh (ISIS) forces. Anarchists and socialists from around the world signed up as volunteers, many joining the International Freedom Battalion (IFB), which was modeled on the Abraham Lincoln Brigade (a diverse coalition of left [ranging from anarchists to Stalinist] volunteers to aid the anarchists of the Confederación Nacional del Trabajo [CNT] and Federación Anarquista Ibérica [FAI] against the nationalist forces of Francisco Franco).[6] The comparison is well made; indeed, the situation is strikingly similar, as it brought in confederated battalions from Turkey like the Communist Labor Party of Turkey/Leninist and United Freedom Forces (BÖG), whose participation in the conflict could have dire consequences, given that their home country considers participation in the fight a form of material aid to declared terrorist organizations (the PKK and Democratic Union Party of Syria).

Another volunteer company was the International Revolutionary People's Guerrilla Forces (IRPGF), an explicitly anarchist militia that joined in the fighting with recruits from around the world. They say: "Our role is twofold; to be an armed force capable of defending liberatory social revolutions around the world while simultaneously being a force capable of insurrection and struggle against all kyriarchal forms of power wherever they exist.[7] We do not enter conflict zones with intent to command but rather, while retaining our autonomy as a collective, to fight alongside other armed groups in solidarity with those who are oppressed, exploited, and facing annihilation."[8]

These organizations sought common cause, collaborating in the ongoing military struggle against ISIS, sometimes alongside the Syrian Democratic Forces (SDF), sometimes in direct military command. They acted in solidarity with the Rojava project, the destruction of ISIS fascist forces, and that the Kurdish people be free from persecution. Likewise, the protection they could afford Rojava was a direct result of the global solidarity effort that helped to influence the decisions of those around them. The region has faced decades of economic hurdles, underdevelopment, and hyper-exploitation, alongside attacks from Turkey (not to mention Syria and Iraq, among others), so the creation of an external movement acting in solidarity was critical. It was also never viewed as a form of charity, because people around the world saw Rojava as a crack in neoliberalism and statecraft. And since the people in Rojava agreed with this perception, it was possible to forge a symbiotic relationship between those building a new society on the inside and those trying their best to defend it from the outside. Their participation in the Rojava revolution, and the conflict from which it was birthed, was not simply an alternative to building revolutions at home, but a part of the same struggle. Through their support, and sincere participation, the people of Rojava fostered an internationalism with the potency to launch revolutionary politics on a global scale.

We Assume We Will Lose

As the bombs began to drop on Afrin in October 2019, many reacted as if this international, collaborative project was merely a memory, dashed by U.S. betrayal and the nationalist war machine of Turkey, or perhaps something that happened "out there," rather than being within our grasp.

"I think that the incredible strides that the Kurds have made in achieving a society that is feminist, egalitarian, non-sectarian, ecological, is such an extraordinary accomplishment and provides such a unique model, in particular in direct democracy, that it is something that everyone who, again, considers themselves a progressive or an activists should seek to preserve," said Debbie Bookchin, who was doing international solidarity work for the region, when I spoke with her in November 2019: "[We should] also look to [Rojava] as a model of how we can build a social movement in this country that actually goes beyond protest and beyond voting for a good Democratic Socialist candidate and starts to really empower people on the local level. And the Kurds have shown us *exactly* how this can be done."[9]

The reality is that the Rojava revolution could be summarily destroyed, at least in the form we know it now, by any of a range of intrusions. Turkey's brutality has continued to escalate as constant shelling kills civilians in the hundreds and thousands, and the conflict has already led to the internal displacement of more than 400,000 Kurds. ISIS then started seeing a resurgence in the area, reversing the gains made by the SDF, YPG, and YPJ. Because the United States has left the Kurds so vulnerable, they have been forced to turn to an earlier enemy—Assad's untrained military forces—for support and so they have returned to the very Ba'athist fold that has historically rejected Kurdish autonomy. And all of these: economic starvation, mass killings, stratification as a solution to increased instability, are eschatological. Each factor works in concert with the other to suggest that this moment of Rojava's revolution is only for a moment. A brief glimmer before the rest of the world collapses onto it with the weight of our circumstances. This story has continued into 2020, with starts and stops, and it seems unclear how the future of the region will play out.

So, there is desperation when we talk of Rojava, when we tell stories of the crimes against the people, and, even more profoundly, when we talk of their victories. But the deep well of sadness that attends this conversation forgets one key fact: the situation was always dire, always uncertain, always stacked against them.

A War Society

Rojava is a society birthed in struggle against the far-right and the austerities of capital. The revolution did not emerge from the best of times or from a series of social democratic reforms that leveled the playing field, or via social movements with access to money and resources. It emerged, by any measure, from some of the worst moments, in the midst of a three-way fight between the neighboring states, with the fascist, murdering insurgency of ISIS amassing on all sides.[10]

Historically, the most cogent example of this dynamic was the Spanish revolution, where such instability enabled the anarchists of Catalonia, Andalusia, Valencia, and Aragon the autonomy to collectivize agriculture and industry. The Spanish Republic was formed in 1931 in a progressive turn from the years of monarchical rule, and in the subsequent years, a turbulent modernization campaign pushed toward addressing the economic crisis in the country. As the Popular Front coalition of left-wing electoralists took the elections in 1936, and the anarchists with the CNT-FAI in the north were building strength, a fascist coup plunged the country into civil war, as the propertied classes backed reactionary Catholic monarchism. Amid this chaos, with fighting on all sides, we see anarcho-syndicalism becoming more than an idea. The anarchists ran factories collectively and created communal farming systems; everything in society was on the table for restructuring, reimaging, or abolition. The anarchists eventually lost, partly because of Soviet betrayal, and Franco would determine the direction of Spain for the next forty years. Nevertheless, for a moment, a whole new world of limitless possibilities existed.[11]

A similar example is the Ukrainian Free Territory during the Ukrainian revolution of 1917–1921. The Revolutionary Insurrectionary Army of Ukraine, led by anarchist Nestor Makhno (the ideological progenitor of the so-called platformist tendency in anarchism) protected what were referred to as "free soviets"—decentralized collectives operating along libertarian communist principles. This was, again, a period of civil war and social revolution, in which the "White Army" of the Russian czar engaged in protracted battle against the Red Army, along with the anarchists who joined the fight (who adopted a more hands-off approach than that of the Bolsheviks). Once the White Army was defeated, the Soviets turned on the anarchists and crushed their burgeoning society, leaving us with nothing more than a flash that has stayed with social movements as both a blueprint and a portrait.

Our history is littered with such examples. The May 1968 student uprisings in France, which took over urban space and tried to reconstruct their communities, with Situationism behind their eyes, amid austerity, rather than affluence. The Argentinian factory recuperation movement of the early 2000s coincided with massive economic collapse and job loss, and necessity rather than just cold ideology led to the takeovers. The Cascadia "free territory" was created in Oregon in 1995 as activists outside Eugene fought against the sale of ancient forests for timber. During a year-long siege, they created a protest camp that became a community, out of the State's reach.[12] Even the Zapatista uprising in 1994 was a direct result of the economic assault of the North American Free Trade Agreement (NAFTA), along with the Mexican state's repression of southern Indigenous sovereignty and self-determination.[13]

When we say that Rojava is a revolutionary society, we mean it quite literally. It is a war society. It exists, as we know it now, in the eye of the storm; they are building a utopian vision while facing encroaching violence. There has never been a moment when the Rojava experiment was safe; there was no time when it was guaranteed the right to see through its vision. The ideas that the PYD and PKK brought into the cantons were the result of decades of guerilla war in the mountains of Turkey. Struggle is at the heart of the vision for Rojava, the story it tells about itself. It is an idealism that comes from a living experience of oppression, and every moment of Rojava's existence has been built on that struggle—the wars from which it emerged, and its own internal fight to remake itself while confronting the oppressions in its own society (and all others as well). Rojava is at war, and it has always been.

The Danger of Remaking the World

Revolutions are difficult to make and maintain. The easy path would be to continue with some version of the status quo, to find reforms that make sense and that offer the illusion of incremental improvements. Revolutions are risky. They usually fail, and even where they don't, a lot of heartache and trials lie ahead. History is not linear, with determined end points, but a trail of unanticipated upheavals: 1871, 1917, 1936, 1968, 1980, 1989, 1994, 2011, 2013, 2020, and a lot of others in between. A revolutionary society wants more than we have had before, more than has ever seemed possible to grasp. So we make the choice to fight for something, to suffer and sacrifice, because we are willing to roll the dice. Because we want more.

Revolutions express our passion for a life worth living; comfort and stability is sacrificed for the hope of better days. In Rojava, every moment matters. Even seemingly mundane parts of society are imbued with meaning because they are at war, not only with the invading armies but also with their own past. The ways armies are trained, bridges are built, and food is grown are all being reimagined, and are all areas of struggle.

A revolutionary society is expected to have pushback, because if the flames of revolution spread, it becomes a direct threat to power. One cannot expect such a society, which exists by virtue of taking back property and resources, to be granted amnesty by those who legally owned those resources before.

"Everybody I spoke to had a very revolutionary sentiment. It's just a horrendously difficult situation. As it always will be, it was what I realized when I was there," said Dr. George Hagglund, who had just gotten back from a medical convoy in Tel Temir in Rojava in late 2019:

> If we do the same thing on the West Coast, do you think it's going to be easy? Do you think the rest of the world is going to support us? Send us weapons and applaud us? No, it's going to be the exact same situation. It's going to be like Republican Spain. They're going to embargo you. They're going to refuse to send you weapons but arm the other side. The exact same situation as what we're seeing in Rojava. And, of course that's difficult. And, of course, that makes a revolution complicated. But the people said that they expect dark times ahead, but they are not prepared to give up their self-governance.[14]

The fight to defend oneself and one's community is part of a process of liberation. The Internal Security Forces of Rojava (Asayish) would beg you not to call them *police*. They provide community protection services, and those who serve have to learn nonviolent conflict resolution skills and feminist theory before they can even think of picking up a gun. In the future, they hope to offer Asayish training to everyone, breaking down the need for a professionalized class of law enforcement and making community self-defense collaborative. They are even implementing transformative justice approaches to harm in support of the vision of eliminating the carceral state. Even when this threat has ended, the weight of capital and imperialism will continue to loom, as will conditions of scarcity, sectarian conflicts, and social conditioning. Struggle will continue because that is the very meaning of a revolution. There is no end in sight.

"For believe me!—the secret for harvesting from existence the greatest fruitfulness and the greatest enjoyment is: to live dangerously!" wrote Friedrich Nietzsche in *The Gay Science*, meaning that it is only under strife that we become our best selves. "Build your cities on the slopes of Vesuvius! Send your ships into uncharted seas! Live at war with your peers and yourselves!"[15] What if the shadow of the mountain is simply the realization of the battle that is in front of us—one that is inescapable if we want to move the immovable? The challenge of Rojava is inevitable, because it is in direct proportion to what it has set out to accomplish: nothing less than rewriting the rules of civilization. Of course it will be an uphill battle. To acknowledge this fact gives no cover to the nations (and Jihadi terrorists) who are encroaching on the cantons. The war that made the revolution possible may be the same one that invites its messy end, almost as though the world was promised a temporary landscape from which to make their future work.

It is an open question as to whether or not a new world can be birthed without a massive conflict that destabilizes the old, but there is no debate as to whether or not war is required to change ourselves. Each piece of the society around us, every horror and dream, is reflected inside us. A war society is defined not only by its military clashes, but by what happens when we are forced to live without stasis and to let that moment of flux be hopeful, rather than just tension and anxiety. To make war is to absolve ourselves of stasis, to say that the safety of the status quo is no longer worth it because something greater has been imagined.

According to Berivan Qerecox, who works with the Women Defend Rojava campaign from Kongra Star in Kobanî,

> What is happening before our eyes is clearly an attempt at ethnic cleansing and an attempt at stopping the society here from existing. Whatever they say, whatever they pay lip service to, the fascist Turkish state's goals are nothing less than that... In one sense there is a very real and very immediate threat. In another

sense, I do think it's important to understand that the experiment here and the project here is much, much wider than just about one place or about some land and not something that could just be destroyed overnight. It is not tied to certain seats of power that you could just come and destroy and bomb and then the organization will, in itself, be gone. The real meaning, the real heart and soul of what is happening here, is about people day to day, dedicating themselves to working hard to reimagining how human beings relate to each other and how we create the systems we live under. And you can't just stop those people doing that overnight. And in the future that might look very different, but these values have lasted a really long time. They were around before the autonomous administration was able to take the space, to build the structures of self-organizations in Northeastern Syria. And they will be around for a really long time in whatever form the future takes.[16]

The gravity of the situation is a call to action, rather than a sign that all is lost. If we give up now, then this will only have been a window into what could have been, a story we will continue to tell for the coming decades in reading groups or at conferences or in our own personal laments and revolutionary longings. We have so many visions of these revolutionary possibilities (after all, we still remember Catalonia). We don't just want another moment in time. And we can do that: not just by acting in solidarity and support, but by living our lives in a state of war. This means committing to the same struggle, not by romanticizing a fight thousands of miles away, but by engaging in the here and now as a single global project. There is nothing inevitable about the collapse of Rojava, because there is nothing inevitable about the world in which we live. We remake our world daily, and we can build something awe inspiring or we can let it burn. The very real nightmare of Turkish attacks—and the unlikelihood of building a new world in the shell of the old—should never dissuade us of our hopes. It was always unlikely that the imaginary could actually be real. And it certainly was always a war zone.

Bring the War Home

What the people in Rojava want, as they have said over and over again, is to bring the ideas of democratic confederalism to the rest of the world. The greatest act of solidarity is to organize at home, to confederate globally, to challenge power, capitalism, and the State, and thereby make a new world possible.

Philosopher Michael Hardt has a famous story about this, which he retells while rowing a boat through Central Park in the 2008 documentary *An Examined Life*. In the 1980s he was a part of a procession of young leftist students and radicals who traveled to Central America to try to support the revolutionary movements, such as the Sandinistas and the uprisings in El Salvador. I remember stories of older organizers, told to me when I first started organizing, about how they went and picked coffee for a year under the idea that their presence might stop American-backed militias (spoiler alert: it didn't). While the people appreciated the support, what they really wanted was their American comrades to go home and make revolution, since, in reality, if the insurgencies in Latin America were successful they would still be crushed by the might of American imperialism and global capitalism.

The reality is that Rojava can only serve as a window when it is the only revolutionary society on the map. There can be no "anarchism in one country"; this is a global system with international consequences, and States dedicated to the status quo. The most important act of solidarity is to make the Kurdish struggle—which is to create a wholly new society—our own. This is what we can do to support the confederation, and that means getting to know your neighbors, creating projects that matter, and having a real stake in your community.

According to Debbie Bookchin, the lessons of Rojava can be applied at home:

> By creating local assemblies, assembly democracy where power is devolved to the local level. Where politics is reinvented. Where politics is not something that is done by a professional class who

you have to put your faith in and hope they do the right thing or make the right decision, but politics is a thing which is done by ordinary people in their everyday lives, who build a dual power, a new society within the shell of the old. And that means not only the things that have already been done on multiple levels successfully by the left like creating alternative educational institutions or co-ops or tenants' rights organizations, but also getting involved politically at the local level to send people into city councils so they can further use that position to further strengthen the local assemblies so that we really give people a sense of empowerment and create a sense of community and build a society based on mutual aid and cooperation.[17]

This is, in essence, to bring Rojava's successes to other countries. This would come with a commitment to struggle, to build connections that extend like tributaries across communities; to meet people where they are at; to locate the problems and build solutions; and to know each other and have a stake in one another's survival. It won't be easy. There is no promise that we will be successful. And the stakes are incredibly high. While the society in the cantons emerged within a particular warscape, the terrain of conflict is far larger, and it extends beyond borders and into our own lives. So, to commit to that war is to commit to the life that comes by way of this crisis of civility: not merely to recognize the battle as tragedy, but rather to embrace life amid the conflict that arises when we fight for each other. Revolutions occur as pressure mounts and cracks appear in the surface, and this is increasingly the day-to-day reality of life in a society of crumbling infrastructure, disaster capitalism, and mass extinction.

We live in a war society already. Let's do it differently this time.

The Continuing Appeal of Antisemitism

The jarring sight of the swastika is what makes the video of a Nazi flag being unfurled in the background of a March 6th, 2020 Bernie Sanders rally so breathtaking. Even shrouded in darkness, emblazoned against a nondescript sea of people, everyone knew what it was and why it was there. Sanders's run for the Democratic presidential nomination is significant for a whole host of reasons, not the least of which is that he is the only truly left-leaning candidate in decades, but he is also the first Jew to stride within reach of the White House.[1] The image of the swastika means "not welcome here," a message to Jews that, far from abating, the curdling rage sitting under gentile society is lying in wait.

At the time, this sight wasn't particularly surprising since it came on the tail end of a string of antisemitic attacks. Across 2019's Hanukkah season, dozens of violent assaults took place, particularly on Orthodox Hasidim in New York: a nightmarescape of crushing beatings, bombings, vandalism, and threats. For people living in the dense Jewish areas of Brooklyn or Upstate New York, there was discussion about going "underground," hiding Jewish events, or even leaving the country.[2] Orthodox Jews are often the focus of attacks, not necessarily because of the particulars of their orthodox faith but because they are identifiable, everyone knows they are Jews. The most publicly bloodthirsty spectacles of this series have been the synagogue shootings, a trope so persistent in recent history that it is a "go to" act of terrorism for white supremacists aching to take nihilistic revenge. Eleven people were murdered at L'Simcha in Pittsburgh, another one at Chabad of Poway, and five stabbed at a rabbi's home in Rockland. While there has been a notable upsurge of attacks in recent years, these numbers are not outside the norm. The reality is that physical spaces marked as Jewish, whether a community center or a religious congregation or even a Shoah museum, are dangerous. It is frightening to be Jewish. For many Jews, signaling their distinctiveness—letting those around them know—is a part of the tradition of being Jewish. In Europe, the terror could be even more real as many Jews increasingly avoid wearing kippahs while synagogues and Jewish centers regularly have to be sealed up like fortresses because violence is expected wherever Jews congregate.[3]

The violence, however, rarely makes antisemitism more visible. Instead, it often appears to people as a series of extraordinary events instead of part of the normal experience of Jewishness. In reality, the pogromatic attacks on Jews are only the tip of the iceberg; underneath the water is an entire infrastructure of blame, denial, and rage pointed towards Jewish people. Conspiracy theories that locate the seat of power in shadowy figures (usually with a familiar canon of names), accusations of "dual loyalties," the disbelief in Jewish experiences, as well as double standards and the refusal of inquiry, are a common part of how even the political left negotiates antisemitism. It is acknowledged only in the bloodletting, rarely in the casualness with which it is employed, or how it continues to shape attitudes, institutions, and identities.

Antisemitism is an archetype that truly motivates people; always present if rarely discussed. The feeling is that there are people who look like us but are not us, who are perverse in their motivations, who undermine strength through their cunning, and that there is a world of backroom deals made not because of the reality of class and power, but rather due to a subversive evil force. Antisemitism drives Western stories; even when the specific character of the Jew is replaced, the same logic and emotion remain in the subtext.

Liars

Kevin MacDonald has been called the "Karl Marx" of antisemitism, and this is an apt title since he has united all antisemitic strains of thought into one unified theory, eclipsing all others. The field of evolutionary psychology has long been tainted by pseudoscientific claims, like the correlation between race and IQ or the inherent predictive nature of gender roles, but MacDonald thought he would take his field a step further. Leaping out of a prolific career in research and publishing, once he got tenure at the University of California at Long Beach, he decided he would author a trilogy of books on Judaism. He argues that Judaism is a "group evolutionary strategy" that Jews created in order to fight with gentiles over resources. He says Judaism is a binding agent, it helps to create a tribal mentality and to develop breeding patterns that, through eugenics, create a "high verbal intelligence." He says that Judaism is an ethnic tool created so that there was an underlying ideological mechanism to help Jews, as an ethnicity, to fight for survival in an otherwise hostile world where they were a microscopic minority.[4]

MacDonald's books trace what he sees as Jewish involvement in social movements, particularly those against racism and in favor of immigration, feminism, and other forces that he sees as endemic to the decline of Western man. He focuses heavily on the Frankfurt School, which he labels as "cultural Marxism." He believes people like Theodore Adorno or Erich Fromm were able to influence all of Western society by applying the destabilizing effects of Marxism to broad social understandings. He focuses primarily on the idea that the Jews of the Frankfurt School "strongly identified as Jews," with the thought that the movement is essentially a Jewish one enacting a Jewish plan on the rest of society. Adorno's classic, *The Authoritarian Personality*, is re-canonized as a Hebraic text that attempts to pathologize Western gentiles and their "natural" feelings of kinship, tribal loyalty, and caste.[5]

While he does identify leftist ideas (particularly antiracism) as emanating from Judaism, he also suggests that the Jewish proliferation of these ideas is fundamentally dishonest. He suggests that

Jews, with their ascribed tribalism, are actually highly ethnocentric and racist. They apply the standards of antiracism to everyone else as a bait and switch; the Jew wants gentiles to drop their tribalism while they continue to maintain their own. The same, he says, is true of feminism, queer rights movements, and most other movements, with the underlying script suggesting that Jews created these alleged social viruses to destroy non-Jewish people.[6] Since antisemitism, a logical manifestation of white nationalism, is harmful to Jews, Jews attack white ethnocentrism. MacDonald goes a step further in suggesting that Jews are responsible for non-white immigration (particularly the U.S.'s 1965 Immigration Act), since it further undermines white society. The high intelligence he ascribes to Jews has therefore allowed them into places of power to rule over the now-fragmented, multicultural society. MacDonald then alleges that Jewish ethnocentrism and intelligence has allowed them to take over seats of power in politics, finance, and Hollywood, all because they intentionally want to orchestrate the mechanisms of our society.[7]

This is where the concept of "Jewish Power" comes from. White nationalists claim they are simply questioning the "undue influence" that Jews have in modern society. The Jewish Question, or the "JQ," is the question of how this happened, what it means, and what to do about it. MacDonald is a white nationalist who edits the *Occidental Observer*. He sat on the board for the American Freedom Party and has presented at Richard Spencer's National Policy Institute conferences, so he has a very clear idea of what he thinks should be done. Whites, he says, evolved in "high trust" societies whereby they come to have a "pathological altruism" that makes them reject their ethnic interests in support of non-whites through things like immigration and affirmative action.[8] These white people are simply too nice and caring. Jews will then use this amiable Aryan quality to destroy them through non-white immigration and the eventual genocide of the white race. MacDonald writes about other "peoples" who have ceased to be—such as the Visigoths—and says that these could be the twilight years of the white race, particularly if the Jews get their way.[9]

One of the core aspects of MacDonald's analysis is that Jews lie. They lie about who they are (they look white, but, of course, they can't be); they lie about their intentions (they want you to be antiracist while they will stay racist); they lie about their allegiance to the U.S. (but their true allegiance is to Israel); and they lie about why they allegedly support "mass immigration."

Distrust is one of the key ways that people understand Jews; suspicion of their claims, even when the evidence is clear (and especially when testimony and experience are all that is available).[10] When the swastika was unfurled at the Sanders rally, some people—and this is true both on the right and the left—suggested that it could have been a publicity stunt by the Sanders campaign. A certain talking point had circulated suggesting that both Joe Biden and Bernie Sanders were "old white men," erasing Jewishness from the equation (and sublimating actual politics to identity). Perhaps Sanders wanted to undermine this perception by reminding everyone of Jew hatred?

We know a lot of the jargon that the Alt Right developed on its message boards and podcasts. The (((echo))) meme was the best known of these, a symbol they encase Jewish sounding last names in to amplify MacDonald's assertion that they "echo" through time because of their vastly undue level of influence in societies.[11] The Happy Merchant is another; a sweaty, hook-nosed Jew rubbing his hands together in usurious glee.[12] A less discussed example is "Whatcha doin' rabbi?," the suggestion that antisemitic hate crimes (and potentially all hate crimes) are just ploys by Jews to gain publicity and tools they can use to guilt the goyim and amass more power. The idea is that when a swastika shows up at a Jewish event, for example, maybe it was actually the rabbis themselves who put it there. This is a common allegation in the white nationalist sphere, but that same conspiratorial thinking "echoes" far beyond this group as well. Where Jews are concerned, no presumption of malicious lying, no trickery or dishonesty is off the table.

This portrayal of the Jew is the archetype of the liar, the person whose power is derived through one's own bewilderment. The qualities that we ascribe to the abstract image of the liar are the same that are assigned to Jews in ridicule, so they exist in the same space of undifferentiated disgust. And there is a lot of lying taking place to draw from in the world. We live in a moment when fact and fiction have merged, when news is difficult to discern, when "deep fakes" are on the rise, when the real may be a mirage. And then there is a people known to be liars, whose alleged lies have "echoed" through history, and whose dishonesty, so it is said, knows no bounds.

When logic, explanation, and narrative fail, we grasp at prepackaged falsehoods, and "the Jews" become the answer to all unanswered questions. So, when distrust becomes common, it is easy to point one's finger at the Jew as the reason why.

Usury

Populist movements require a figurehead to push against, an elite for the "pure" people to oppose. Systems themselves are not good enough, they may inspire instability and logical revulsion, but by the nature of their abstraction, they rarely inspire rage. We hate *people*: the pharma-bro who jacks up the cost of HIV/AIDS drugs, the GM CEO who lays off Flint auto workers, or the property manager issuing evictions on Christmas Eve. And capitalism makes this easy, because it churns out these identities en masse; it is a culture where cruelty is so rewarded that it recrafts humans into haunting spectacles.

"The people" are the people by virtue of not being "the elite," and it is through that bifurcation that we come to know ourselves. This was the positioning of class that Marx explained, a subject created through both the class's experience of wage labor and its inability to own the means of production. But populism adds another element: the elite and their perversity. Part of what gives the anger its energy is the association between the elite and despised qualities: indulgence, decadence, weakness, and their reliance on manipulation rather than strength. Class antagonisms are not enough for the populist surge, the rich have to be seen as taking on both the tyranny of rulership and the qualities posed as the antithesis of a "pure" worker, who is often characterized as strong, honest, and hard working.

The caricatured image of the Jew offers a nexus that can unite these threads.[13] The Jew is characterized as the "Financier," the person who would not do the work himself yet would fund and profit from the work of others. The caricature of the money lender is so persistent that it is likely the best-known stereotype about Jews. In *The Merchant of Venice*, Shylock is seen as a bloodthirsty financial vampire, feeding off of the legitimate work of the community he is embedded in. Shylock has become such a symbol of how the West views Jews that the name is now quite literally an antisemitic slur used regularly to defame Jews as money grubbing.

The Jew's perceived propensity for unethical money dealing is wrapped up in the idea of usury, which means high-interest money lending, yet almost always coded as "Jewish money behavior." While many were religiously prohibited from lending money with interest, some European Jews became money lenders because the professions available to Jews were those deemed "un-Christian" and/or dirty (like tanning leather). While most medieval European Jews lived in poverty, they were often blamed for extracting wealth from gentiles.

Usury is, by many measures, the common way that money is managed in late capitalism, but in the antisemitic narrative it is also how Judaism is connected with financial exploitation. In a conversation I once had with fascist occultist Augustus Sol Invictus, he told me he had recently given a talk on usury. I suggested that this was, likely, antisemitic. "No, not antisemitic. Just against usury. What, are you pro-usury?" he quipped. Usury is often connected to Judaism through the Talmud's accused permissiveness towards such loan practices (a mischaracterization), often ascribed to Hebraic law, which antisemites believe treats gentiles differently from Jews.[14]

This concept emanates from the antisemitic falsehood that the Talmud proclaims that gentiles are not fully human in comparison to Jews, and instructs Jews to deal with them dishonestly, to manipulate and rob them, to feed their vices so as to make money that can enrich the tribal community. This is the core of the antisemitic claim that the Yiddish word "Goyim," which in fact just means gentile, actually means "cattle." The idea being that Jews think gentiles are the equivalent of livestock. This is at the heart of the medieval (and often resurrected) claims of "blood libel," that Jews use Christian or Muslim children as part of some occult blood ritual during Passover, suggesting that non-Jewish blood be used for extractive purposes instead of being treated as sacred, as Jewish blood would have been.[15] That the Talmud's first rule says to "trade in good faith" doesn't seem to matter; reality plays little role in the caricature made of Jews.

Jews are then the archetype of the demonic capitalist, not because capitalism is not demonic, but because the negative stereotypes of Jews are then combined with those of the ruling class. The Jew is portrayed as essentially weak, lacking in the physical strength it takes to do "real work," like that in a factory or on a farm or to work with your hands. The Jew character lacks any strong sense of masculinity (if they are a man), and instead wins victories through trickery and manipulation, not the determined clash of wills. The rich Jew is therefore seen as ugly and wins social status and sexual validation through their manipulation of money and people, not through the awarding of such spoils by virtue of their objective superiority. The happy merchant stereotype exemplifies this, but such images also play into the common portrayal of the capitalist class as physically deficient and lacking qualities that "real workers" would have.

Ultimately, the character of the Jew is the personification of control. While managers may be perverted by the system, the Jew perverts the system itself. That system is either imperfect, and made worse by the Jew who manipulates it, or was created by the Jew in his own image. Capitalism, particularly ultra-globalized neoliberalism, is the pure essence of this since it commodifies humans and destroys their natural tribal allegiances to each other by turning everyone into objective profit centers wherein preferences and prejudices are interruptions to market potential. The Jew stokes this thinking in the broader public, but, since they lie, they maintain their tribal allegiances at home. The Jew benefits from the destruction of national borders since, as the progenitors of this form of capitalism, it helps them extract profits, create more wealth, and transform people into consumers. Communism is only the other side of the coin, also seen as a Jewish perversion whereby they go through a different political route to meet the same ends of internationalism, anti-nationalism, and the destruction of sovereign people's and hierarchies.

"Notice the Israelis: a fundamentally secular society. They no longer need Judaism because they have soil. The real Jew is a wanderer, a nomad. He has no roots, no attachments. So, he 'universalizes' everything. He can't hammer a nail, plow a field. He can only buy and sell, invest capital, manipulate markets. He takes the life of a people rooted in soil and turns it into a cosmopolitan culture based on books, ideas, numbers. This is his strength." These lines were spoken by a young Ryan Gosling in the movie *The Believer*, where he played a Jewish man who rejected Judaism and became a neo-Nazi skinhead.[16] The movie was held from release for a few years, partially because 9/11 made people less friendly to a film about bomb plots at synagogues, but also because people were unsure if they wanted someone making the more articulate version of the same arguments later found in *The Daily Stormer*. Gosling's character, Danny, later states: "Take the great Jewish minds: Marx, Freud, Einstein. What have they given us: communism, infantile sexuality, and the atom bomb? In a mere three centuries since these guys emerged from the ghettos of Europe, they've taken us from a world built on order and reason and hurled us into a chaos of class warfare, irrational urges, and relativity, a world where the very existence of matter and meaning is in doubt. Why? Because it is the deepest impulse of the Jewish soul to unravel the very fabric of life until nothing is left but thread, nothing but nothingness. Nothingness without end."[17]

The Jews are seen as the enemy of everything fixed and orderly; they exist in a world of abstractions, unlike the proper Aryan performance of labor, value, and meaning unencumbered by intellectualism and modernity. Accepting this image of the Jew requires a complex matrix of ideas and assumptions, a blend of fact and fiction, real anger and stoked identitarian scapegoating. When those are combined into a toxic stew, the antisemitic caricature of the Jew solidifies. Stranger still, Jews are ascribed to be both enemies of materialism and its champions. If a Jew is characterized as focused on economics, either capitalist or communist, they are too materialist because they abandon the soul of a "people." If a Jew is accused of philosophizing and mental gymnastics, then they are the enemy of scientific reason and truth. No matter how it is framed, Jewishness is characterized as embodying the absence of what is right, true, and self-evident.[18]

"It is indispensable for us to undermine all faith, to tear out of the mind of the 'goyim' the very principle of god-head and the spirit, and to put in its place arithmetical calculations and material needs," says the antisemitic forgery *The Protocols of the Learned Elders of Zion*, best understood as a compilation of every antisemitic allegation made against the Jews. "In order to give the GOYIM no time to think and take note, their minds must be diverted towards industry and trade. Thus, all the nations will be swallowed up in the pursuit of gain and in the race for it will not take note of their common foe."[19]

According to the *Protocols*, the Jew is then the force of modern progress; capitalism and communism are a two-headed serpent, both headed by the Jew. They order the world through materialism rather than spirit and identity. The forces of modernity are the result of the Jew's plotting, not the complexity of the forces that move society forward or backward. The idea that the *Protocols* are the minutes of the Zionist World Congress meeting of 1891, a meeting to plan for world destruction, is ludicrous on its face.[20] A person's willingness to believe something so far-fetched does not lead someone to antisemitic conclusions but requires that this thinking was already present. As Umberto Eco writes, "it is not the *Protocols* that produce antisemitism, it is people's profound need to single out an Enemy that leads them to believe in the *Protocols*."[21]

"[The *Protocols* are] just a literary representation of what the leadership of the Jewish community would be saying if they were all meeting together and taking notes. And it's very plausible in that sense...there definitely is a Jewish conspiracy. And it's not all that secret, and it's very, very old," Greg Johnson, the editor of the white nationalist Counter-Currents Publishing, told me in an effort to reclaim the meaning of the *Protocols* while acknowledging its forgery.[22] When facts discredit antisemitic theory, they will just tell you those facts never mattered in the first place.

Crypsis

What drives white nationalists maddest is that most Ashkenazi Jews are white. Or, as they would say, "appear white." Whiteness for them is not a social construct but instead a bio-historical legacy. As Richard Spencer has said, whiteness and its cultural legacy of the "heritage and peoples of Europe," is a grand legacy mythologized into a glorious memory, one distinctly threatened by modernity. Jews, on the other hand, want to destroy that greatness (as they represent modernity itself), and since they appear—or are mistaken to be—white, they have a unique advantage in doing so.

The word *crypsis*, used in white nationalist circles, is a non-word that connotes a particular feeling about how and why Jews supposedly hide their Jewishness. The idea is that Jews pretend to be like you (but are not like you), so that they can achieve their end. A particular example of this is the alleged prevalence of white Jewish antiracist activists, particularly in key moments like the Civil Rights Movement. It is not enough to explain that the history of Jewish oppression led many to get involved in left-wing and antiracist movements; instead it must be pernicious (and full of the aforementioned lies). They then speak *as* white people, or *for* white people, but subsequently *against* white people.

This comes from the image of the Jew as an outsider, or perhaps a wanderer; one who does not belong and does not want to. Suspicions about Jewish people come partly from this supposed outsider nature. They have, historically, lived in communities partly removed from the larger society from which they belong. This outsider perception comes partially from Halakha (Jewish law), and partially from the religious injunction to indicate distinctiveness, all of which is exaggerated and attacked by antisemites. All ethnic and religious communities have a certain level of "apartness" from their surrounding communities, which is due to the systemic oppression and violence leveled at them from the larger society. Jewish distinctiveness could easily have been seen as the tapestry of a larger society, but instead was seen with suspicion.[23] The image of the Jews as the "chosen people," which simply means they were chosen to first introduce ethical monotheism, was only made more severe when Jews did not announce themselves in public. Jews are accused of flirting with this suspicious apartness to create the image of Jewish self-supremacy, something that, like Passover rituals, was intentionally misunderstood to mean an anti-Gentile sacrifice.

The image of tight-knit Jewish communities with their placement on the outskirts of gentile towns and cities (a reality enforced by antisemitism), created easy points of scapegoating: Jews dwell just outside of your community but are still a part of it. Jewish distinctiveness has roots in Halakha as well as the realities of antisemitism, and one is not reducible to the other, but the way that separateness played out and was addressed by the surrounding society keeps its roots in the pernicious distrust Christians manufactured for their Jewish neighbors. *They* dress and worship differently, but could still blend in. As a result, the image of Jewish difference was given outstanding importance; was seen as cryptic, supposedly hiding the communities' Jewishness and therefore its ulterior motives.

The Nazis also claimed that Jews burrowed into the countries they entered until they brought people to the point of destruction through financial collapse, inter-European conflict, godlessness, sex, or anything else, really. In that era of false race science, it was critically important to indicate that the fault lay not just in their alien religion, but in their genes. They could look like any German (except when portrayed in antisemitic comics), but they were not just like any German. The Nazis justified the Yellow Star as a way that ordinary Germans could finally see the alien in their midst. The (((echo))) is a modern version of this, letting everyone know that a wanderer lurks in our midst, someone who pretends to participate in our shared heritage, but who does so disingenuously.

Like all other features of antisemitism, there is a particular utility to this. In a world where destruction feels imminent, where we are all vulnerable to exploitation and cruelty, it makes sense that we would have a Judas in our midst, someone who seemed like a member of our family but turned out to be one of *them*. The concept of "scapegoating"—of transferring blame to a singular object, person, or people—is often used in discussions about antisemitism, and there is a reason for this. The psychological process of transference, the shifting of blame externally, is a reflex that plays out socially in scapegoating when a people are under siege, or simply believe they are.[24]

And within that dynamic, a racialized narrative makes sense to the antisemite—the role of the Jew, a seeming outlier to how race and ethnicity play out, becomes a central part of understanding tribal experiences. Jews of color, of course, do not fit into this narrative, but it was never meant to be consistent.

Jean-Paul Sartre noted this about the logical fallacy at the heart of not just antisemitism, but the antisemite: "Never believe that antisemites are completely unaware of the absurdity of their replies. They know that their remarks are frivolous, open to challenge. But they are amusing themselves, for it is their adversary who is obliged to use words responsibly, since he believes in words. The antisemites have the right to play. They even like to play with discourse for, by giving ridiculous reasons, they discredit the seriousness of their interlocutors. They delight in acting in bad faith, since they seek not to persuade by sound argument but to intimidate and disconcert."[25] Indeed, it was logic itself, the world of the mind in which the Jew thrives, that got us in all this trouble to begin with. To cleanse ourselves, we have to revert to the role of the violent enforcer, the brutish mob that will make the wrong things right, not out of argumentation and analysis but guttural emotion.

Antisemitism is a revolt against reason because someone understands rationality as what got us into the current mess. Rationality is modern, it is bourgeois and enlightened, all the things that are endemic to the caricature of the Jew and their assumed place as an agent of cosmopolitanism and social turmoil. To revolt against reason and give in to impulse is to reject intellectualism. This is the process by which antisemitism relieves the bigot of the burden of reality, the assertion that crushing complexity is not symptomatic of the world but only a pathology perverting it. The historic role forced on Jews by antisemitic Christian Europe, as perceived "middle agents of capital," has created an image of Jews as the symbolic arbiters of the system of abstract capital, consumerism, and commodity, and the rage against the alienation of modernity has a face to strike with fury. This is the return of magic and mystery, the re-sacralization of the world, regressing from the failed promises of the Enlightenment. There is both a psychological and social process here, whereby antisemitism offers the permission to mobilize bigotry in service of anger against conditions of oppression, from spiking rents to lost jobs and foreign wars.[26] Antisemitism is anger pushed onto a particular type of person because it *feels* right, not because it is justifiable; to move into the arena of pure feeling is to abandon the highbrow mentality that we associate with the upper classes. This is anti-elitist mode of antisemitism, which identifies a ruling caste and chooses stereotypes of Jewishness as its dominant character.[27]

And this need—to transfer your experience from the abstract to the individual, from the unreachable to the personal—is always there. There is an undying need to save ourselves by ridiculing others, and when we are disempowered, that displacement spins out on each other rather than those responsible. In that world, where impulses are to be trusted and facts are to be ignored, the figure of the rich alien will always inspire guttural rage.

Modernity

In Germany, in advance of the Holocaust, Jews were identified with the word *asphalt*, as were cities. The two were one and the same, as industrialism pushed people into the alienating urban landscape, which created a nostalgia for what agrarian feudal life was like. Jews were agents of this modernity; they were accused of propagating this wave of modernization because it was in their rootless cosmopolitan nature. The essential nature of Germanics was said to be rooted in the soil, but Jews failed to attach to the soil because it was not encoded in their genes or spiritual selves.[28] When Joseph Goebbels announced in 1933 that the reign of "Jewish intellectualism" had come to an end, his audience knew what he meant without him drawing a line. This was the era where the complexities of capitalism were coming into its full force: speculation, financialization, complex social relationships stemming from there forward. It happened at the same time as a complex social phenomenon, the rise of Marxism as a political force, the abstractions of modernity impending down on the German public. These conditions gave rise to the Volkisch nationalist and romantic movements of the nineteenth century, and helped to set the stage for the nationalism of the early-twentieth (as well as the brutality of German colonialism). Judaism has often been used as a marker for the boundaries of non-Jewish identity, which is to say that Jews and Judaism are used as an untrue archetype for what a given people believe their opposite is or what they find pernicious and threatening. David Nirenberg, in his book *Anti-Judaism*, says that in the West, "across several thousand years, myriad lands, and many different spheres of human activity, people have used ideas about Jews and Judaism to fashion the tools with which they construct their reality of the world."[29] As they are passed from generations, these ideas often mutate per the needs of those who are mobilizing them, but antisemitism evolves as a concept for how to explain the world and doesn't have a direct connection to Jews (which is why antisemitism can be strong in regions that have almost no Jewish people). Judaism then becomes "more a moral and epistemological category than a people," and as Europe moved into a modern way of being, the features of that modernity—from the development of financial capitalism to the abstractions of modern art and science— were labeled as fundamentally "Jewish."[30] Christian Europe has become "Judaized."

Part of why Jews were attached to "modernity," this manufactured concept, is that they flourished in its arrival. Historian Dan Diner coined the term, "Jewish Modernity" to signal the post-emancipation cultural movements ascribed to Jews, from the Yiddishland world of art and poetry to the flourishing Jewish revolutionary movements.[31] Jews were well represented inside socialist and anarchist movements (we need not explain why oppressed people often become radicals), which can be considered a part of the experience of constructing a modern Jewish identity. Jews were allowed into professions that they previously were not, and professions that they may previously have existed in became more important. The "mobility, circulation, commercial exchange, acculturation, exile and multilingualism" that had been ascribed to Jews became an archetypal metaphor for the binaries between tradition and modernity, degeneracy and strength, Jew and German.[32] Artisans and others dispossessed by a shifting world could not make sense of these changes, and so the appearance of Jews who were now more visible in social life had an explanatory power. Jewish success was just intolerable.[33]

One of the reasons the Holocaust is ascribed uniqueness is that the destruction of European Jewry lacked a utility. It gained little for the German state or ruling class; little in the way of territory, military might, or capital. Nazi antisemitism, which was the culmination of the turn away from traditional Christian antisemitism to a biologicalization of this earlier model, was that the "extermination of Jews seems to not have been a means to another end," as Moishe Postone wrote in 1986.[34] Postone was a Frankfurt Marxist of a different order, committed to understanding the historic role of antisemitism in developing National Socialism and, ultimately, Auschwitz, an institution that held a type of modernity in its own right. Nazi antisemitism took its notes from Christianity and attributes power to the Jews. It's different than other racisms in the expansive power it ascribes Jews through their "mysteriously intangible, abstract, and universal" nature.[35] This Jewish power works through proxies to destroy the assumed universal shared health of a people, who otherwise would have been living a strong collective life if the Jews had not deracinated them with abstractions. This complex power ascribed to Jews is that of the commodity, "the abstract domination of capital, which— particularly with rapid industrialization—caught up in a web of dynamic forces that they could not understand, became perceived as the domination of International Jewry."[36] The struggle against the imposition of modern capitalism was diverted to antisemitism, the belief that the overwhelming confusion of capital was the result of a particular minority in the midst.

As society changed, communities tried to make sense of the social shifts and ascribed the cause to an "Other" that had historically been accused of conspiratorial attacks on the social fabric. This creates a model for what Werner Bonefield says makes antisemitism "different from racism [in] that it has a direct relationship with 'modernity's' attempt at reconciling its constituting contradiction, that is the class antagonism between capital and labour."[37] Jews make up an abstract "society," a perversion of the natural "community" of which it is not a part. Since this community finds its shared natural status in the interplay of blood and soil, it sees the "other as a parasite whose objective is to oppress, undermine and pervert the 'natural community' into a society based on the accumulation of abstract and intangible values."[38] The abstractions of capital, its ability to rip through "traditional" German life with intellectualism, financialization, and "asphalt," is then patterned onto Jews because of their forced role in Christian Europe (as money lenders). "National anti-Semitism not only uses and exploits these historical constructions but, also, transforms them: The Jew stands accused and is persecuted for following unproductive activities."[39] All social relationships are biologicalized, essentialized, identity reified, and forced onto Jews so that they are shackled to the accusations of bio-capitalism, the personification of what is believed to have robbed Germanness of its beautiful essence. The struggle of National Socialism was not just of the German Nazis against the world for power and control, it was to free themselves from the shackles of what they determined to be "Jewishness": the destructive complexity of the modern world. They were willing to lose the war since it was a proxy for a bigger fight that motivated German venom.

This comes partly from what Moishe Postone called "structural antisemitism," which is social forces that create ways of thinking in a population where antisemitism slots in perfectly. Marx understood this, and explored it in essays like "On the Jewish Question," where he saw behaviors as being essentially Jewish, such as greed and market manipulation.[40] This was, of course, the result of structural antisemitism itself. Marx could not free himself from the stereotypes of Jewishness and believed that it was simply something endemic to Judaism that we had to emancipate Jews from. This was not new to Marx, and it arrives from what David Nirenberg calls "Anti-Judaism," whereby people define themselves through the inversion of what they say Judaism is, or Jews are. Jews are then products of the accusation: they are carnal when Christians are spiritual, they are abstract when "true" Germans are of the soil, they are conspiratorial when the Gentiles are honest.[41] This is why antisemitism can exist as a powerful social narrative even in societies were there are almost no Jews. "Antisemitism does not 'need Jews'... The Concept of 'Jew' knows no individuality, cannot be a man or a woman, and cannot be seen as a worker or beggar; the word Jew relates to a nonperson, an abstraction," writes Bonefeld.[42] Jews are the personification of a world made complicated and frightening because it is emotionally satisfying to attach ideas and conditions to people rather than to accept abstraction. Antisemitism is built into the fabric of Western society, our conception of value, dignity, and even liberation (particularly the resistance to capital), is tainted by antisemitic constructs that single out perceived Jewish qualities or institutions associated with Jewry, taking impulses towards disruption and creating a Jew-shaped target. This bigotry surpasses ideological borders, tainting left-wing anticapitalism as well, where it can be an expression of the fight against the artifice of the capitalist world.

Golem

One of the most persistent stories of Hebraic folklore is that of the golem, a robot created of clay or mud that can act out the will of the people behind creation. The story traces back to the Talmud, which reveals that Adam was originally a golem who God blew a soul into. But the most archetypal story of the golem comes from the golem of Prague, where Rabbi Juda Loew ben Bezalel allegedly created a golem in the sixteenth century from the sticky clay of the banks of the Vltava to defend the ghetto against antisemitic attacks. This is likely the version of the golem most people know—a vengeful monster of Judaic rage—and this fits well with the crushing medieval allegations against Jews of attacking their surrounding community. Jews poison the wells, kidnap and sacrifice Christian children, perpetuate the plague while keeping themselves sanitary. The golem has been so persistent that, as fascism was arising in Europe, and the German-American Bund started raising the specter of pogroms in the U.S., many Jewish leaders turned to "golems" of their own: Jewish mafia figures, Murder Inc., and others who would use violence to target the leadership of the fascists.

The golem was both friend and enemy—it can rebel and destroy. In Wegener's *Der golem, wie er in die Welt kam* (1920), Rabbi Loew's assistant brings the golem back to life in order to punish him for oppressing the rabbi's daughter, with whom he (the assistant) is having an affair. The golem sets his house ablaze and even threatens the whole ghetto. Similarly, Agnon's golem relies on a wordplay between modernity and rebellion, where the golem is a pretty violent soldier—the idea here is that the text itself is a golem that is given life and then develops a mind of its own.

And among the surrounding community the golem is often seen as less creation of Judaism than of its pure essence. The Jews' malevolence is not just self-serving, it is vile and demonic for no reason. The Jew is evil incarnate because evil needs no justification, and as our conception of what evil is evolves, so does its placement within the Jewish people.

Volcano Demon is a phrase from the Alt Right lexicon, popularized by *The Daily Shoah*, which they apply to the Jewish God of the Torah. This antisemitic joke has a long history; it is the idea that Judaism was a desert cult in which Yahweh was in fact an earlier demonic force and has arisen through the people who worship him. In this gnostic reading, Yahweh competed with other gods, or the one-true god, and the Jews were his evil servants, giving him power through their cruelty and sacrifice (especially of their foreskins). Christianity was then their greatest ruse: it was Yahweh's expansion into the non-Hebraic people, where their worship would give him power. They often cite what they see as the demonic agenda of the Old Testament god, followed by the rabbinical laws in the Talmud. Jews have then been cast as the agents of this evil god for centuries, undoing the divine inspiration of the Aryan people with their perversions. James Russell's book *The Germanization of Early Medieval Christianity* argues that the early imperial Christianity of Europe was less a true Christianity and more a manifestation of early Germanic paganism, where their culture, ideology, and spirituality was simply imprinted on Christian mythology. The Christianity we know today, with its occasional signals to human rights, is actually the erosion of its Germanic heritage. Russell's book is heavily cited by the far-right, particularly by folkish

Asatru (the racist form of Nordic Paganism), as an example of their meta-genetic pagan roots and their rejection of the Judeo-Christian influence—a foreign religion that wants to turn Aryans against their kin, an act of destruction perpetrated by Jews.

"Some religion! This wallowing in filth, this hate, this malice, this arrogance, this hypocrisy, this pettifogging, this incitement to deceit and murder—is that a religion? Then there has never been anyone more religious than the devil himself. It is the Jewish essence, the Jewish character, period!," reads Deitrich Eckart's pamphlet "Bolshevism from Moses to Lenin," which is written as a conversation with the Fuhrer and used as Nazi propaganda. The conversation traces what it sees as the Bolshevik tendencies inherent to the Jewish people throughout history, making this "disruption" a natural feature. Bolshevism was characterized as a Jewish revolution against Western nations, and even today many white nationalists refer, without irony, to the final goal of communism as the "Dictatorship of the Jew." Bolshevism is then considered the natural instinct of Jews to disrupt and destroy strong Aryans so they can issue control. This supposedly comes from deep within the Jew, whose God is to be pleased by the destruction of all that is right and good.

Nazi-Hindu mystic Savitri Devi considered Jews to be a conquering force in Europe, and thought they undermined pagan sensibilities with their alien god. To her, they were a force of retrograde imperialism, a people who were watching with glee as Aryans around Europe were bowing to a Semitic god rather than the gods that they had birthed in their once-great civilization. Jews and their wretched monotheism had poisoned Aryans, turned them into cruel, unfeeling people who did not see sacredness in the Earth and its animals because of their separation of the sacred and profane. Radical traditionalist fascist theorist Julius Evola saw Christianity, which sprung from a universalized Judaism, as inherently destructive to the west, with its "lunar" concepts of "brotherhood, love, and collectivism." He saw Judaism as particularly pernicious when secularized, and believed it to be a force for the destruction of civilization. Francis Parker Yockey, the author of *Imperium* who helped to define post-war fascism, believed that the Jews had perverted Western society with their materialism, their usurious concepts, and their opposition to absolute ethics, and thought that, since the Enlightenment, they had seized their opportunity to essentially stage a coup on Western culture.

Miguel Serrano went a step further with what has now been called Esoteric Hitlerism. Starting with Carl Jung's earlier assertion about the presence of the gods in the psyche of particular peoples, he asserted that those were actually spiritual forces underlying all of creation. Hundreds of thousands of years ago, the gods of creation were challenged by a malevolent demiurge who tricked them into material creation. This demiurge is Jehovah, the god of the Torah, and the Jews then stole the "birthright" of the Aryans, the descendants of the true gods of creation. The Jews were said to be a "bastard race," an amalgamation of other peoples, lacking in purity, who created their laws, history, and religious expansion on the denial of the Aryan's spiritual place. The Jewish religion, and their false god, is built on fortifying the destruction of that which is "true," by twisting the natural spiritual instincts of man in an effort to conquer them by way of their golem, the god of their despicable book.

The Talmud is a book of rabbinical teaching and Halakha—religious law—is the interpretation of Judaism. The Talmud is seen as the instructive text of Judaism (though this is ahistorical and non-universal) and—according to antisemites—teaches Jews to hate and destroy non-Jews, and is legalistic, petty, and manipulative—qualities they then ascribe to Jews. This is the "true" Bible of the Jewish people, as bestowed by the priestly caste and authorized by the vengeful Jewish god. While the Christians eventually worshipped a god of forgiveness, the Jewish god was about ethnic warfare and genocide. The Jews did not have the graceful second act of the Bible, only Torah, and this characterizes the evil by which they operate.

At the same time, the (allegedly) forgiving nature of Christianity is also placed at the feet of Jews. Christianity universalized Judaism, made it for everyone, allowing all to be equal through the majesty of salvation. "And have put on the new self, which is being renewed in knowledge in the image of its Creator. Here there is no Gentile or Jew, circumcised or uncircumcised, barbarian, Scythian, slave or free, but Christ is all, and is in all," reads Colossians 3:10-11. The allegation goes that this mentality universalized salvation, breaking down the national boundaries that existed before, where different cultures had their own pantheon, rites, and rules, which they believed were natural expressions of their ethnic identity and faculties.

Judaism, through its proxy in Christianity, then marched through Europe, undermining their national identities and imperial instincts through Christianization. This runs in contrast with other claims, for instance that Christianity was Germanized, or the history of bitter Christian bigotry and colonialism—but consistency and reason are not the point. The European New Right, a fascist intellectual movement that began in France in the 1970s, suggested that Christianity was at fault for the failures of modern liberal society, and that it should be rejected in favor of an ethnically derived paganism that could better realize our natural differences.[43] "Christianity = The Original Cultural Marxism" was a meme used by the white nationalist heathen organization Odinic Rite. The faults of Christianity are then found in Judaism, yet more as a trick than a feature. Judaism inspired the universalism of Christianity, but it did not share it, and hence the claim that Jews want diversity for non-Jews, while maintaining tribalism for themselves.

Christian antisemites, particularly in the extreme variety found in neo-Nazi movements and Christian Identity, take a slightly different road. The original Israeli religion was pure and bestowed by god, but it was not the Jewish religion as we understand it today. Instead, they say that this was a heretical deception introduced by modern Christian institutions, like the *Scofield Reference Bible*, that suggested that the Israelis of the Old Testament are the ancestors of the Jews of today. The idea that their Christianity has an origin in Judaism is intolerable, so they suggest that the Jewish religion was a cult that, while appropriating some of the religious elements of the ancient Israelites, did so for its own despicable and tyrannical ends.[44] They explain these ancient people in a couple of ways: They could be the Khazars, a separate people who perverted the Hebraic religion with their occultism and have posed for centuries as the Jews of the Bible. In this story, which has become popular with everyone from white nationalists to groups like the Black Hebrew Israelites, the Jews are in fact a separate tribal group that has created its own perverted temple religion and usurped the historic legacy of the "true" Jews, who could be anything from all-white Europeans to African-descended peoples.[45] The key point here is that the Jews we have today are lying about their own importance, and "chosenness," and diverting attention from those who should be identified as heroic.

In its more extreme version, they are the literal descendants of the Devil through what is called the "dual seedline theory." This suggests that Eve was actually impregnated by the Devil in the Garden of Eden, that Cain was the result of that union, and that the "Mark of Cain," which was cast upon him as punishment, was dark skin. Jews then grew their line through the ultimate sin for the white "Adamic" peoples: miscegenation. The true Israelites of the Bible were not the ancestors of the people we call Jews today—who are the natural enemy of white Christians—but the ancestors of all white people, who migrated up into Europe and started Western Civilization as the "lost tribes of Israel." Jews maintain a cosmic war against whites; people of color have no souls, because they are, in fact, animals; and white genocide is the tool used by the Devil to destroy the soldiers of Christ.[46] This is the motivating ideology that sparked the creation of the Patriot militia movement with Posse Comitatus in the 1970s, much of the revolutionary violence of The Order and Aryan Nations in the 1980s, and continues in certain backchannels of the movement today.[47]

No matter what the founding myth is, the Jew is unnatural for reasons that are more than self-interest. Their spiritual nature is in direct opposition to that of the saved; they inspire fear, hatred, and revenge as a spiritual instinct; and they are successful when the rest of the world fails. There are those who believe this literally, those who use it metaphorically, and those who simply feel it in their gut.

The desire is there to single out a responsible party, to create a cohesive narrative about the modern world to explain deprivation and despair. If you idealize the past, and present the modern world, with its failures and contradictions, as a contrast to that, then you have the appearance of a fallen people. Then you can place blame:

enlightenment, secularism, multiculturalism, modernity. And to give this process a culprit, to fill the audience with dread and horror and targeted venom, you turn it into a person. To explain the complexities of our society and to simplify and channel the disgust it inspires, you have to put an eternal enemy at the center. The ruling class is too vague, institutions too impersonal. The Jew is then constructed as the intersection of all of these things, and because Jews have been painted with this same brush for centuries, it is easy to reaffirm their role as the agents of these contemporary forces that are the cause for all this suffering.

A People Who Shall Dwell Alone

Around the time the swastika appeared at the Bernie Sanders rally, a series of reports about members of Britain's Labour Party participating in antisemitic forums with fascist collaborators surfaced. Several suspended members of the Labour Party had been attending conspiracy forums called Keep Talking, including a one by antisemite and David Duke collaborator, James Thring, where he claimed that no one was killed at Auschwitz. Controversy came earlier when a Labour Party member created a Facebook group called Palestine Alive where they published Holocaust Denial and the idea that Jews were responsible for 9/11.[48] Former party member Peter Gregson spoke at the meeting with Thring, and he had been previously suspended after his organization, Labour Against Zionism and Islamophobic Racism (Lazir), received accusations of trafficking in antisemitic conspiracy theories.[49]

The Labour Party has been dogged by claims of antisemitism over the past few years, and has largely been dismissed by the left as a cynical Tory plot (there is some truth to this), but this ignores what is a not just a problem in Labour, but in the entire left. For various reasons, both neglectful and intentionally malicious, antisemitism is a continued presence on the left, and the inability to locate and confront it means it can't be fully eradicated and inoculated against.

Antisemitism on the left is ephemeral, less than obvious, difficult to clarify, hard to pin down. While rarely becoming explicit, it exists often in the margins: the core of the problem is in the left's refusal to look for it, to see it as important. It is easy to paint with broad strokes, as so many centrist books on antisemitism and establishment organizations have done, but the reality is that antisemitism on the left lingers as a contradiction to the left rather than a core feature. Radical politics are made up of people who bring conflicting experiences and biases in them, and those can inform discourses that are, on their face, there to upend inequality itself. The role of antisemitism on the left has a persistent legacy that is often ignored or denied, and this has shadowed the history of anti-capitalism since the nineteenth century as Christian anti-Judaism evolved into the complex social phenomenon of antisemitism that painted the modern world as a Jewish disease.

Criticizing, or outright opposing Israel is not antisemitic, and the idea that it is should be wholesale rejected. Opposition to Israel is a logical continuation of the movements against nationalism, colonialism, authoritarian oppression, all of which are existing in what is continuing the Nakba over 70 years since it began. The issue of antisemitism in these movements is not in their fabric, it is in where they creep out of bounds and into something else. Antisemitism on the left is something that right-wing scholars and Israeli politicians have built their careers on, but they wholesale mistake where it actually comes from and instead try to denigrate movements towards liberation as something naturally dangerous for Jews.

Antisemitism on the left can be said to be borne of utility, and rests in two distinct areas: conspiracy theory and particular types of anti-Zionism. For conspiracy theorists, both the explicitly antisemitic and the coded variety, this is done to explain the current crisis of capitalism and provide people an Emmanuel Goldstein to vent their rage at. The continuing appeal of antisemitism is in its ability to spark anger, to simplify narratives, to name culprits. For anti-Zionists, the outrage that many feel about the crimes of Israel are so raw that they some feel as though they can ignore the boundaries of antisemitism out of anger and fear over the oppression of Palestinians. Anger can be expressed as bigotry, and this anger sometimes permeates the left as we try to reckon with colonialism, occupation, and racial nationalism. This does not mean that the opposition to Israel is the antisemitism, but that antisemitism can creep into the discourse if unchecked.

There are a couple of realities that only further compound the complexity of these feelings. Israel is waging a permanent colonialist war of oppression, only stoking an even more violent form of nationalism to ethnically cleanse an Indigenous population. Israel also has its finger on the trigger of a PR weapon, ready to fire accusations of antisemitism at anyone speaking against its crimes, and right-wing politicians and pundits never tire of using antisemitism as a battering ram against their opponents. Even more frightening, the claims have been used as a cover for an intensifying Islamophobia, the growth of movements like PEGIDA and the English Defence League, and is leading to the radicalization of the far-right "Settlement" movement in Israel.[50] This toxic mess only serves to further delegitimize claims of antisemitism, and while Israel is building alliances with far-right antisemitic regimes around the world, we are losing our ability to create a workable antiracist solution to confront the issue. At the same time, violent explosions of antisemitism are increasing, and the left, the place where racism and white supremacy is supposed to be confronted, has a widening blind spot.

The left's difficulty in addressing antisemitism comes from multiple directions, from collaboration with movements that have antisemitic roots, the inclusion of populist anti-capitalist arguments, and the unwillingness to challenge antisemitism when it arises mid-struggle. Spencer Sunshine outlines eleven ways that antisemitism is conveniently responded to on the left, including denying what is happening, attacking the accuser, claiming the antisemite is being persecuted for Palestinian solidarity, saying the accusation is "Zionism," calling the claim a smear or guilt by association, redirecting or making a bait and switch, asking for unattainable proof, making a false equivalency, or citing a Jew that agrees with them. The point is to avoid accountability when behaviors are labeled as antisemitism, therefore rejecting the notion that anything needs to be changed, examined, or confronted.[51]

Inside of left spaces, antisemitism is often rendered invisible, assumed to have been a relic of the past or the property of only the most genocidal reaches of the far-right. But this perception can help ensure an approach that is, in and of itself, antisemitic. In left spaces, double-standards are common for Jewish movements (particularly issues related to Zionism), litmus tests for Jews around hot-button issues proliferate (demands to know Jewish people's position on Israeli policies), and the willingness to allow antisemites (particularly from national liberation movements) or conspiracy theorists (such as "9/11 Truth") to be a part of movements. During the height of the antiwar movement, "9/11 Truth" and antisemitic speakers alleging that Jews were responsible for 9/11 were reasonably common, and a distinct part of the "coalition" that had formed.[52] In Occupy Wall Street, the criticisms of finance capital often resulted in the focus on Jewish figures with catchy last names (that often started with "R"), reverting to antisemitic conspiracy theories that redirect legitimate class anger to archetypal images of secret Jewish cabals.[53]

The argument around where the line is, when rhetoric becomes antisemitic in confronting Israel's crimes, has continued for decades. And during these contentious discussions, people of Jewish descent have consistently rung the bell of creeping antisemitism into left spaces. When a person raises the specter of racism and oppression, whether institutionally or interpersonally, the left has, at least in rhetoric, made it a priority to believe them. Belief is part and parcel of listening to marginalized voices and learning from them, a corrective for years of erasure. When it comes to Jews, belief is not the tendency, and instead, allegations of antisemitism, both sincere and in bad faith, are taken with a grain of salt.

The experience of Jewishness, which includes the lived oppression of antisemitism, is seen as suspect, and one is only believed after hoops are jumped through. If we look at major leftist publishers and publications, how many articles and books are defending against accusations of antisemitism? How does that compare to the numbers of essays that sincerely take on the challenge of addressing antisemitism? This disparity is not a form of silencing since, in response, the non-Jewish left actively defines all the things they believe to *not* be antisemitic. This creates a profound distance for Jews inside social movements, where their experience does not feel validated by the groups they are aligned with. In an antiracist movement dedicated to greater equality, Jewishness was supposed to be defended, and Jews protected. If this turns out to be untrue, where do they go next?

Antisemitism can even be seen as an incredibly potent motivator inside social movements, inspiring fervor and building fanaticism. The anger about the ethnic cleansing of Palestine can sometimes outstrip the prohibition on ethnic or religious bigotry, it can outweigh our revulsion of antisemitism by comparison. In light of war crimes in Gaza and occupation in the West Bank, what is antisemitism? Does it matter? Or worse ... is it justified?[54]

The uncritical support for the voices of those affected by Israeli crimes is a double-edged sword. On the one side, the support raises the voices of the most erased by the conflict—Palestinians trying to survive amid decades of colonial occupation. On the other side of this sword are some Palestinian movements that see the struggle for land in explicitly racialized and antisemitic terms, something often explained away by the left as the passions of those experiencing violence.

The latter is not unique to Palestinian movements since conspiracy theories and latent bigotries often exist amid movements for liberation; all people exist with uneven consciousness, with conflicted and confusing narratives about who is committing these atrocities and what will make them stop. And the lack of perfect politics is not a reason to abandon solidarity, if we did then there would be no social movements at all. But when transposed to our political rhetoric this narrative can leave the most biting antisemitism intact, and when mixed with litmus tests, demands for isolating Jews, and shouting anger, the focus can shift from Israel to Jews to an individual Jewish person in a matter of minutes. The Intifada was both a righteous uprising and fertile ground for antisemitic attacks, and it has to be seen in its complexity, not by reducing national liberation movements to two-dimensional caricatures of pure heroism. The reality is that most political movements fail to live up to our aspirations, and that does not mean they should lose the support of the international left community, but it does mean that their full picture, flaws and all, has to be made evident.

The world is filled with old Jewish phrases, anecdotes, parables, and proverbs, and many of the ones we know come from the uniqueness of diaspora Yiddish, a language filled with humor and irony. "The world will never forgive the Jews for the Holocaust," is a new one, but it echoes a historical theme. The Jews will never be forgiven for what they made us do to them. Once, when I was a young boy, my father hit me in the face. Afterward, he approached me shaking, eyes filled with tears, ashamed of what he had done. But more than ashamed: angry. He told me he was angry with himself, but I never really believed him. He stared at me with a kind of contempt, as if I had been responsible for his violence.

If Jews are tied to all ills, from capitalism to communism to colonialism, and these institutions emerge from them, from their manipulative nature to their nebbish tribalism, then the anger of the world rests on their shoulders. The antisemitic archetype of the Jew has features you can focus on, your rage can intensify, you can blame and scream and warn others. And when the story you tell, the myths you use to explain the world, catch up to your emotional reality, which connects economic and social crisis with the image of a Jew, then a spark occurs. It would be wrong to say that we work backward from ideology and reason, but instead we are often searching for explanations that match up with our gut instinct. Structural analysis is not emotionally resonant enough: you need a face and a name on which to focus your anger.

We trust our emotional common sense because it is there to guide us in decision making. But the reality is that this instinct is molded by the world around us, it is built by subtleties and conditions of social relationships. Bigotry and bias are a part of that, the result of a vastly unequal world built on white supremacy. So, when we are in search of answers, we often work backward from our conclusions, particularly about who is to blame. We may not have identified the Jew as the enemy, but instead we may have imagined the capitalist as someone composed of the stereotypes that have been historically used to marginalize Jews. The picture of a sweaty-palmed liar, a person looking to disrupt our wholesome lives, someone warned about for centuries in everything from whisper to scripture. That quest for answers and the process of blaming are not simply held by the unenlightened of the political right, but by an entire society, and when push comes to shove antisemitism is an easy fall back for a political movement trying to make sense of itself.

Despite the narrative that Israel's defenders propose, nationalism is not the solution to antisemitism. A collective approach to liberation is the only functionally useful way to address antisemitism, as it sees this oppression as bound up with the experience of Palestinians and the global explosion of Islamophobia. These forces are intertwined, and retreating to exclusionary enclaves will do nothing to undermine the fundamental drivers of antisemitic violence, nor will ignoring the voices of Jews who raise the issue.

Nation

Antisemitism echoes throughout history. For hundreds of years, despite differences, there are core stories and impulses that return again and again.

Antisemitism holds a continuing appeal to each generation, a built-in answer and motivator that is so easy to return to. This is, largely, why contemporary white nationalists make their claim to the "Jewish Question," suggesting that there is something inside Jews, and the culture they create, that makes them passionately disliked by everyone else. "You are disliked—you people, you have been disliked for three thousand years, you have been disliked so much that you have been hounded from country to country, from pogrom to purge, from purge back to pogrom. And yet you never ask yourselves why you are disliked," said Holocaust denier David Irving in a speech that has often been cited to prove the motivations for his "revisionism."[55] It is, again, not us, but them, that are causing dislike of them. But there is something persistent about antisemitism, something that is so ever present and so unceasing that many Jews have become resigned to its durability.

Antisemitism's appeal is similar to that of nationalism; it drives emotion into the center of an oppositional struggle for power, it names names and rallies the troops. Antisemitism provides a satisfying narrative and validates internal turmoil. It undoes the complexity that often exists in the shifting sands of liberation movements. Antisemitism transforms the struggle against inequality and oppression into spiritual terms, where the anger is pure and the people are bound together by it. Even when the name isn't spoken, we know that there is a person responsible. It could be all Jews, or one Jew, or even the idea(s) of the Jew, but there is a force there that we are united in an apocryphal Armageddon against.

Jews are a useful stand-in as the cause of everything we have lost, and it has been a lot. Falling wages, lost family members, a failing biosphere, a crushing alienation, a life too ordinary, mundane, and tragic. Like any form of entrenched bigotry and racialized oppression, to get rid of the instinct to blame the Jews we would have to unthink our narratives, confront our histories, and challenge our assumptions. This is difficult, and with antisemitism it often appears as though it is either not worth it or that antisemitism still resonates. The Jew is the caricature that we make of our enemies and we need to dehumanize them as a tactic of war, and to dehumanize ourselves so we are able to fight.

While modern liberalism tries to push back against antisemitism through its commitment to logic, either by showing the silliness of conspiracy theories or by conditioning people to the presence of Jews, antisemitism is, fundamentally, about the revolt against logic. The liberal fantasy is that bigotry is simply rooted in ignorance and if people were exposed to reality and diversity, say getting to know some Jewish people, they'd be cured of this sickness. The problem is that bigotry in society is also a component of our emotional selves, it thrives even when we try to logic our way out of it. And so logic feels suspect because of the strength of our emotional attachments.

Sociologist Arlie Hochschild spoke about the creation of our personal "deep story," the internal narratives we apply to our experiences in order to satisfy our feelings. She was talking about the Tea Party movement, which, while claiming to be a response to material issues like taxes, was much more about the myriad feeling of loss happening among whites. "Given the experiences we've undergone, we have deep feelings. These shape our 'deep story,' and this is an allegorical, collectively shared, 'honor-focused,' narrative storyline about what 'feels true,'" writes Hochschild. "We take fact out if it, judgement out of it. A 'deep story' says what happened to us from the point of view of how we feel about it."[56]

Irrational rage comes from the undirected impulses of people. It is how their anger comes out unmediated and undirected. Antisemitism is a narrative that gives the irrational rage direction, it validates it and turns it away from politics and into an anti-politics of conspiratorial revenge. At the heart of antisemitism is a story that makes no sense, and for the antisemites it is the decision to reject the search for meaning in favor of the heart and the fist. To give in to the anger of our lives and the image of who is responsible: the petty, foreign, meek, manipulative "other" that is disrupting the "we." While not everyone "names the Jew" when acting on this impulse, it is the desire to reject complex evidence in favor of the individualized conspirator that drives the continuing appeal of antisemitism.

All bigotry is about violence, who is safe from violence, who we take measures to stop violence against, and who we decide to enact violence on. Antisemitism is no different, and is often expressed through spectacular acts of violence. Mass shootings. The Holocaust. Historical expulsions. Forced conversions. Jewishness is, in many ways, defined by the resistance to this violence, its biting need to survive. MacDonald wanted to call this resistance a "group evolutionary strategy" to give it a pernicious edge, but Jews have forged an identity of community defense to stay alive. The ability to hold traditions and to find one's self with the help of another, all while a fire circles the gates, is a core part of this story. Judaism is caked in fear, every kippah a dangerous target.

Judaism is about a people who know themselves by the scratches they leave on the floor, by the ability to continue against all odds. Jewishness is about the choice between being hidden and celebrating in public amid threat. It is a chambered round in the 9MM next to my bed, the panicked memory in the middle of the night, the changed last name and questioning glances and little memory of a shared past. It is the reason that our records were blotted out or burned, or why my father never owned a copy of the Torah. How are we supposed to build an identity out of Jewishness that is not surrounded on all sides by fear? Diaspora meant more than displacement to the corners of the Earth; it meant the dislocation from the ownership of who we are.

There has to be a consensus that antisemitism does exist and that it is persistent, despite all odds, because we have failed to understand its function. In a culture of disbelief, of impossible standards of proof, of aiding and abetting of the bigoted, antisemitism will continue. Without active agents poised on its destruction antisemitism will only blossom again and again. Because we want it to, because it makes the unbelievable make sense. Without antisemitism we just have to live with our hate, and it could destroy us. It's much easier to name our enemy.

Chase the Black Sun

Super Male Vitality

What I always heard was that when a loved one dies, the things that annoyed you about them, maybe even that enraged you, usually fall by the wayside. My father died in 2013, and while I miss him with a persistent passion, I've never been so fucking angry. I remember things from my youth, things I excused away at the time, but that stick with me today. You can never truly hold your parents accountable because, by the time you confront them, they are rarely still the person who committed the infraction. And sometimes you never get to confront them, because they die.

My Dad never seemed particularly comfortable in his masculinity. Though he would constantly antagonize me with provocations to behave like a man, he oddly never seemed like he did so himself. My Mom would say that he wasn't exactly a "man's man," but that never stopped him from demanding it from others or acting with some of the most egregious arrogance towards women. He spent his whole life passing between masculine stereotypes, from his time as a Marine to a family patriarch, but with his thin frame, slight tone, and often meek presentation, his masculinity seemed more aspirational. For years, I had trouble locating what the discomfort was, but now it seems almost as though he knew he had a role to play and spent his whole life in frustration trying to act the part.

He was always completely mystified by gender. One time, when I was visiting from college, he explained to me that men and women had different kinds of brains, which is why men were better at riding motorcycles. When I asked him what kind of science would have studied cognitive structures and motorcycles, he looked embarrassed, like he had again failed to bond with me. All he had was a masculine script that he couldn't figure out and that the rest of us didn't want to.

His most toxic behaviors were those that were distinctly not masculine by any stereotype. Instead of being able to take criticism, when his feelings were hurt, he would lash out at others, yelling and throwing tantrums. Likewise, the qualities that we loved about him were present more when he stopped trying and went with his instincts, which were to be kind and warm and to drop the expectations he had of others. His toxicity was less in his ability to be masculine, and more in the privileges assigned to him in the masculine role. He would explode when his status, intelligence, or authority was questioned. When my father had an affair, or I should say *another* affair, my brother confronted him. He blew up, acting as though we had broken rank and saying that the women in his life had betrayed him by "getting fat" and not doing what he wanted sexually. Masculinity as an amalgamation of qualities—commitment, refusal to adapt, stoicism, et cetera—never seemed the issue, but the promises of the patriarchy were.

My father spent his later years apologizing in private for the things he'd done, and I don't doubt he was sincere. He would break down, offer regret for how he handled things, and talk about my mother as the "true love" who saved him. He walked her through the end of their lives, through cancer, and did it with a kind of tense devotion. But as I got older, and I tried to live out some of the lessons of commitment and stoicism that he seemed to embody when I was young, I realized just how little of this role he had a capacity for.

There is an infectious quality to the promise of masculinity, particularly at its most toxic. Masculinity is characterized not just by a hardness and immobility, but also by a lack of desire for vulnerability and adaptability. There are traces of this in every bit of gendered programming we come across, but it becomes more explicit as men believe themselves under threat by femininity or diversity or simply when other people demand equality. Fascism makes the implicit explicit and calls on existing hierarchies to be consciously stratified. The resulting shift in society has been to turn men into frothing advocates for the patriarchy.[1] Masculinity is promised to men as their inherited right, as access to control, but also a script about what they are going to be like. The real genius of the new world of far-right grifters, like advertising wizards for the last hundred years of American consumer capitalism, was their ability connect a built-in sense of inadequacy with a hyper-realized version of the promise society makes to men every day. Fascist insurgents always promise men that they will become heroes, if only they can be transformed by the fire of racialized violence.

Groups like the Wolves of Vinland, a male-tribalist organization, take this model even further, telling men that the promise of their patriarchal authority is built into the connective tissue of the natural world and that their feeling of anxiety is the proper reaction to the "attack on men" that the modern world has devised. The founder of the Wolves of Vinland, Paul Waggener, made a name for himself as a new kind of leader, selling his model of tribalism through a series of interlocking businesses all built on pulling as much money out of recruits as possible. Through a project called Operation Werewolf, which was equal parts pagan instruction, workout regiment, and self-help manual, Waggener strung men along a pathway to "Total Life Reform," a process billed as their last chance to reclaim health, happiness, and masculinity, which he framed as so revolutionary it could literally break apart empires.

As I sneaked into the Operation Werewolf "Elite" forums, and into the program itself, I wanted to figure out exactly why Operation Werewolf had struck a chord with men around the world and why it was attracting recruits in astonishing numbers. What was it about Paul's mythology that attracted so many, particularly when his violent fascist politics were just an inch below the surface? As I started my research in their private forums, among their piles of arcane literature and the constant string of the leaders' commandments to the "operatives," I followed along with the Total Life Reform program to try and understand why something so nakedly absurd and hateful had such a hold on a growing subculture of men.

***

In a lot of ways, likely intentionally, the product that Operation Werewolf is selling is Paul Waggener himself. Waggener and his lifestyle brand, Operation Werewolf (OPWW), are fond of using the phrase "cultivate an aesthetic." Their aesthetic comes from his description of the Wolves as an organization built around personifying the "Germanic hero" archetype, a bit of German idealism rephrased for the working class. What this really means is to set goals based on the image of someone or something you admire, such as Odin's astonishing strength or Erik the Red's fortitude in the Sagas. Waggener's aesthetic is layered. On top of bulging muscles so meticulously defined that he built an ideology out of his weight training regimen, he is painted with runic tattoos, including "WOLVES" across his throat in a brutal jailhouse Old English. He is usually seen wearing shirts of his own design—if he's wearing a shirt at all.

Waggener's underlying ideological principle is *intentionality*, which derives from his decades of Germanic mysticism and his own conception of Nordic magic. As he outlines in his book, *On Magic*, this can be boiled down to the use of "will" to exercise change in the world, and usually involves ritualized methods to enforce concentration, goals, or to set intentions in your mind.[2] He has even created a "branding" guide (which he sells for $47), in which he trains his Operation Werewolf followers to create a brand and connect with consumers.

All this is to say that the hulking masculinity of every pose is planned, each word is chosen to elicit a particular response. In Waggener's branding seminars, he uses archetypes—he is a Jungian after all—and he talks about the archetypal customer that a brand is attempting to connect with.

Waggener has applied his core principles to the host of projects that make up Operation Werewolf, but there is a principle that runs even deeper—one that undergirds not just the appeal of the program and the movement, but Waggener himself. His archetype is that of an isolated and idealized masculinity, not just as a phenomenon that exists and is prized, but one that you too can experience! Waggener's model for himself, and what he offers in the form of t-shirt designs and a vigorous weight training ritual, is about (re)claiming a primal masculinity, a force that runs under the surface of the world and is so powerful that it can crack the foundations of the empire.

A bit of history. The Wolves of Vinland began in 2005 as an Asatru social club for Waggener, his brother Matthias, and a few of their friends; they were basically, a crew of guys who wanted to practice Nordic paganism with the edginess of a motorcycle club.[3] The Waggener brothers were teenage neo-Nazis in Cheyenne, Wyoming, with a crew they called the 17th Street Psychos.[4] They are the sons of an Anglican pastor who eventually left the church to become an Orthodox priest because of the "creeping liberalism" in the church.[5] The Waggeners eventually drifted away from the skinhead crews and settled into the black metal and biker scene of Lynchburg, Virginia, where they wanted to build a tribal group that was defined by its exclusive nature. They would set requirements for their guys: they had to train, couldn't be fat, had to be capable of violence, had to prioritize the group, and had to maintain distinctiveness of gender. The racialism was implicit; they defined themselves as "folkish," the idea that the Nordic pagan revival is only for the people who are descended of Northern European blood stock.[6]

The Wolves of Vinland's fascist bonafides are unquestionable. They have attracted the membership of white nationalists like Kevin DeAnna; fascist male tribalist writers like Jack Donovan; staff members at *World Net Daily*, American Renaissance, and *the Daily Caller*; and they even had a member prosecuted for torching a Black church.[7] Waggener's own philosophy is built on scientific racism—the belief that people of different races have different levels of intelligence and personality patterns—and his spirituality is an expression of his belief in racial nationalism. Through his published work and videos, Waggener advocates for men preparing themselves for violence and for building racially exclusive enclaves where they enforce their power as men. He does this in connection with the larger project of the Alt Right.

In Operation Werewolf, he has sanitized out almost every one of these talking points in order to recruit a wider swathe of non-white men, offering a "tribalism for all peoples" model and avoiding any definitive white nationalism in branding materials. Operation Werewolf became a touchstone for white nationalists around the world who were looking for a cool branding model that offers plausible deniability to accusations of white supremacy while also venerating all of their key ideological impulses. Former skinheads around the U.S., including from the violent neo-Nazi gang American Front, are flying the Operation Werewolf flag, and there are organizations around the world that are mimicking the model set by the Wolves. Operation Werewolf is Waggener's Trojan Horse.[8]

Waggener eventually branched out and started writing about his experiences with the Wolves, about the sanctity of male spirituality he found in weightlifting and combat training, and his desire to help men to create their own crews. The Wolves of Vinland had expanded, and Alt Right writer Jack Donovan was now among the ranks, but others were encouraged to build their own cults of strength. This the mission of Operation Werewolf: "At its core, this is what Operation Werewolf truly means, to make war on weakness and complacency, first through the act of physical overcoming and the obtaining of strength on a visible, outward level—so that the would-be hero can pass through those Gates of Iron and apply their principles to every area of his being, in a legendary act of Alchemical transformation. We call this process Operation Werewolf. MIGHT IS RIGHT," says Paul in the first issue of his zine *Iron and Blood*.[9]

Operation Werewolf became part of the many-headed hydra of Paul's self-help business empire, which ranges from his many books to his brand-building services to his weight training programs. Men pay for an initiatory system that trains them how to become more total men, to build a male tribe, and become heroes of their story. They get the opportunity to be more like Paul.

Physical training is at the center of this, considered a "transferable" experience that builds fortitude in the man by making him experience pain.[10] This pain builds a body to be admired; physical strength becomes a cultivated aesthetic that others should admire and emulate. To do this, Paul stripped out almost all the racialist language from Operation Werewolf and recruit men of color as well, only expanding his reach.

***

"You know every time we talk about them you stand in a fighting pose," my wife teased. I was telling her about a particularly exhausting bit of Wolves research. I had just finished one of Paul's books, and was on to the next one. "It's sort of like you're flexing when you talk about them."

I laughed, embarrassed, but she wasn't exaggerating. I actually noticed that, when I was watching their videos and taking notes, I ended up working out longer and harder. I felt like I had to prove something. I'm not sure to whom, but I had just listened to a series of bodybuilders talk about measuring your self-worth by the number of plates you could press... And the more I tracked Operation Werewolf, the more pronounced this feeling became. I felt the tug of accountability, like someone was watching to see if I didn't meet my goals. A mountain had formed, and I had to climb it; I had to be better, be stronger.

My wife, Alexandra, called it "intoxicating masculinity," a quest for maleness that isn't cerebral, but rather is felt. Operation Werewolf is a dangerous project normalizing fascist politics inside a subculture that promises self-improvement but stokes violence instead. And the core of it spoke to subcultures of men who were searching for something—not just identity, but a sense of having improved themselves or gained value somehow. Being masculine and the need to fulfill masculine gender norms are a subtext running through many cultures' stories about what it means to be a man. Being masculine supposedly comes with a set of rewards, and many men unconsciously strive for it. Masculinity is ubiquitous and has a coercive effect, even when the entire reason you are watching the display of toxic masculinity is to participate in its destruction.

***

The idea of a "men's group" is not a novel concept; various incarnations of romanticized men's groups have popped up from time to time. Men's only clubs went back into vogue in the U.S. during the mid-twentieth century—a reaction to increased gender integration—and fraternal organizations have been a consistent feature of society for centuries. The idea is to segregate men into a space where they "can be men," because mixed company poisons the experience of isolated maleness. The men's movement of the 1960s and 1970s, particularly the mythopoetic men's movement, sought to apply some kind of New Age spirituality to this gender essentialism, trying to revive the "deep masculine" with everything from Jungian archetype visualization to sending white guys on "spirit quests." The men's movement was split on different things: some saw themselves as an adjunct to the women's movement and fought toxic masculinity through men's mentorship, others openly saw women as the enemy. All of these groups hoped to find something deep inside, something that was lost and could be uncovered through performative apartness.

While the phenomenon of the "men's group" is certainly more fringe today than it used to be, their rarity of these groups may fortify their appeal. These organizations, each with their own cultural particulars, promise to elevate male recruits by enhancing something that is inside them already: their essential masculinity. This is how a whole range of recruitment strategies work, whether large-scale groups (like the Marine Corps), the religiously specific (Promise Keepers and other men's-only Christian groups), the violently anti-feminist (Men's Rights Movement) or those specifically for sex (Pick-Up Artists).

Operation Werewolf (OPWW) is not wholly new in its ability to tell a story about what one's masculinity can be, what one can be-come from it, but it presents a different version of call for a disaffect-ed twenty-first century man. Waggeners' vision of a "revolutionary masculinity" is all the more seductive as alienation and angst are constant features of a vastly unequal and stilted modern world. His vision will tear down walls and force you to be "free."

The most involved a man can be in OPWW (and it should be clear, it is for men only) is the Elite Performance program, which amounts to a series of private message boards that men pay to access. At the end of a three-month period, the men go to an event called Conclave, which is held at Ulheim, the Wolves' sacred space in Virginia. There, they are put through endurance tests and other spiritual rituals.[11] If they pass, they pay more money and move to the next level, and so on, as they "progress" through the Werewolf network, and build their own tribes. I got into their message boards without being noticed—since their entry process is little more than paying—and signed up for their Performance program. Their internal communication hub was the place to go deeper with the research, but it was also the place I could see how the men felt. They were encouraged to stay strong but also be vulnerable, to share their dreams and what held them back. This is where they were to admit how they had failed—in the gym, at work, in their marriages.

It was easy enough for me to slip into the forums, make an ac-count, and find a way into the program, but it was harder to explain was why I was doing it. On the one hand, this was a look inside the social space that Operation Werewolf was creating, so it had a real practical utility. Digging into a far-right group, deep into the mem-bership and literature is what I do, part of a journalistic mission to expose them. In this case, something clearly appealed to these men, and I needed to better understand it, so I committed to following the program's daily routines. I would do the workouts, read the rune guides, follow (to a point) their strange investment strategies, and try to sincerely answer the question, "Why is this appealing to a growing guild of men?"

The American white nationalist movement was excited when the Wolves of Vinland first came to their attention. Early Alt Right figure and Youth for Western Civilization founder Kevin Deanna had been a member since the group's early years, and remained so as he continued to write for the *Radix Journal*, American Renaissance, and *VDare*. He had brought to Wolves' events people like American Renaissance staffer Devin Saucier and *Daily Caller* writer Scott Greer, so inside the group the racial element was crystal clear. After Jack Donovan first wrote about the Wolves for his website, then became a member, they gained more attention across the Alt Right media sphere. Their movement loved the image that the Waggeners presented: a tribally focused group who toned down the explicit racialism in public and expected all their members to have stellar fitness and personal/professional lives. Wolves of Vinland was the antithesis to the image of the toothless Klansman or the skinhead with a tattooed face, but it was still accessible and proletarian.

The Alt Right love affair slowly faded when the Wolves continued to operate on their own terms, and with Operation Werewolf, Waggener further toned down the racialism. While the program has clear far-right, nationalist elements, Waggener has tried to make it appeal to men of every ethnic background.[12] This is along a separatist "nationalism for all peoples" mentality, and it is why he supported groups of non-white men forming Operation Werewolf groups around the world. People of color wouldn't be invited into the Wolves of Vinland, but they are welcome to have their own group similarly modeled. As the Wolves developed, they crystalized what they were about, dropped even more of the political-activist baggage of the larger white nationalist movements, and Waggener set to proselytizing this "new" way of living.

Waggener created a cottage industry of zines, then books, that outlined his philosophy, how he combined runic magic and old-school powerlifting, and they were all tinged with his disgust for the "modern world." His philosophy was heavily influenced by fascists like Julius Evola and Oswald Spengler, and he romanticized a mythic pre-modern past where men lived out healthy lives by virtue of their earned strength. With Operation Werewolf, he finally had a cohesive brand, a set of guiding principles, and a financial framework that allowed him to make money. Now there are gyms around the country building on the Operation Werewolf model of exclusivity and "outlaw" aesthetics.[13]

What is offered as a product to be sold is embodied in the people themselves, and Paul Waggener in particular. Crafted from steel and hardened masculinity, made useful through the mastery of violence. The Operation Werewolf Elite program is dressed up self-help, with everything from how to clean up your diet to anger management techniques lifted from mindfulness seminars. Paul requires Operation Werewolf recruits to train in a martial art, and Matthias Waggener is the Jiu Jitsu coach of the two, running Devotion Jiu Jitsu in Lynchburg. When they come to Conclave they must fight—fighting is not a suggestion, it is required.

Eternal

The promise of Operation Werewolf, and by extension the Wolves of Vinland, is not just about getting fit, hanging with a group of friends, or in its practical utility as a self-help program. It is about the supposed eternal nature of the kind of masculinity it promises to awaken. When the Wolves of Vinland first started getting some attention, an associate of theirs was arrested for trying to burn down a historically Black church. Paul was certain to tell reporters that his group was an "Odinic Wolf Cult," which sent liberal reporters screeching. Nothing could have been a worse/better representation of the Wolves.[14]

Waggener was being sincere. His beliefs about mythology and archetype trace back to the mythic Indo-European peoples, and a theory that both Europeans and much of Hindu South Asia had common ancestry because of commonalities in their languages. It's a theory that has been part and parcel of white supremacist literature over the years, including the gnostic Nazi idea that there was a "pure" race of whites who inhabited Hyperborea at the North Pole. This common-ancestry theory places a certain amount of white racial ownership over Hinduism, and would reimagine the caste system in racial terms.

The image of the wolf reappears throughout mythology across many cultures, especially those Waggener attempts to group into a singular narrative of his "people," the rebellious figures on the outside of society.[15] The "wolf cult" protects from the outside the people of their society, those rebellious men who refuse the rules of the dominant culture, usually despondent with decadence, and set on bringing down "their world" with their radical traditional lifestyles. They are barbarians protecting the people at the gates, men who abjure themselves from the comforts of popular culture to live a life of warriors.[16]

This alleged spiritual notion is a perennial concept that appears in all cultures, potentially at all times (or at least cyclically). Julius Evola's "Traditionalism" was founded on the idea that there is an underlying spiritual "tradition" that sits underneath all the worlds of religions (think Chomsky's "Syntactic Structure" but for spirituality), and that it, over time, degenerates as the culture moves away from its spiritual hierarchies and social roles. It starts in the Golden Age, ruled by the Brahmin, and over the centuries moves through the Vedic Cycle of Ages until it gets to the Kali Yuga, the Dark Age. This is the period when materialism has taken over and the hierarchies have broken down, when men have lost their true nature, and multiculturalism and modernity reign. Evola called for "men against time" to emerge, warrior philosophers who would stand against modernity as they await the return of a Golden Age where their strength would be valued. These warriors would not just "stand before history yelling stop," as conservatives have for generations, they would fully retreat and pray for (or even actively accelerate) the collapse of liberalism. Evola's thought influenced fascist terrorists in Italy in the 1970s, leading to a string of bombings and killings known as the Years of Lead as "radical traditionalists" tried to push liberal society over a cliff.[17]

Far-right historian Oswald Spengler saw the cycle of ages from another vantage point, believing that civilizations rise and fall in a predictable system, heavy from their own excesses. Fascists believe we now live at a point when Western culture has been weighed by its consumerism, sexual perversions, lack of ethnic identity, and inability to express strength, and men have been lost to their power.

Men's ability to create tribal allegiances is not valued, their physical attributes are seen as suspect, and their "natural" masculine instincts admonished as "toxic." There is another way: to stand against time and act as a defender of what is right.

The theory of the wolf cult doesn't just place us in the Kali Yuga, though Evola's concept features heavily in the OPWW mythology. The current state of the Kali Yuga is blamed for "modern, liberated women," Type II diabetes, and everything in between—all signs that we have lost our true path and an indicator that becoming an Operation Werewolf Operative can set you free.

A significant part of the Wolves literature and rhetoric is based around the impending collapse of civilization. This collapse is ideologically built into the concept of the Kali Yuga, because once civilization collapses, the true Golden Age replaces it and the cycle begins anew. This is similar to the most toxic messianisms of American evangelicals who pray for the Rapture because suffering is pre-ordained, and we should just get it over with because the worthy will inherit greatness on the other side. The Wolves themselves incorporate other millenialist traditions: a little bit of survivalism, a dash of militia conspiracy theory, a heavy dose of rural fetishism, and delusions of grandeur. The world is about to fall to pieces, maybe financially or perhaps from the weight of its own excesses, but however it happens, we will return to the underlying Tradition that remains once these temporary detours, like liberal democracy, have fallen away.

Testosterone

The Waggeners recommend that the "most revolutionary thing you can do is get on the bottle"—to inject testosterone.[18]

Paul tells a pretty common story, of being stressed out, missing sleep, and getting poor results in the gym. He went to the doctor and found that his testosterone had "tanked," was down to about four twenty. A healthy range is anywhere from 250 to 900 (this could be debated), and so he set out to correct the problem. But after months of monitoring he finally decided to get injections, which brought him to a "high to maximal [sic] normal," which he says is over a thousand. In a YouTube video that amounts to steroid apologism—a common conversation in modern weightlifting culture meant to undermine conventional thinking about the potential risks of anabolics—the Waggeners go on to discuss injecting testosterone. They go so far as to recommend that their operatives connect with them directly because they contracted with a medical provider in Colorado who can get their levels tested and provide testosterone injections, all legal and aboveboard.

As time wears on, OPWW's obsession with testosterone has intensified. They've released articles about test boosting, complete with strange myths about what can increase your hormone levels (everything from cold showers to smelling random women in public places, which they suggest causes men's testosterone levels to increase due to the potential for sex [it should go without saying that this is false]).[19] "Probably, you shouldn't roll up on random women and smell them, although I have used this technique in the past to pretty good success—but simply interacting and talking with females that are potential sexual mates raises your test," writes Waggener in one of his guides.[20]

Another recent focus of OPWW is men's declining testosterone levels over the past few years. There is some truth to this, as average testosterone rates have been falling the last twenty years for reasons that are not fully understood. Lower testosterone could be a result of unwanted body weight from poor food access and choices, sedentary jobs, or simply because more men are raising kids (which can reduce testosterone levels somewhat). Whatever the reason, Paul finds the situation intolerable.

"A world full of weak, submissive, unaggressive post-men enslaved to pleasure, defined by products, and contemptuous of heroism makes the system run smoothly," writes Operative 413, a member of the Wolves who helps run Operation Werewolf, suggesting that when men are stripped of their testosterone, they become the blank "consumers" that the "system" wants. "For that reason, those who try to build something outside this consumerist system, to promote different values, will find themselves hated by the systems' propagandists. To be a man is to be a threat. To pursue physical strength, to try to increase one's testosterone, and to practice a diet and lifestyle that will further those ends is to revolt against the modern world in the most literal sense."[21] The Wolves even sold patches with the chemical formula for testosterone on it.

"As men, our worldview, how we feel. . .is directly linked to our hormone panel, ala testosterone. If our testosterone levels are low, we are going to perceive the world in a particular way," says Paul. "If your test levels are crashed you are perceiving the world like a fucking female." There is no shame in them injecting testosterone (and they say that if you are concerned it that's just a sign that you have low testosterone) because the modern world is built to lower men's hormone levels. "It's easy to fall into conspiracy theory and think this is all part of a conscious plan by shadowy elites who want to destroy men. In the West, that's certainly what media coverage would suggest. However, the more horrifying possibility is that this *isn't* happening by design but is simply an outgrowth of modern life," says Operative 413.[22]

What he means is that phytoestrogens, a chemical mimicking estrogen, is prevalent in our environment; it's in everything from consumer plastics to soy (hence those "soy boys"). Phytoestrogens are said to interfere with men's testosterone production and are a common explanation for low testosterone levels as explained by Naturopathic physicians. This was explained to me when I first had my hormone levels checked. I had a similar story to Paul's. I had gained some weight after going on some psychiatric medication, wasn't getting good results in the gym, and my sex drive had tanked. My testosterone was middling: low, but not pathologically so. While a regular medical doctor probably wouldn't have suggested testosterone, my Naturopath did, and so I went on TRT.

The reality was that upping my testosterone to a "high normal" certainly improved how I felt, gave me better results from training, and made me less prone to stress, but it had no effect on how I saw the world. Why would it? Ideologies do not come from within; they are belief systems developed through subjective experiences.[23] The phytoestrogen narrative is particularly useful to Waggener because it doesn't just explain why "modernity" (an elusive concept that is almost always a proxy for something else) is at war with masculinity, but it can be manipulated to do so in archetypal terms. The Gods of Waggener's religious system are, essentially, metaphors for the cosmic forces of the natural world. The myths are not literal stories, they are parables, which one can learn from by interpreting them in mythic terms. The phytoestrogen narrative takes on a mythic quality but it is simply a consequence of modernity. Modernity attacks masculinity, and it does so with a flood of consumer products and food that interrupt testosterone.

Testosterone is a naturally occurring hormone that is beneficial to the body in a multitude of ways, from bone density to blood pressure. When it is fetishized as the key component of "maleness" it conflates health benefits with masculinity. The suggestion is that by increasing your masculinity, you make yourself more emotionally fit, healthier, better. The two (masculinity and testosterone) become one in the far-right imagination, suggesting that one can inject some mythic "maleness," and so the transformation seen in the gym is not just the result of a medical intervention, it comes from a man increasing his maleness. This is a magical pathway to a singular vision of success: the pure masculinity, coursing through your veins, and radically improving your life. The reflexive power of this can be astounding as operatives compare testosterone, anticipate its effects seeping out of their bodies and into their relationships and communities and bank accounts.

Male Fantasies

The most common joke on the right (and the left, for that matter) about the Wolves of Vinland is that they are live action role playing (LARPing). These guys call themselves a wolf cult, they go into the woods and smear themselves in black paint, sacrifice goats, and howl at the moon. I spoke with Katie McHugh, a former *Breitbart* staffer who dated WoV member Kevin DeAnna, who said that his participation in the Wolves was eventually what split them up. "I couldn't be raising our kids and having him going into the woods every weekend to perform secret occult rituals," she said.[24]

OPWW is not particularly offended by the LARPing joke because, in a sense, it is absolutely true. They are living out a certain fantasy of maleness, which so many the men in their circles aspire to. These men want to validate their insecurities and social difficulties by framing themselves as innately correct in opposition to the rest of the world, which is degenerate.

In 1987, Klaus Theweleit published *Male Fantasies*, his landmark book about what he called "fascist male imprinting and socialization" of the Freikorps, the reactionary civilian militia that declared war on the communist and socialist working class in Germany in the wake of the First World War. Theweleit highlighted the psychological effects of war in the creation of masculine identities and violent fantasies towards women and other affected peoples.

Are the male fantasies of the Friekorps reflective of the fascist turn, or do they forecast it? In the book's foreword, Barbara Ehrenreich wrote that the fascist fantasy "springs from the dread that (perhaps) lies in the hearts of all men, a dread of engulfment by the 'other,' which is the mother, the sea or even the moist embrace of love."[25]

For that which is loved first—woman and mother—is that which they must learn to despise in others and suppress within themselves. Under these conditions, which are all we know, so far, as the human condition, men will continue to see the world divided into "them" and "us," male and female, hard and soft, solid and liquid—and they will, in every way possible, fight and flee the threat of submersion. They will build dykes and against the "streaming" of their own desire. They will level the forests and pave the earth. They will turn viciously against every revolution from below—and every revolution starts with a disorderly bubbling over of passion and need. They will make their bodies into hard instruments.[26]

The fantasies of the Freikorps are an indulgent orgy of genocide, of violence against women's bodies in a way that "reproduced" itself but was not wholly disconnected from the rest of patriarchal socialization. These men experienced the traumas of war (which also produced a warrior, as Ehrenreich noted), but it was also an extreme casing for male identities. The oppression of women, specifically its violent indulgences, is the heterosexual male body reified through its induction into sexuality, whereby social power becomes private desire. This was the ingrained identity that had been romanticized during what Enzo Traverso calls "the European Civil War," meaning the brutal first and second World Wars. At the end of the nineteenth century, along with the volkisch racial movements, came the masculinist German youth movement called the Wandervögel, or "migrating birds." This movement coalesced around the myth of the Männerbund (a men's fraternal organization), which was supposedly an archetypal formation of men that goes back millenia in the history of the Germanics.[27] The male archetype became defining for the revolt against modernity and the new generation, and the soldier became the center of this maleness.

Masculinity became synonymous with strength, courage, virility, energy, will to action and solid nerves, but also moral uprightness, generosity, beauty, nobility of spirit and idealism. Summarized in this way, the masculine ideal was inevitably opposed, as an absolute and irreducible antinomy, to all symptoms of "decadence": weakness, cowardice, immortality, ugliness, monstrosity. These evil and despicable markers were then focused, as we have seen, on Jewish and homosexual "outsiders." Effeminate features—an unbridled sexuality, an excess of nervousness and intellectualism at the expense of physical activity—were the characteristics of individuals "outside the norm," who weakened the body of the nation and condemned it to inexorable decline.[28]

The *Männerbund* is how Waggener refers to his project of male tribalism, which inspires many of the individual "tribes," including a group called Wandervögel in New England.[29] The mythology is constant because today's fascism is a resurrection of fascism's past; while we have shattered earlier incarnations of their cult, we have done little to undermine what causes it to form in the first place.

Because the Wolves believe their masculinity is "eternal" and "true" and derives from the "scientific" sources of hormones and bodies, the masculine values ascribed to it are likewise deemed correct. As John Stoltenberg writes in his essay "Rape Ethicists," about the formation of "male" identities, the assumption of the naturalness of masculine roles comes with a certain set of convictions:

> · an unfailing belief in one's own goodness and the moral rightness of one's purposes, regardless of how others may value what one does;

> · a rigorous adherence to the set of behaviors, characteristics, and idiosyncrasies that are appropriately male (and therefore inappropriate for a female);

> · an unquestioning belief in one's own consistency, notwithstanding any evidence to the contrary—a consistency rooted, for all practical purposes, in the relentlessness of one's will and in the fact that, being superior by social definition, one can want whatever one wants, and expect to get it.[30]

Stoltenberg traces this male identity to the possession and victimization of women, which are blamed, used and abused through the assignment of feminine roles in proximity to male roles. That violence is then deemed "normal," with a whole history manufactured to support it.

Judith Butler's elaboration of "gender performativity" always sat at the front of my mind as the Waggeners discussed masculinity. The idea of gender as a discursive script did not seem far off, and perhaps one the Waggeners would even partially agree on some level.

As a public action and performative act, gender is not a radical choice or project that reflects a merely individual choice, but neither is it imposed or inscribed upon the individual, as some poststructuralist displacements of the subject would contend. The body is not passively scripted with cultural codes, as if it were a lifeless recipient of wholly pre-given cultural relations. But neither do embodied selves pre-exist the cultural conventions which essentially signify bodies. Actors are always already on the stage, within the terms of the performance. Just as a script may be enacted in various ways, and just as the play requires both text and interpretation, so the gendered body acts its part in a culturally restricted corporeal space and enacts interpretations with the confines of already existing directives.[31]

The aesthetic portion of the Wolves is an extremist forthright performance. It is instructive and discursive, reflexive and propagandistic, meant to affect both the performer and the spectator. Wolves' rituals, both the esoteric pagan ones and the simple ritual of posing for the camera, are meant to not only influence and convert those seeing them, but to have the same effect on *themselves* as they push to more thoroughly embody the ideal they are romanticizing. OPWW teaches you what masculinity is, how you perform it, why you must, and what it takes to achieve it. This performative masculinity derives, in part, from the self-improvement modality of esotericism, the need to impose your Will back onto yourself. This implies a certain "unnaturalness" of these masculine ideals, since the vision of masculinity they are offering supposedly comes from within. But it doesn't actually work that way since they need to share their script, otherwise no one would know they were deficient. If gender was implicit, there would be no reason to build it through this process. If this gender performativity requires a constant repetition of particular acts (rituals, you might say), then Waggener is the Wolves' spiritual guide. This is his lifehack for how to become the kind of man he thinks you should be: by acting it out so completely, and by creating a series of cultural signifiers his followers can embody, their sense of gender and self will literally be transformed.

A good portion of the Wolves' propaganda is in how they present themselves, particularly their own bodies. For a group founded on denouncing modern institutions like social media, their Instagram accounts are cultivated with the attention of an advertising agency.[32] Far-right researcher Matthew N. Lyons talks about how the message of male tribalism, from current and former Wolves, includes writing and organizing, but also "the aggressive use of [their] own physical image."[33] Members are covered in tattoos, not just symbols, but "forbidden" symbols of Nordicism most well known for their association with Nazism. These are worn not just with pride but with the belief that they will strengthen the wearer of the tattoos while reflecting an inner vitality. Everything from their clothing to their posture displays their outlaw brand—part Viking, part mystic, part 1%er, part savage survivalist. It is a synthesis of all manly ideals, rolled together into something strikingly edgy and hard to ignore.

I met Augustus Sol Invictus after he sent me a series of bizarre and desperate pleas to meet after I published an article about him.[34] He declared me something of a worthy adversary and wanted to meet in person. I finally met him at a Panera Bread, where he alternated between compliments and accusations of pernicious tactics. He then attempted to impress me with his fair-minded answers but, frankly, he seemed lonely.

After the meeting, he headed to Jack Donovan's short-lived tattoo parlor inside a Clackamas, Oregon, powerlifting gym, to get the "fasces" tattooed on his back. The symbol originally hung over the Roman senate and became better known for its use by the Italian Fascist Party. He told me about how he had been "fight training" and lifting heavy, and that is when I felt like I knew him. Acne scarring painted most of his face, and there was a meekness that filled the cracks. In his videos, he had a pained accent, somewhere between Scarlett O'Hara and George Wallace, but with me he was just a nerdy kid finding ways to tell me he was strong. Shortly after our meeting, he was chased out of a local bar by black-masked antifascists wielding 2×4s.[35]

At the time he was a Libertarian Party candidate for senate in Florida and was best known for being a Thelemite and drinking goat's blood in a ritual he kept talking about in interviews.[36] He is an attorney who had represented members of the neo-Nazi American Front in a court battle, and over the following months, he descended even more openly into the violent fringes of white nationalism. Despite having biracial kids, he became a favorite inside the accelerationist circles of Atomwaffen Division and The Base, finding any excuse to rap hyperbolic about apocalyptic violence.

His version of masculinity was harsh, violent, and unobtainable. His speeches constantly reinforced "men being men" and enacting their masculine roles, but his life rarely lived up to the expectations of masculinity he cultivated in his political persona. When Invictus finally went to visit the Wolves of Vinland, they allegedly stripped his clothes off and taped him to a tree in an act of cruel hazing—even they were tired of all his patriarchal posturing.[37]

In 2020, Invictus was jailed twice, both times for physically assaulting women. Over the previous two years, story after story emerged of him terrorizing his ex-wife by beating and kidnapping her. "To conceal the bruises from the public, he regularly punched me in my stomach and in my head so hard it caused me to see flashes of light," she read aloud in a pre-trial statement.[38] He was let out on pre-trial release because of the COVID-19 crisis.[39] Shortly thereafter, he menaced another woman, and was immediately back behind bars.[40]

Before far-right agitator Andy Ngô became a household name for his constant pearl clutching over what he calls "antifa" (and he calls everything "antifa"), he got a series of high profile retweets for revering masculinity at a distance: "I understand why masculinity is under attack because I used to attack it. I once rejected all things masculine because I was bitter that I couldn't be a protector or leader. I let my jealousy of strong men turn into hatred and resentment. It was a miserable way to live."[41] In the time that followed, he made a name for himself by attacking trans people, questioning womens' stories of abuse, and using every masculinist stereotype possible to mock gender rebels. His answer to his feeling of masculine failure was to venerate the most toxic of masculine behavior, to sow favor with other men or simply to make money.

This story is both about the qualities that we ascribe to masculinity and how those qualities are shaped by their proximity to the men trying to perform them, and the toxic privileges and power they hold. There is violence in the role of oppressor; it doesn't take confidence, musculature, or skills to enact it, and the absence of all of those can sometimes even exacerbate it. Operation Werewolf appeals to a male fantasy where patriarchy calls the shots.

Violence is the Force That Gives Us Meaning

"No, what I'm asking is if you are saying kill him? Not hurt him.

Shoot him in the head and kill him," John asked, handing his .45 to me.[42] After some drunken confrontation, and a series of previous squabbles, a local kid, high on methamphetamines, had tried to run my mother off the side of a country highway. I would like to say that the total sense of rage that descended on me was just concern. But it wasn't. It was a personal slight, an insult not an offense, and I had to do something about it.

I had known John for a long time. We had been in martial arts together. He was an early MMA prodigy. John had graced the cover of magazines and won competitions before he copped a cocaine habit. Eventually he couldn't stay sober enough to weigh in, let alone compete. When he was sixteen, John got in a street fight and broke a kid's neck, landing himself into a diversionary program for violent teens. Rumor had it, and we have little facts to go on, that he tried to escape from a psychiatric hospital and was sent to a boot camp program in American Samoa. John was beaten, shocked with cattle prods, and forced to eat dogfood, and his grandpa bribed the management with $100,000 to sign his papers and let John go home. The actual story was he likely just served a bit of time in county, but he never let reality get in the way of a good story.

John was a product of the region. We lived in a rural tourist area, known for drug and crime stereotypes. When real violence was sought to solve a problem, John was a good go-to. Fighting wasn't enough for a threat on my family, pulling guns and asserting myself had to be.

"Umm...well, no, I think we should just scare him," I said.

"What the fuck is wrong with you? You don't use guns to scare people. You use them to kill people."

When I was sixteen, John commandeered a house. First, he threatened the people who rented there to leave, go somewhere else. Then he threatened the property management company into signing a piece of paper saying that he was, in fact, the lease holder. He ran it as a drug den for three months before moving on to the next hustle. He walked through walls. Years later I would walk in on him injecting heroin, desperately crying for me to not tell his wife where he was.

He eventually started competing again, winning a series of MMA fights in bouts that lasted fewer than a couple of minutes. His secret was injecting Human Growth Hormone, pig and horse testosterone, and freebasing seconds before the fight began. After he had arranged a series of fights in our coastal hometown and ticket sales went poorly, he dragged his wife and kid into the living room and made them watch as he shot himself in the head.

Violence felt like the fog we lived in, because it was always present. It was the protective shield that carried us, particularly when it involved drugs or petty theft. But the money meant little in comparison to the violence itself, which provided status and ecstatic experiences. Violence punctuated life. It was not comfortable, but it defined the culture. I idolized these kids when I was a teenager, not because I wanted to be like them, but because violence projected a sense of identity. Protection from their violence was exclusive, it made me elite, even if I couldn't own up to its promise. This was raw masculinity. You didn't have to look perfect. In fact, these were some of the ugliest guys I've ever known. Their violence afforded them a certain authority in a world otherwise out of our control.

***

Jack Donovan, a former Wolves of Vinland member, has a famous tagline from an article he wrote: "Violence is golden." The concept is simple: violence gets you what you want, it is the imposition of will.[43] Operation Werewolf is delicate on the specifics, but not on the mission. "If we are to live lives of action, every word and deed becomes a spell of creation or destruction—shaping the malleable fabric of the world around us, changing our environment to reflect where our will is applied, and how," says Paul.[44]

In this formulation, the world is violent, at least the proper non-modern world, and therefore so are men. A man's use of violence is determined by need, and only a weak, feminized man of modernity would assume that he should be safe from violence. Instead, a life lived *all the way alive* is one that incurs the threat of violence.[45]

The "tribal" format of the Wolves of Vinland, which is packaged and sold as a DIY program through Operation Werewolf, is a tribal formation based on the ability to enforce toxic masculine standards. This enforcement is understood through one's ability to enact violence, to agree culturally when that violence is to be used, what the violence means, and what level of violence is acceptable. Operation Werewolf recruits are required to start training in martial arts, usually some form of Jiu Jitsu or American boxing.[46] When they come to Conclave for the first time, they have to fight.[47]

"Violence is multi-level and it creates an in-group versus an out-group mentality," says Shannon Reid, a criminologist who studied Alt Right gang formations and discusses how violence both initiates participants and creates a mythic quality that pulls people closer. "This is why the 'wannabes' in any subculture are always the most dangerous, because they want to impress established members. So the storytelling and mythology becomes something that helps build their identity and is sort of being central to the in-group/out-group dynamic and group ethos that binds people together."[48]

The Kali Yuga lacks many of the systems that enforce individual power through violence, and are replaced by the passive systemic violence of the state. Chivalry is a code about the proper uses of violence, often implied by an insult, which is a threat to status. Without the constant threat of violence, the Wolves believe men get weak and begin to lack an essential maleness, lowering their testosterone and rebuilding their identity along the feminine lines. If the masculine ideal is intoxicating, violence is a carnal explosion. An easy answer to complicated problems, a means to an end and a reason all its own. There is a visceral sense of power in the ability to enact violence, and when that power is seen as an essential good, then the institutions that undermine its use can seem to be thwarting pure living.

Androphilia

At what point does the celebration and admiration of a "fit" male body become sexual? Answering that question may be where some of the tension with Jack Donovan began, and when the homophobia of the organization became more pronounced.

Jack Donovan was the Wolves of Vinland's most recognizable member from 2013 to 2018, when he unceremoniously left the group with little explanation. Donovan's entry to the Wolves was a big deal because he was, for the right at least, the "go to" author on maleness. The fact that he was a gay man writing for white nationalist publications about the problems of femininity always seemed like a ruse, but he was utterly sincere.

Donovan first published his manifesto *Androphilia* in 2007. In it, he asserted that the gay identity had little to do with same-sex attraction and was instead a sort of cluster of behaviors or ideas that he thinks are harmful to men. The gay subculture, influenced by women and feminism, turned queer men into effeminate leftists and denied them their proper roles as true men who would work in concert with other men. While he supported some degree of union between queer men, he did not agree with gay marriage since this was a "civilizational" institution that promulgated families. Instead, his gay relationship was a "mars/mars" attraction whereby two masculine men were attracted to each other by virtue of their maleness, and the sex naturally followed.

While his book was well received in some masculine gay circles, he wanted to make a clean break with that scene entirely with his 2012 follow up, *The Way of Men*. This was his true manifesto about what men are, and why "being a good man" is different than "being good at being a man." The four "tactical virtues" that Donovan assigns to men are strength, courage, mastery, and honor, and one must commit to live by the first three in the pursuit of the approval of one's male peers. For Donovan, masculinity happens inside men's bodies: the masculine presentation, particularly its enforcement of norms through violence, he believes, are the natural manifestation of the chemical cauldron of the cis-gendered male body.[49] Donovan sees pure masculinity as an inverse of modern consumerist society, with its emphasis on safety, consumptive commerce, and the use of simulation—from watching TV to masturbating. Manly virtue comes from true competition, the expectation of male peers, and the ability to perpetuate survival—not to live up to moral codes, which are specific to an "in group."[50] For men to be men, they have to push past the limits of modernity, which they think elevates the feminine over the masculine.

Donovan sees true masculinity as only truly possible when paired with tribalism. This is why he wrote in favor of white nationalism, which he said he himself did not claim but was enthusiastic about because it enforces boundaries based on a tribal identity.[51]

"If your ethnic heritage or race is something you feel strongly about ... then this may be your starting point," he wrote in *The Way of Men*, in his guide for starting a gang.[52] Donovan sought out Paul Waggener so he could write about the Wolves, and found that they were the tribe he had been looking for. "When it comes to forming us it is better to have a group of men on the same page about the issues that are important to them. If you have decided after reading this book that you want to return to the way of men, then the men in your gang will have to be committed to opposing the globalist masturbation society, hollowing out the state, and reviving a culture of honor."[53]

Donovan joined the Wolves in 2015 and started building a Männerbund, a male tribal society, in Cascadia, the bioregion of the Pacific Northwest (he lived in Portland, Oregon).[54] With Casacadia the Wolves had three locations at this point, including one in Cheyenne (where Matthias lived) and the headquarters in Lynchburg (where Paul lived). When they met, Paul felt like Jack had been watching them, the Wolves were doing what Jack was writing about, and their ideas began to merge into one cohesive sense of male tribalism and ethnic identity.[55] While Donovan tried to avoid talking about the racialism, it was there as he spoke at the white nationalist conference American Renaissance, at the National Policy Institute, and in writings for websites like *Radix Journal* and *Counter-Currents*. His book *Becoming a Barbarian* is an openly racist tract, suggesting that "identity is everything" and that men need to know themselves by reverting to racial nationalism and a fight against other peoples. Donovan tried to insulate himself by saying that it wasn't white tribalism, but just tribalism itself, a point that echoes what the European New Right terms "Ethnopluralism." This was a "right to nationalism for all peoples," and the idea that by supporting "third world nationalism" and movements like Black nationalism they could insulate their own reactionary ethnic nationalist movements.[56]

"I support White Nationalists . . . I think people should be able to organize and advance their own interests just like every other group of people," writes Donovan in his essay "Mighty White," where he parrots most major Alt Right talking points, from the idea that people naturally like "their own" to fears about the upcoming white American minority status.[57] "Because stereotypes aren't going away, because humans are tribal, and because we're a group that is well on its way to becoming just another minority, we have every right to organize as a group and take care of our own. I'm pro-white because I am pro-me."[58]

Donovan's talk shifted and became identity obsessed, and his sense of manhood (and that of the Wolves) followed. Men were men by their ability to maintain the boundaries and success of their tribe, which safeguarded their identity. Colonialism and imperialism were simply the successful conquest of your identity over another, something natural and normal in a world tinged with blood.

"Most Western men are hesitant to allow themselves to think tribally. Western men, especially white Western men...don't know how to become the kind of men who can become members of a tribe," said Donovan.[59] The acceptability of ethnic identity as this tribal barrier was implicit at this point, and Donovan was hanging with the core of the Alt Right and white nationalist movement with little objection. "Without outsiders, there can be no insiders. Without them, there can be no us."[60]

"Donovan presents a vision of a man who is fully in touch with his will, comfortable with his desire for other men, unapologetic about his body, and unconcerned with what anyone thinks of him. In his books we see this aesthetic turn into an entire ethic, a religious redemption of the masculinity which bourgeois feminism sees as the primary cause of oppression," writes Rhyd Wildermuth in an essay about the how anti-civilizationism of the Wolves can appear seductive.[61] He locates Donovan, and the Wolves, as offering an "*oppositional* aesthetic" to modernity, presenting their image as the only thing capable of unseating the empire, by which he means the current global system ranging from governments to corporations to social structures. What Donovan offers is largely the aesthetic, a window to an emotional reality of fantasy and aspiration. "Donovan's aesthetic attempts to escape this, but it cannot. What Donovan portrays is crafted just as any other selfie is, posed, selected, filtered and cropped, uploaded into The Feed for us all to see. It is an antimodern aesthetic made possible only by the modern, a resistance to Empire generated by Empire like Orwell's Emmanuel Goldstein waiting with Big Brother's pre-scripted revolt," says Wildermuth.[62]

There is an open fascism in his worldview, which Matthew N. Lyons suggests is in line with the "violent male camaraderie at odds with 'bourgeois' family life, glorification of the masculine body, exclusion of women, and sometimes even homoeroticism (which was captured in *Male Fantasies*)."[63] Donovan's essay "Violence is Golden," which says that violence is a necessary feature of success and identity, is foundational to the Wolves and has echoed through the entire manosphere.[64] Donovan is fine with this, and thinks of himself as a renegade "playboy," who while defending the hetero-ideals, chooses not to be of them.[65] He calls the "political position" of his books as "anarcho-fascist," a term he loosely means to be the quest for male gangs to destroy the orders of liberal democracy and fight against the weak in their own interests for dominance.[66] In *A More Complete Beast* he uses Nietzsche to argue that men can and should absolve themselves of compassion for the broader society and behave like conquerors, bastardizing the texts so that they mirror *Might is Right*.[67] Donovan has desperately tried to separate himself from the Wolves and the Alt Right, saying that it was "a dark time" in his life, yet he has not renounced any of his positions from that time.[68]

The Purification Rundown

A suspicion of pleasure is a persistent theme of the far-right. Johnard Spencer argued that there are two dominant images of dystopia in Western literature: *1984* and *Brave New World*. In *1984*, a gothic fantasy of totalitarianism plays to the hyperbolic indulgences of liberals and conservatives alike who view all revolutionaries they encounter as authoritarians bent on oppressing them. The more compelling narrative, he argues, is *Brave New World*, where the world is held hostage by sexual and euphoric pleasure seeking.

In the Operation Werewolf lexicon—where metaphor is everything—weightlifting is the perfect analogy. Weightlifting is a ritual where you offer up your own time, pain, and suffering (what else would a trip to the gym be?), and in return you are granted strength of body, an enhanced physical ability, improved health and longevity, and the rightly won sexual interest of a high-status mate. This is the path of stoicism whereby suffering is correlated with achievement, so much so that you can measure success through the associated personal discomfort and loss.[69] When you overcome the hurdle, the barriers of pain, it is because your Will has become so strong that it can shatter the walls. A weaker man could never have achieved this. You are right to get what you want, what you deserve.

Waggener defines *transformation* through the image of the Black Sun, a symbol from alchemy that became a centerpiece of the Nazi appropriation of pagan and occult semiotics. The Black Sun is the fire that burns away your weakness, a chemical agent that is meant to transform you as you sacrifice hedonistic desires for something greater. Pleasure, on the flip side, is seductive and frightening. You can see the men who give in to pleasure, their flesh fat and their muscles weak. Instead of eating food to fuel their physical alchemy, they eat for pleasure. Their time is spent socializing or, worse, in activities that show little material result (like videogames). On a deeper level, pleasure is the path of sexual degeneracy, which stands in direct contrast to the traditional family that is the root of all conquest and civilization. Drugs are an even further bridge. It should go without saying that pleasure prohibitions are rhetorical, not actual, and the Wolves are regularly seen parading around sexual partners and engaged in ritualized frenzies of alcohol-fueled ecstasy, but they would never let reality get in the way of a good story (degeneracy for me, not for thee). Or a heroic myth.

While pleasure is the signifier, it is passivity that is the real enemy. Casual entertainment, whether it is experienced in the body or the mind, is about spectatorship or giving in to the immediate at the cost of the distant. When you masturbate to pornography you are simulating something that, in life, they would say takes achievement, mastery, and status. Instead, pleasure seeking hacks the mainframe of the universe's reward system, making you feel good for doing nothing.[70] Suffering leads to true greatness, pleasure should derive from that achievement, and the great advancements of Western civilization result from this equation.

Pain is how we know we have entered the heroic realm, the path of Odin, and it is actively sought by Operation Werewolf recruits. The workout routines are designed not just to be effective, but to be painful, as that pain will forge the body and mind into a hardness that equates to greatness.

***

As I followed "Total Life Reform," Operation Werewolf's Elite program, different challenges were offered up. Each week you get a series of five posts, a new one on each weekday. "General" covers overarching self-help concepts, "Mental" is different "pop psychology" tidbits like mindfulness, "Temporal" is about making money and investing, "Spiritual" is about the runes, and "Physical" (the most important of the group) is workout advice and programming. As time went on, they started creating benchmarks and extra goals to establish bigger gains. Each morning recruits are to get up and start the day with meditation and visualization, usually to identify goals and focus on reaching them. Then they should add discomfort (i.e. pain) into their day, with the understanding that the benefits of pain are twofold: the strengthening of the mind through the strengthening of the body. They recommend things like doing pushups every hour, which I chose to do, creating a constant stream of agonizing body pain, all on top of the increasingly dense workouts.

I decided to do the program to get a sense of its appeal, but it is not hard to understand why constant self-flagellation can be addicting. The constant commitment to pain is a reminder that you are doing something, and the discomfort conjures an image of what the weeks of work could result in. Every hour I would hit the ground, not just to put myself in a few seconds of pain, but to revel in what that pain represents: a vision of myself transformed. The pain became tied to an image of my body, recrafted, hardened, powerful. I looked forward to this because the pain was bundled with meaning: I was overcoming. This feeling was largely masturbatory (push-ups don't make you a millionaire), but the self-satisfaction that comes by constantly meeting benchmarks is an intoxication of its own, and I constantly forced myself into a process connected to an idealized image of my achievement.

Push-ups are not exactly a problematic routine (people rarely say that doing push-ups set them down a dark path), but it was reminiscent of the world of Alternative Medicine. With each new treatment, which may or not be based in actual science, the patient starts to see more and more ailments to address. Take these tablets, drink this tea, do this exercise, visualize a healing light. The responsibility becomes so great it can overwhelm you. Sometimes pain results in more strength, sometimes it is just pain, and at worst it results in trauma.

But if the pain is a signifier that you are in the process of becoming, then the pain becomes a pleasurable reminder that this stage of your life is only transitory. When you chase the Black Sun the pain is your old, weak self being burned away. By reframing your experience, even the clunkiest bit of self-immolation becomes a joy.

Fenrir

It is almost a misnomer to call the Wolves white nationalists, and often counter this accusation by saying they are "Wolves nationalists,"[71] essentially meaning that their tribalism is not centered on the broader race, even if their tribal affiliation requires racial homogeneity. Following Evola's line, they see nationalism as a form of modern inclusivity. They follow what they see as the "natural" hierarchical order of things, where tribal men bond together on a shared identity.

As the "Empire of Nothing," with its consumerism and effeminacy, fades or collapses, it is their tribal model that will inherit the earth, and they will refuse to apologize for fighting tribally.[72]

Operation Werewolf itself is not a particularly novel idea: create a group for men (only), give them "very manly" things to do (working out and competition), and then something positive is destined to emerge. This model is distinctly working class and founded on white nationalist identitarianism, but it follows a common pattern that has existed for centuries.

The appeal is obvious: it's a kind of enhanced friendship. In a fraternal organization, particularly one that exists on the fringes like an outlaw club, you can rely on your "brothers" for anything. In the Wolves of Vinland, Paul talked about how he never missed a meeting, in rain or ill health, and if a brother called him in the middle of the night to help him in a fight that he started, he would tell his wife he had to go and he'd hop on his bike.[73] This is an unwavering loyalty, the kind of dependability few people have in the fragmented relationships of modern anti-communities.

In 2013, my father died suddenly of a stroke. This would have been painful on its own, but he was my mom's primary caretaker. She was in the final months of a years' long battle with stage 4 cancer. I moved home, rode through the frightening last six months, and then watched my romantic relationship and friendships dissolve in the wake of this time. People don't tell you how much a big crisis can separate you from what would normally be a support system, but it is logically and emotionally difficult to actually be with other people amidst the disaster. Since their deaths, it has been hard for me to make and keep friends; it was as if I had to relearn how to build supportive relationships and I never quite got to where I had been. The idea of a group with a built-in roster of fanatically committed friends is more than appealing. It's like religious propaganda. Its narcotic effects would be felt immediately; the perfect antidote to loneliness.

The fraternal organization provides friendship with so much more, offering positive reinforcement to tribal identities. They validate your biases, celebrate your boundaries, and romanticize being on the inside as opposed to the rest of the world on the outside. Being in a clique feels great, but being in a cult feels even better.

"It's just a fraternal organization, really," my friend told me about a local Trojan skinhead crew that were decidedly anti-Nazi and anti-racist. Throughout the '90s this particular crew had been one of the most instrumental forces booting Nazis out of spaces up and down Oregon's I-5 corridor, but they weren't heavily interested in politics beyond that. It was, for all intents and purposes, literally a boys club: they like clothes, music, and hanging out.

"We don't just let dudes in the group get away with bullshit though," my friend told me about his crew. "If we hear a guy is abusing his wife, we get her out of there, set her up in her own place, kick the shit out of him, and make sure he gets his shit straight and starts acting right."[74]

There is a version of a men's group that has an even more appealing nature: the one that supports men in improving themselves and holds them accountable to their promises. There is a tinge of self-improvement and accountability in most fraternal organizations, and the far-right has a twisted version of this as well. Operation Werewolf repackages a lot of "mindfulness" techniques, explaining that men should take responsibility for their emotions and not make, for example, their partners responsible for them feeling a certain way. A "real man" takes proactive steps to deal with his anxiety and depression, not wallowing and blaming. They go on to explain that to do this effectively you create a tribal band of ethnic brothers to stand against modernity.

Part of the intoxicating appeal of the fraternal organization is that this group of people, with the same problems as you, will allegedly support you in getting *better*. Better, stronger, faster, happier, kinder. All of these qualities have a similar trajectory since the point is to acknowledge that we have fallen short and would like to become something greater than we are now.

The first time I was invited to a "men's group" it was explained to me in the least appealing way possible: "We get together and call each other out on our bullshit," an acquaintance told me, explaining it was a group where men supported each other in essentially "killing

the patriarch in our head." I tried to avoid saying that there was literally nothing I wanted to do less than attend his group, particularly
since I do think addressing toxic masculinity is incredibly important.
A lot of these groups take the form of recovery and accountability organizations, modelling themselves on transformative justice projects
and acknowledging and unlearning abusive behaviors. Some of them
are meant as adjunct to social movement spaces, where patriarchal
dynamics usually play out just as they do in the rest of the world,
despite people's vocal admonishment of them.

While a worthy endeavor, these groups often lack the element
that would inspire a deep commitment from those participating: *a
way they feel as though it will improve their lives.* The politics of moral accountability only go so far, and to take people the rest of the way they
have to be able to identify a reason to transform: a solidarity model
of change. They have to feel that by unlearning toxic patriarchal behaviors it won't just improve the world around them (though it will),
but will also markedly improve their own lives. This was what was
offered by people like John Stoltenberg, who followed the antiracist line of rebellions against "whiteness" to men against masculinity:
"We are all human beings. We be who we be. We are who we are. Yet
we are also inhabitants of categories that we have been made into.
We have had no alternative, for there are those who insist angrily
upon being white, and those who insist angrily upon being men. But
keep heart, and keep on. Because these identities need not be us. We
have a choice. They need not be our selves."[75] The point was that the
rejection of masculinity was not just an act of moral atonement, it
was intended to help men as well. The toxically bounded versions
of masculinity we are taught are stifling, tearing apart our ability to
bond and share, eliminating our capacity to create sound relationships. It is no wonder that the Wolves' gang accountability sounds
like love and devotion to the men who are attracted to it.

In a primer for men looking to challenge the patriarchy, adrienne
maree brown discusses the ways in which the default approach that
men have to relationships is toxically co-dependent: men are not
encouraged to have friends, get professional help, or to even feel
their feelings or notice that the toxic masculinity they are trying to

enact is pathological. "Believing that masculinity is a factor of mental, physical, emotional, economic or other superiority that results in doing less labor and having more power is disease," writes brown. The challenge she poses to this is about men engaging in the active work of dismantling patriarchy, both for themselves and the people they love, through a series of actions that amount to a real change of life: sharing responsibilities, taking responsibility, and acting with responsibility.[76]

Nora Samaran cites the experience of people socialized as men as a crisis of "attachment style," where the skills of proper bonding are neglected and then they often do not know "how nurturance and comfort look and feel."[77] An intervention has to be made, particularly if men have never had other men to learn the skills of nurturing and healthy bonding, and it has to be done by other men for three reasons:

1. Men understand the experience of being a man and can therefore communicate nurturance through the language of that experience.

2. Women cannot be responsible both for healing men and defending themselves against men's violence.

3. Since men are raised to be in emotional "solitary confinement," talking about feelings with other men is in and of itself a radical act of transformation.[78]

The men's group is an essential part of this healing space, or improvement space if you prefer. Samaran asks how men can form a group like this, which is the photographic negative of a question that Operation Werewolf attempts to answer. How do you find a group of men that will help you be a better person? If your answer is exclusionary violence, the Waggener's have the program for you. But if you want the opposite of a culture of violence, which Samaran identifies as nurturance, you have to connect with men invested in such a process.[79]

"By supporting patriarchal culture that socializes men to deny feelings, we doom them to live in states of emotional numbness. We construct a culture where male pain can have no voice, where male hurt cannot be named or healed," says bell hooks, looking at the confrontation that has to happen with a culture of systemic hurt in men.[80] There is an impulse to walk away from this because, well, why should anyone spend their time healing the ones who hurt them? This is a fair point, and one that draws on a need to develop a cultural space for men that encourages it, but it is also a reminder of just what it is going to take if the change is really possible. As bell hooks notes, "Self-help books galore tell us that we cannot change anyone but ourselves. Of course they never answer the question of what will motivate males in a patriarchal culture who have been taught that to love emasculates them to change, to choose love, when the choice means that they must stand against patriarchy, against the tyranny of the familiar."[81] Both of these promises indulge a type of intoxication, that a community can be built from a common experience (of identity) and that coming out of the other side you will be made (more) whole. This gets to the core of what the appeal is because we are looking for bonded roots, something most of us are missing. I do not live in a close-knit social space, and I often feel estranged from even my closest friends. The interdependence of tight friendships is often supplanted with anxiety and loneliness, and there is no roadmap to squashing the strangeness. So it makes sense that when a promise of community is made, people listen.

Men's groups could be a part of the answer, but the appeal is really what needs to be reckoned with. Rightly or wrongly, there is something offered there that is hard to replicate in another kind of space. And men can help each other through this process, and the men sitting behind their computer and staring at utopian promises from message boards recognize this. There are a number of men's groups that exist to confront this alienation, and challenge patriarchy. The Mankind Project has existed for several decades and facilitates over one-thousand groups that combine Jungian psychology and mind-body practices in an effort to unlearn the damaging masculine scripts; a kind of mythopoetic of its own creation.[82] Evryman has a similar model, and they hold outdoor retreats to increase "masculine emotional intelligence" and break down masculinist stereotypes.[83] Part of this is the process to locate a "non-toxic masculinity," the hope that there is still something salvageable underneath the violence and entitlement that many experience as masculinity.

The Challenging Male Supremacy project has a similar intention, and trains men and masculine identified people to join the battle against patriarchal domination and to create a model for men to actively participate in the work to end intimate partner violence.[84] The Coronavirus pandemic that began in 2019 ushered in a number of correlated personal crises, such as loneliness, alienation, and depression. This was especially true for many men who had to confront the disconnectedness that masculine obsession often cultivates, which is why some men started creating WhatsApp channels and social distance check-ins in an attempt to create a space for vulnerability and support, which was missing in their lives even before the disease hit the world so hard.[85]

And all of these examples offer something of an intention, and maybe an approach, and are bent on "remaining men together," not without their problems, but with the intention to try something not built solely on accountability, but also on community love and care. At their best, they start to support men in confronting their alienation, at worst they are self-help groups that promise the world. The goal is not just retraining (though it is that as well), but building an alternative structure, both for relationships and for some type of masculinity.

Inequality

The earliest publishing efforts that would evolve into Operation Werewolf were a series of crude zines called *Iron and Blood*, which had the same frenetic black metal aesthetic that has marked the rest of Paul's output. It had a certain fractured, anarchist-inspired look, complete with talk of "liberation" and "rewilding," but with a darker edge too.

"Only the inferior would want equality," said a middle panel, complete with the equal sign with a slash through it, which would come to adorn a lot of Operation Werewolf swag—a way of separating themselves from the liberal consensus that humans are equal.[86]

"Genetics only count for excuses. You can use them to explain why you are a shuffling puddle of adipose tissue, or why you prefer the gender pronoun 'xher,' but not to set yourself apart in the realms of ancestry or culture—depending on what that ancestry is. YOU ARE ONE with the circle of flabby, scabrous hands that surround this rock in a great ring of mediocrity and self-pity, your corpulent bodies oozing putrescence like a field of cancerous meat that goes on forever," says Paul in his essay "You Are Not Equal."[87]

"I don't want to fucking convert people into the wolves and try to make them strong. I want strong people to find their way to the wolves... The weaker all these people get the easier it will be for all of us to take what we want from them," said Paul. "Embrace your chronic victimhood cause I'm going to make you a real victim motherfucker when I decide I want what you have. Then they are going to know what it means to be unsafe in their personal space."[88]

They believe that hierarchy is natural to the world, and the more horizontal social standards emerge the more that sloth, weakness, and sub-par performance is celebrated as heroic. They instead have a standard that must be upheld; an excellence they have determined, usually combining the meritocracy of extreme free market capitalism with a Mixed Martial Arts octagon.

Rhyd Wildermuth's look at the Wolves tried to unpack exactly why Operation Werewolf fills a hole in many men's desires, and concludes it is done by going after very real desires and reframing them in their own worldview.

Readers for whom the notion of sweat, brawls, and "accepting no weakness" is off-putting should be reminded that it is supposed to repulse you. They are not writing for you. Just as Jack Donovan is not baring his torso for the civilized urban feminist. They are not attempting to build an inclusive ideology, but rather they are cultivating difference and exclusion.[89]

Equality is positioned as a modern invention (fundamentally feminine) that keeps superior men like us down by reducing accomplishments to mere happenstance, negating the real struggle from which greatness emerges. Part of egalitarian social projects is the faith participants have that everyone benefits from a more equal and just society. By reinforcing superiority, and an aggressive blaming of people labeled less fortunate, solidarity between peoples is broken. All the better, since Paul says a man's allegiance is never to the world, only to the tribe.

> Tribalism is the way that humans have always existed. There is always going to be tribalism... Tribal nature is to be xenophobic because it creates an inside and an outside. And I think that's extremely healthy. And I don't care if you agree with it—it's always going to be that way. And people who are hoping for a utopia where everyone is holding hands and all want to get along and are the same color beige... I think those people are evil. I think that's the most horrifying and boring and soulless world... That's what monoculture wants. They want everyone to be the same beige color.[90]

The logical path in the far-right is identity materialism: your fixed identity dictates who you are, social systems allegedly erupt from that idea as do social conditions. This is a strange paradox for Operation Werewolf, which proposes that each person has full control over their own level greatness. Nonetheless, this potential for status only emerges from an identity that can be defined by both its difference and its superiority. White men inherit a whole legacy of art, culture, and politics, but not only that. They inherit conquest, genocide, and violence as well, all things that are recontextualized as greatness when a "survival of the fittest" mindset is applied to their identity. The winners win because they are better, or, as the Waggeners love to say, "If they could steal it, it wasn't yours to begin with."[91]

In 1902, Russian anarchist and scientist Peter Kropotkin published an essay collection called "Mutual Aid," which looked at the reciprocity in biological evolution. Contrary to the more viscous interpretations of Darwinism that poisoned everyone in a brutal war of survival, Kropotkin noted the ways that species work together in mutual benefit to survive and thrive over generations. Success, growth, the towering heights of society, are not built in violent opposition to one another, but through cooperation, caring, and mutual benefit. "Practicing mutual aid is the surest means for giving each other and to all the greatest safety, the best guarantee of existence and progress, bodily, intellectual and moral," he wrote.[92]

It is only when success is reframed as "greatness" that the method for achievement changes because the goal is different. The greatness offered by the Werewolf narrative is not about what a person can achieve that is of value, but what they can gain when another person cannot. Greatness here is defined solely by the lack of greatness in others. It's a bait and switch: they are told their success is measured in what they are able to accomplish, but it is actually a curved grading system. Domination is a key component of this, reframing the world as winners and losers, colonizers and colonized. There is no future of mutual victory through collaboration.

"Those who lecture us about our moral obligations have this power because their superior ancestors were conquerors. No doubt, if their powerful ancestors could see their mentally and physically weak descendants, they would have decided it wasn't worth fighting for them," says Operative 413.[93]

Schadenfreude has a visceral power, to drive others before you and to measure your worth against someone's lack thereof. This notion of dominance gets to the heart of the masculine identity manufactured by patriarchy: that men's role over women is deserved, natural, and based on what is lacking in women. Whiteness plays a key role as well, where the only way the accomplishments of their ethnic forefathers could be redeemed is with the idea that the oppressed are losers who got what they deserved. While this plays to the basest part of white mens' psyche, it is a role they have been trained for since birth. The socialization of men is based around not just their role in competition, but in their willingness to take pleasure in others being harmed. Cruelty is recrafted as a celebrated achievement, the conquest of kings and kingdoms that built the modern world. The reality is that the victory is not emotional power, but rather the victimization of their opponents. Famous studies that encouraged and rewarded cruelty, like the Stanford Prison Experiment, are echoed in the vision of male heroism that Operation Werewolf builds on.[94] The other side of the promise of being strong and courageous is that you could potentially have the capacity to victimize others, and therefore be a man of legend. In the increasing state of social crisis, the desire for this model of being only becomes more intense. The romanticization of collapse comes from the idea that you will dominate when the social structures are abolished, that underneath, at the end of the day and despite it all, you were actually able to achieve.

The claim that inequality is natural gives it a sense of permanence. "In the natural world hierarchies spring up ... there's always going to be a hierarchy in any group of animals," claims Paul in an early conversation with Jack Donovan. The far-right makes this claim about ecology, transmuting their own philosophic concepts onto natural phenomena, but this claim simply does not add up. But in claiming so they build on the mythology and provide credence to the rest of their argument: that you are who you are by virtue of those who fail to measure up. Collapse will then reveal the "natural hierarchy" (which you *obviously* would be at the top of), and you can act as the vanguard of a more naturalistic civic religion that will replace the old world.

We Don't Need It (Build Your Own Body Cult)

The appeal of Operation Werewolf is in the things it promises: success, power, identity, attractiveness, health, happiness. The ideological function of it is to pair those things with other ideas, such as hierarchy and bigotry, creating a narrative that one is the path to the other. This gives men (particularly white cis men) permission for their supremacy, and tells them their pathway to true liberation is through it, not in destroying it.

As white supremacist organizations shifted to much of the insurrectionary "white power" model of street violence and spectacular terrorism starting in the late 1970s, the idea that white nationalism was actually just a cultic phenomenon began to float inside of pop psychology. Instead of white nationalism framed as ideas and radicalization, in which racists were responsible for their actions, white nationalism was reframed as a sort of sickness that an unwitting participant was infected with. Maybe the same "de-programming" functions that worked with people leaving the toxic remnants of the Human Potential Movement (to which Operation Werewolf owes so much) could work on people who were essentially "tricked" into Nazism. There was a kernel of truth to the fact that neo-Nazi skinhead gangs were recruiting young poor kids from broken homes, one key aspect was ignored: the sickness wasn't planted by the group, it was only cultivated by them. White supremacy is the acidic chemical that corrupts our development, it redirects the process by which we form a sense of self. The ideologies spouted by white power gang members are certainly something they were taught—from lies like the Zionist Occupation Government to disproved pseudo-science about race— but these are only intensified versions of the messages society had sent them since birth. We are poised for white radicalization since white identity is itself a construct built and maintained by colonialism and supremacy, and it that reseeds itself as systemic injustice underneath all social institutions continues to prosper.

Operation Werewolf has a similar reseeding effect, and since it (somewhat) tones down the explicit racial rhetoric, the heroic patriarchy is designed to wash over participants without objection. We don't need to be told these stories about the kind of man want to be, because we always wanted it. These images were flooded around us, in every image of a masculine ideal, in the childhood bullying that forms our gender boundaries, in the alienation we feel from our partners and our community, in the caustic way we continue to learn to be men. Operation Werewolf just gave it a name and a well-worn path to follow.

Many fascist movements work by merging disparate narratives. For the "ecofascist" movement, that narrative is looking at the current destruction of the natural world and suggesting that "modernity," a construct that for them means everything from advanced

technology to cosmopolitan multiculturalism, is to blame. By merging multiple concepts into one narrative, it leaves only their answer
for survival and overcoming. Multiculturalism *must* be responsible
since it arrived at the same time as fossil-fuel extraction, so they
must be inextricably linked.

A similar process takes place here, where fitness, self-improvement,
pagan spirituality, close relationships, and rebuilding your life must all
come from their vision of the "Odinic path." It's offered as a path out
of the alienation inherent to capitalist society. OPWW only becomes
more appealing when it is framed as a do-or-die cult.

What is unmistakable about Operation Werewolf is how truly
unnecessary it is. The four pieces that make up the general program
(General Orders, Physical, Mental, Temporal) are little more than
self-help tropes packaged in action movie rhetoric. We can build
a group of friends who workout together. We can get together and
build a spirituality that merges the modern and the ancient and try
to find wisdom in the past and our ancestors and from the mythic
power of storytelling. More than this, the loss of a close community
is an actual tragedy, and so we can approach that missing piece with
intention. The power of Operation Werewolf is in its ability to frame
our own fears and desires through their narrative, thereby reinforcing men's most toxic imprinting. But as with social movements, or
the "left" (whatever that means), one of the clearest ways to undermine them (as well as with direct opposition) is to build something
beautiful that builds us up and undercuts the conditions by which a
fascist movement grows in the first place.

The idea of an esoteric body cult is easy to dismiss, but this likewise dismisses the people who it speaks to. There are radical versions
of these: from Starhawk's Spiral Dance or the reclaiming of the Wild
Woman archetypes, not to mention the radical revivals of Sufism,
Kabbalah, antiracist heathenry, and a whole complicated mess of
people building mystic spiritualities. "Our struggle then must begin
with the re-appropriation of our body, the revaluation and rediscov-
ery of its capacity for resistance, and expansion and celebration of
its powers, individual and collective," says Silvia Federici, discussing the reclamation of a non-technological, non-commercial body

experience.[95] She presents dance as the option, others hit the gym or ritualize sex, but the process is the same. There is an impulse to re-sanctify the body, to engage in a spiritual practice that sees the body as a thing to be shaped and worshipped and to guide us into the future. The point here is that no one owns these impulses, and people can build what they want on their own terms. Operation Werewolf offers only falsehoods dressed as solutions.

Another issue is what does a non-toxic masculinity look like, and how would something like that be achieved? Operation Werewolf is only one version of the modern financial grift promising to train men to be men. What would a masculinity be if it was stripped of the toxic violence that people like Jack Donovan allege is its core? Would it simply cease to be? Or is Donovan correct?

The state of masculinity is an open question, as is whether or not masculinity is even a worthwhile concept to begin with. The bigger issue is maybe not the specific traits we ascribe to masculinity—since anyone can have these—but it could be that packaging them together as an identifiable label called "masculinity" is the problem. To change men, or people who identify with masculinity, there has to be a commitment to them and by them. This has multiple faces: accountability, skill building, challenge, fortitude, new and complimentary ways of being, rituals, bonds, traditions, strength. The image of men today has been forged in the absence of love, or in its inverse, where violence takes the role that nurturance and caring should. The unmaking of this is its own kind of trial by fire, one that is centered on the very thing the previous identity is lacking. In her book *The Will to Change*, bell hooks locates this in a certain kind of love, not unconditional, but absolute.

> To create loving men, we must love males. Loving maleness is different from praising and rewarding males for living up to sexist-defined notions of male identity. Caring about men because of what they do for us is not the same as loving males for simply being. When we love maleness, we extend our love whether males are performing or not. Performance is different from simply being. In patriarchal culture males are not allowed simply

to be who they are and to glory in their unique identity. Their value is always determined by what they do. In an anti-patriarchal culture males do not have to prove their value and worth. They know from birth that simply being gives them value, the right to be cherished and loved."[96]

There is a transvaluation that can take place with the "masculine" qualities that reposition them, seeing their value transposed from their assumed maleness. Managing emotions rather than emotional impulsivity paired with suppression, strength of fortitude and character, stoicism when necessary, vulnerability that comes from the strength to survive pain, the ability to care for someone else through responsive adaptation, and, at its core, the ability to take responsibility. Operation Werewolf promises these sorts of personal adaptations yet attaches them to an entirely toxic male identity built on domination. We can, and should, seek to grow on our own terms, free from the narratives of masculinity that have not served us. If we see masculinity as a proper construct, a cluster of aspirations and traits, then we can reconstruct it the way we see fit—perhaps even beyond masculinity altogether and toward a different kind of person.

"It is true that masses of men have not even begun to look at the ways that patriarchy keeps them from knowing themselves, from being in touch with their feelings, from loving. To know love, men must be able to let go the will to dominate. They must be able to choose life over death," says hooks, which clashes with the Wolves appeal.[97]

Operation Werewolf's threat is that it can move recruits along an ideological process, the only logical conclusion of which is white violence. A man may be attracted to the project for its programmatic effects, but actually has their own white supremacist inclinations massaged along the way. Confronting part of this is easy: you counter-organize the organization and disrupt its ability to grow. But what about what made it attractive in the first place?

There is not a clear-cut answer to this since part of this returns to some of the most deeply laid hierarchies in society, but there are other driving forces that bring about its rise. Fascism studies scholar Robert O. Paxton called the conditions by which a revolutionary struggle emerges, such as social strife or insecurity, "mobilizing passions."[98] Theoretically, this could bring about a left-wing revolution (it certainly has), but when it appeals to a privileged group within the working class (whites who have a better situation than non-white workers), then a different sort of response can be triggered. As Paxton elucidates, fascism is about feelings more than ideology (and more about action than words), so it is important to unpack just what feelings are stoked.[99]

We need to be ready to offer up own answer. To build up communities that are strong, that help people through their difficulties, so they come out stronger on the other side. To help people build a body cult to stay tied to their physicality and health, not to fit the prescriptions of a hierarchical and fat-phobic fitness culture, but to build themselves according to the vision they alone have. To rediscover spiritual traditions, some new and some ancestral, that can connect us to where we are today. To build a real committed and connected cauldron of people who can stay bonded in mutual support. We need an answer that is committed to the eradication of white supremacy, patriarchy, and the privileges that attempt to sell off our solidarity. Toxic masculinity has failed even the masculine, but we don't have any other models to teach us how to live. We can build something new.

Notes

Introduction

1. Michael Barkun, *Culture of Conspiracy: Apocalyptic Visions in Contemporary America* (Berkeley: University of California Press, 2013), 16.
2. Ibid., 18.
3. Ibid., 19.
4. Jesse Walker, *The United States of Paranoia: A Conspiracy Theory* (New York: Harper Perennial, 2013), 202–03; Richard Beck, *We Believe the Children: Moral Panic in the 1980s* (New York: PublicAffairs, 2015).
5. Shane Burley, "'A huge difference': Volunteers mobilise in Oregon fire aftermath," *Al Jazeera*, September 25, 2020, https://www.aljazeera.com/news/2020/9/25/a-huge-difference-activists-mobilise-in-oregon-fire-aftermath.
6. Megan Brenan, "Americans' Face Mask Usage Varies Greatly by Demographics," *Gallup*, July 13, 2020, https://news.gallup.com/poll/315590/americans-face-mask-usage-varies-greatly-demographics.aspx.
7. Bobby Allyn and Barbara Sprunt, "Poll: As Coronavirus Spreads, Fewer Americans See Pandemic As A Real Threat," *NPR*, March 17, 2020, https://www.npr.org/2020/03/17/816501871/poll-as-coronavirus-spreads-fewer-americans-see-pandemic-as-a-real-threat.
8. Quoted by Ben Collins, "Coronavirus conspiracy theories are frustrating ER doctors," NBC News, May 6, 2020, https://www.nbcnews.com/tech/tech-news/what-are-we-doing-doctors-are-fed-conspiracies-ravaging-ers-n1201446.
9. Shane Burley, "I Spoke to the Woman Coordinating Anti-lockdown Protests. She Told Me What They Plan to Do Next," *The Independent*,

May 5, 2020, https://www.independent.co.uk/voices/reopen-america -lockdown-protest-us-states-michigan-oregon-arizona-a9499921.html.

10. Katherine Schaeffer, "A Look at the Americans Who Believe there is Some Truth to the Conspiracy Theory that COVID-19 Was Planned," *Pew Research Center*, July 24, 2020, https://www.pewresearch.org/ fact-tank/2020/07/24/a-look-at-the-americans-who-believe-there-is -some-truth-to-the-conspiracy-theory-that-covid-19-was-planned/.

11. Nicole Lyn Pesce, "Roughly 1 in 3 Americans thinks the coronavirus hasn't killed as many people as has been reported," *Market Watch*, July 21, 2020, https://www.marketwatch.com/story/roughly-1-in-3 -americans-thinks-the-coronavirus-hasnt-killed-as-many-people-as -has-been-reported-2020-07-21.

12. Joris Lammmers, Jan Cursius, and Anne Gast, "Correcting Misper- ceptions of Exponential Coronavirus Growth Increases Support for Social Distancing," Proceedings of the National Academy of Sciences of the United States of America, July 14, 2020, https://www.pnas.org/ content/117/28/16264.

13. Megan C. Hills, "Goop Contributor Kelly Brogan Peddles 'Non- sense' Conspiracy Theories about Coronavirus, Cites 5G and Vac- cine Companies as Real Causes," *Insider*, March 25, 2020, https:// www.standard.co.uk/insider/living/goop-contributor-kelly-brogan -peddles-conspiracy-theories-about-coronavirus-and-cites-5g-and -vaccine-a4397061.html.

14. Paulina Villegas, "South Dakota Nurse Says Many Patients Deny the Coronavirus Exists—Right Up Until Death," *Washington Post*, Novem- ber 16, 2020, https://www.washingtonpost.com/health/2020/11/16/ south-dakota-nurse-coronavirus-deniers/.

15. Resilience, "'Collapse of Civilisation is the Most Likely Outcome': Top Climate Scientists," *Resilience*, June 8, 2020, https://www.resilience .org/stories/2020-06-08/collapse-of-civilisation-is-the-most-likely -outcome-top-climate-scientists/.

16. Intergovernmental Science-Policy Platform on Biodiversity and Eco- system Services (IPBES), "UN Report: Nature's Dangerous Decline 'Unprecedented'; Species Extinction Rates 'Accelerating,'" May 6, 2019, https://www.un.org/sustainabledevelopment/blog/2019/05/nature -decline-unprecedented-report/.

17. Jack Hunter, "The 'Climate Doomers' Preparing for Society to Fall Apart," *BBC News*, March 16, 2020, https://www.bbc.com/news/ stories-51857722.

18. Brendan O'Connor, *Blood Red Lines: How Nativism Fuels the Right* (Chi- cago: Haymarket Books, 2021), 125.

19. Shane Burley, *Fascism Today: What It Is and How to End It* (Chico: AK Press, 2017); George Hawley, *Making Sense of the Alt-Right* (New York:

Columbia University Press, 2017); Alexandra Mirna Stern, *Proud Boys and the White Ethnostate: How the Alt-Right Is Warping the American Imagination* (Boston: Beacon Press, 2019).

20. Em Steck, Nathan McDermott, and Christopher Hickey, "The congressional candidates who have engaged with the QAnon conspiracy theory," *CNN*, October 30, 2020, https://www.cnn.com/interactive/2020/10/politics/qanon-cong-candidates/.

21. Shane Burley and Alexander Reid Ross, "Conspiracy Theories by Cops Fuel Far Right Attacks against Antiracist Protesters," *Truthout*, September 18, 2020, https://truthout.org/articles/conspiracy-theories-by-cops-fuel-far-right-attacks-against-antiracist-protesters/.

22. See "The Fall of the 'Alt Right' Came from Antifascism" and "A History of Violence" in this volume.

23. Author interview with Spencer Sunshine, November 16, 2020.

24. Shane Burley, "Anti-Fascist Group Targeted for Murder by Far Right Won't Back Down," *Truthout*, May 25, 2020, https://truthout.org/authors/shane-burley/.

25. Chris Schiano, "'Bowl Patrol': Dylann Roof Fans Hope to Inspire More Mass Shootings," *Unicorn Riot*, January 8, 2019, https://unicornriot.ninja/2019/bowl-patrol-dylann-roof-fans-hope-to-inspire-more-mass-shootings/.

26. Rosa Schwartzburg, "No, There Isn't a White Genocide," *Jacobin*, September 4, 2019, https://jacobinmag.com/2019/09/white-genocide-great-replacement-theory.

27. Shane Burley and Alexander Reid Ross, "How to Defeat the Cretinous 'Great Replacement' Theory at the Heart of the Christchurch Mosque Attack," *The Independent*, March 18, 2019, https://www.independent.co.uk/voices/christchurch-attack-new-zealand-shooting-brenton-tarrant-great-replacement-a8827966.html.

28. Josia Brownwell, "'One Last Retreat': Racial Nostalgia and Population Panic in Smith's Rhodesia and Powell's Britain," in *Global White Nationalism: From Apartheid to Trump*, eds. Daniel Geary, Camilla Schofield, and Jennifer Sutton (Manchester: Manchester University Press, 2020), 161 68.

29. Zoe Hyman, "Transatlantic white supremacy: American segregationists and international racism after civil rights," in *Global White Nationalism*, 192–204.

30. O'Connor, *Blood Red Lines*.

31. Luke Darby, "What Is Eco-Fascism, the Ideology Behind Attacks in El Paso and Christchurch?," *GQ*, August 7, 2019, https://www.gq.com/story/what-is-eco-fascism; Also see "Wolf Age" in this volume.

32. "Mapping Paramilitary and Far-Right Threats to Racial Justice, *Political Research Associates*, politicalresearch.org/2020/06/19/mapping

-paramilitary-and-far-right-threats-racial-justice.

33. Shane Burley, "The End of Violence: 100 Days of Protest in Portland," Verso Books blog, September 28, 2020, https://www.versobooks.com/blogs/4862-the-end-of-violence-100-days-of-protest-in-portland.

34. Shane Burley, "Trump and the GOP are using Kyle Rittenhouse in last-ditch 2020 voter strategy," *NBC News*, October 4, 2020, https://www.nbcnews.com/think/opinion/trump-gop-are-using-kyle-rittenhouse-last-ditch-2020-voter-ncna1241940.

35. Quoted by Peter Wade, "Trump calls for 'Retribution,' Not Justice, in Portland Shooting, *Rolling Stone*, September 13, 2020, https://www.rollingstone.com/politics/politics-news/there-has-to-be-retribution-trump-endorses-us-marshals-killing-suspect-1058875/.

36. Benjamin Carter Hett, *The Death of Democracy: Hitler's Rise to Power and the Downfall of the Weimar Republic* (New York: St. Martin's Press, 2018), 235.

37. Author interview with David Neiwert, November 17, 2020.

38. Shane Burley, "The Right Wing Is Trying to Make It a Crime to Oppose Fascism," *Truthout*, April 9, 2019, https://truthout.org/articles/the-right-wing-is-trying-to-make-it-a-crime-to-oppose-fascism/.

39. Author interview with Effie Baum, May 31, 2020.

40. Ibid.

41. Author interview with David Rose, August 13, 2019.

42. Robert O. Paxton, *The Anatomy of Fascism* (New York: Vintage Books, 2004), 41.

43. Author interview with Stephanie Noriega, March 31, 2020.

44. Shane Burley, "Amid the coronavirus crisis, mutual aid networks erupt across the country," *Waging Nonviolence*, March 27, 2020, https://wagingnonviolence.org/2020/03/coronavirus-mutual-aid-networks-erupt-across-country/.

45. Shane Burley, "Trump's Sending in the Feds. Here's What We Saw in Portland." *The Daily Beast*, July 21, 2020, https://www.thedailybeast.com/trumps-sending-in-the-feds-heres-what-happened-to-us-in-portland.

46. Shane Burley, "The Feds Have Left, but the Battle for Portland Continues," *Roar Magazine*, August 11, 2020, https://roarmag.org/essays/portland-fed-police-protest/.

47. Author interview with Stella Fiore, September 15, 2020.

48. Ibid.

49. Author interview with Samantha Brybe, September 14th, 2020.

50. Shane Burley, "Coronavirus fight: Some US worker unions become more aggressive," *Al Jazeera*, May 1, 2020, https://www.aljazeera.com/economy/2020/5/1/coronavirus-fight-some-us-worker-unions-become-more-aggressive.

51. Shane Burley, "What New Orleans' Common Ground Collective can teach us about surviving crisis together," *Waging Nonviolence*, August 20, 2020, https://wagingnonviolence.org/2020/08/what-new-orleans-common-ground-collective-can-teach-us-about-surviving-crisis-together/.

52. Author interview with scott crow, April 2, 2020.

53. Ibid.

54. Robert Evans and Jason Wilson, "The Boogaloo Movement Is Not What You Think," *Bellingcat*, May 27, 2020, https://www.bellingcat.com/news/2020/05/27/the-boogaloo-movement-is-not-what-you-think/.

55. George Robinson, *Essential Judaism: A Complete Guide to Beliefs, Customs, and Rituals: Updated Edition* (New York: Astria Paperback, 2016), 92.

56. Abraham Joshua Heschel, *The Sabbath: Its Meaning for Modern Man* (New York: Farrar, Status and Giroux, 2005), 68.

57. Ibid., 79.

58. See "Introduction to Armageddon."

59. Neil Gillman, *The Way into Encountering God in Judaism* (Woodstock, VT: Jewish Lights Publishing, 2000), 176–83.

60. Martin Buber, *The Way of Man* (London: Routledge, 1965), 33.

61. Walter Benjamin, "Theses on the Philosophy of History," in *Illuminations: Essays and Reflections*, ed. Hannah Arendt (Boston: Mariner Books, 2019), 200.

62. Ibid., 204.

63. Ibid., 208.

64. It should be noted that Benjamin may or may not have actually agreed with this interpretation. But that's okay. We have to break with our past anyway.

65. Author Interview with Joan Braune, November 18, 2020. Joan Braune, *Erich Fromm's Revolutionary Hope: Prophetic Messianism as a Critical Theory of the Future* (Rotterdam: Sense Publishers, 2014).

66. Erich Fromm, *You Shall Be as Gods: A Radical Interpretation of the Old Testament and Its Tradition.* (United States: Open Road Media, 2013).

67. Martin Buber, *Ten Rungs: Collected Hasidic Sayings* (London and New York: Routledge, 2013), 64.

68. Rosa Luxembourg, *The Julius Pamphlet: The Crisis of German Social Democracy* (1915), https://www.marxists.org/archive/luxemburg/1915/junius/ch01.htm.

69. Robert Evans, "Elite Panic: Why the Rich and Powerful Can't Be Trusted," *Behind the Bastards*, November 19, 2020, https://www.iheart.com/podcast/105-behind-the-bastards-29236323/episode/elite-panic-why-the-rich-and-74157341/; Lee Clarke, and Caron Chess. "Elites and Panic: More to Fear than Fear Itself." *Social Forces* 87, no. 2 (2008): 993–1014.

Disunite the Right

1. Richard Spencer, "The Alt-Right Triumphant," AltRight.com, June 30, 2017.
2. Andrew Marantz, "The Alt-Right Branding War Has Torn the Movement in Two," *The New Yorker*, July 6, 2017.
3. Richard Spencer, "Alt-Right Politics–June 24, 2017–This Means War!," AltRight.com, June 24, 2017.
4. While the Alt Right is a "big tent" in its own right, the coalition has defined values of inequality and ethnic identity. Richard Spencer, "What is the Alt Right?" *NPI/Radix*, YouTube, December 17, 2015.
5. Bradford Richardson, "Trump supporters headline free speech rally at University of California, Berkeley," *The Washington Times*, April 27, 2017, https://www.washingtontimes.com/news/2017/apr/27/gavin-mcinnes-lauren-southern-headline-free-speech/.
6. David Neiwert, "Competing Alt-Right 'Free-Speech' Rallies Reveals Infighting Over White Nationalism," Southern Poverty Law Center, June 21, 2017.
7. Richard Spencer, @RichardBSpencer, Twitter, June 16, 2017, "The Alt Light is a collection of outright liars (Posobiec and Cerno), perverts (Milo, Wintrich), and Zionist fanatics (Loomer)," https://twitter.com/richardbspencer/status/875959139582840832.
8. Richard Spencer, "Milo and His Enemies," AltRight.com, March 2, 2017, https://altright.com/2017/03/02/milo-and-his-enemies/. Shane Burley, "As the alt-right breaks with Trump, so goes its moment in the sun," *Waging Nonviolence*, April 17, 2017, https://wagingnonviolence.org/2017/04/alt-right-trump-break/. Brakkton Booker, "Alt-Right Infighting Simmers Around Inaugural 'DeploraBall,'" NPR, January 1, 2017, https://www.npr.org/2017/01/01/507395282/alt-right-infighting-simmers-around-inaugural-deploraball.
9. Spencer Sunshine, "The Growing Alliance Between Neo-Nazis, Right Wing Paramilitaries and Trumpist Republicans," *Colorlines*, June 9, 2017, https://www.colorlines.com/articles/growing-alliance-between-neo-nazis-right-wing-paramilitaries-and-trumpist-republicans.
10. Joshua Green, *Devil's Bargain: Steve Bannon, Donald Trump, and the Storming of the Presidency* (New York: Penguin Press, 2017), 5–6.
11. Kyle Chapman, interview with Author, June 4, 2017.
12. Nathan Damigo, "Is Based Stick Man Not So Based?" AltRight.com, March 28, 2017, https://altright.com/2017/03/28/is-based-stick-man-not-so-based/.
13. Ibid.
14. Josh Harkinson, "Cashing in on the Rise of the Alt-Right," *Mother

Jones, June 16, 2017, https://www.motherjones.com/politics/2017/06/kyle-chapman-based-stickman-alt-right/.

15. Lucian Wintrich as quoted by Andrew Marantz, "The Alt-Right Branding War Has Torn the Movement in Two," *The New Yorker*, July 6, 2017, https://www.newyorker.com/news/news-desk/the-alt-right-branding-war-has-torn-the-movement-in-two.

16. Michael Driscoll, "Lauren Southern, Generation Identity, and the Quest for Meaning," AltRight.com, June 29, 2017, https://altright.com/2017/06/29/lauren-southern-generation-identity-and-the-quest-for-meaning/.

17. Ibid.

18. No author, "Antigovernment militia groups grew by more than one-third in last year," Southern Poverty Law Center, January 4, 2016, https://www.splcenter.org/news/2016/01/04/antigovernment-militia-groups-grew-more-one-third-last-year.

19. Arun Gupta, "Playing Cops: Militia Member Aids Police in Arresting Protester at Portland Alt-Right Rally," *The Intercept*, June 8, 2017, https://theintercept.com/2017/06/08/portland-alt-right-milita-police-dhs-arrest-protester/.

20. Joey Gibson, "Speech at 'Free Speech' Rally," Speech, Patriot Prayer "Free Speech" Rally, Portland, Oregon, June 4, 2017.

21. Stewart Rhodes, "Oath Keepers say IDENTITY EVROPA is not Welcome: 'If they come in today we going to whoop their ass,'" Very Fake News, *YouTube*, April 29, 2017, https://www.youtube.com/watch?v=14J1dCwXh5w.

22. In mid-August, *The Daily Stormer* was denied domain registration from Google and GoDaddy and these webpages were no longer live. This started a dramatic saga for Stormer editor Andrew Anglin as he hopped around the world, running from indictments and using "dark web" sites to host the Stormer. As of this publishing, the Stormer is no longer a consistent force in Nazi media because of its inability to find stable web support.

23. Azzmador, Mike Enoch, and Seventh Son, "The Daily Shoah 164: Vanned in the UK," *The Right Stuff*, June 20, 2016.

24. Sarah Viets, "Neo-Nazi Misfits Join Unite the Right," Southern Poverty Law Center, July 26, 2017, https://www.splcenter.org/hatewatch/2017/07/26/neo-nazi-misfits-join-unite-right.

25. Jason Wilson, "'Young White Guys are Hopping Mad': Confidence Grows at Far-right Gathering," *The Guardian*, July 31, 2017, https://www.theguardian.com/us-news/2017/jul/31/american-renaissance-conference-white-identity.

26. Jason Wilson, "Charlottesville: Far-right Crowd with Torches Encircles Counter-protester Group," *The Guardian*, August 12, 2017,

https://www.theguardian.com/world/2017/aug/12/charlottesville-far
-right-crowd-with-torches-encircles-counter-protest-group.

27. Yesha Callahan, "White Supremacists Beat Black Man with Poles in Charlottesville, Va., Parking Garage," *The Root*, August 12, 2017, https://www.theroot.com/white-supremacists-beat-black-man-with-poles-in-charlot-1797790092. Brendan King, "Protesters pepper spray, beat each other during Charlottesville rally," WTVR, August 12, 2017.

28. Joe Heim, "Recounting a day of rage, hate, violence and death," *The Washington Post*, August 14, 2017, https://www.washingtonpost.com/graphics/2017/local/charlottesville-timeline/. Hatewatch Staff, "Alleged Charlottesville Driver Who Killed One Rallied With Alt-Right Vanguard America," Southern Poverty Law Center, August 13, 2017, https://www.splcenter.org/hatewatch/2017/08/12/alleged-charlottesville-driver-who-killed-one-rallied-alt-right-vanguard-america-group.

29. Jennifer Calfas, "Virginia Governor Delivers Defiant Speech Against White Supremacists 'We Are Stronger Than Them,'" *TIME*, August 13, 2017, https://time.com/4898560/virginia-governor-terry-mcauliffe-church-speech-transcript/. Glenn Thrush and Rebecca R. Ruiz, "White House Acts to Stem Fallout from Trump's First Charlottesville Remarks," *The New York Times*, August 13, 2017, https://www.nytimes.com/2017/08/13/us/charlottesville-protests-white-nationalists-trump.html.

30. "USA: Unite the Right organiser shutdown after blaming Charlottesville chaos on 'anti-white hate,'" Ruptly TV, Youtube, August 13, 2017, https://www.youtube.com/watch?v=4X4qeu5zLVI.

31. Media Matters Staff, "After praising Trump's statement on Charlottesville, a neo-Nazi website celebrates murder of counterprotester Heather Heyer," Media Matters for America, August 13, 2017, https://www.mediamatters.org/daily-stormer/after-praising-trumps-statement-charlottesville-neo-nazi-website-celebrates-murder.

32. Doha Madani, "'Crying Nazi' Christopher Cantwell found guilty of extortion in rape threat case," NBC News, September 28, 2020, nbcnews.com/news/us-news/crying-nazi-christopher-cantwell-found-guilty-extortion-rape-threat-case-n1241263.

33. Justin Ling, "Neo-nazi site The Daily Stormer moves to the Darkweb, but promises a comeback," *Vice News*, August 15, 2017, https://www.vice.com/en/article/gydmdj/neo-nazi-site-the-daily-stormer-moves-to-the-darkweb-but-promises-a-comeback.

34. Jonathan Berr, "PayPal cuts off payments to right-wing extremists," *CBS News*, August 16, 2017, https://www.cbsnews.com/news/paypal-suspends-dozens-of-racist-groups-sites-altright-com/.

35. Doug Criss, "Texas A&M cancels white nationalist rally set for 9/11,"

CNN, August 15, 2017, https://www.cnn.com/2017/08/14/us/texas
-white-nationalist-protest-trnd/index.html. Colin Dwyer, "University
of Florida Denies Richard Spencer Event, Citing 'Likelihood of Violence,'" *NPR*, August 16, 2017, https://www.npr.org/sections/thetwo
-way/2017/08/16/543874400/university-of-florida-denies-richard
-spencer-event-citing-likelihood-of-violence.

Lawsuits are Not Enough to Stop the Far-Right

1. Shane Burley, "The Alt Right's War on Whitefish, and the Growth
   of an opposition," *Gods & Radicals*, February 13, 2017, god-
   sandradicals.org/2017/02/13/the-alt-rights-war-on-whitefish
   -and-the-growth-of-an-opposition/.
2. Ibid.
3. "SPLC sues neo-Nazi leader who targeted Jewish woman in anti-
   Semitic harassment campaign," *Southern Poverty Law Center*, April
   18, 2017, splcenter.org/news/2017/04/18/splc-sues-neo-nazi-leader
   -who-targeted-jewish-woman-anti-semitic-harassment-campaign.
4. Laurence Leamer, *Lynching: The Epic Courtroom Battle That Brought
   Down the Klan* (New York: William Morrow, 2016).
5. Elinor Langer, *A Hundred Little Hitlers: The Death of a Black Man, the
   Trial of a White Racist, and the Rise of the Neo-Nazi Movement in America*
   (London: Picador, 2004).
6. No author, "Victoria Keenan Discusses Run-in with Aryan Nations," *Southern Poverty Law Center*, December 6, 2000, https://www
   .splcenter.org/fighting-hate/intelligence-report/2000/victoria
   -keenan-discusses-run-aryan-nations.
7. No author, "Keenan v. Aryan Nations," *Southern Poverty Law Center*,
   splcenter.org/seeking-justice/case-docket/keenan-v-aryan-nations.
8. "Report: Neo-Nazi site raises $150K to fight lawsuit by Jewish
   woman," *CBS News*, June 7, 2017, cbsnews.com/news/neo-nazi
   -website-raises-150000-to-fight-lawsuit-by-tanya-gersh/.
9. "How the Alt Right was Decimated After Charlottesville," *Anti-
   -Fascist News*, October 25, 2017, antifascistnews.net/2017/10/25/how
   -the-alt-right-was-decimated-after-charlottesville/.
10. Alexander Reid Ross and Shane Burley, "Will the Alt Right Produce
    the Next Timothy McVeigh?" *Alternet*, November 6, 2017, https://www
    .alternet.org/2017/11/will-alt-right-produce-next-timothy-mcveigh/.

The Fall of the Alt Right Came from Antifascism

1. Gregory Conte and Richard Spencer, Video, "The State of the Alt
   Right," AltRight.com, March 3, 2018.

2. ((counterapparatus)), @walmas, *Twitter*, March 6, 2018, twitter.com/walmas/status/971028370497687554.

3. David Jesse, "E-mails reveal how MSU grappled with Richard Spencer's request to speak on campus," *Detroit Free Press*, December 20, 2017, https://www.freep.com/story/news/education/2017/12/20/richard-spencer-michigan-state-university/969080001/.

4. No author, "How the Alt Right Was Decimated After Charlottesville," *Anti-Fascist News*, October 25, 2017, https://www.antifascistnews.net/2017/10/25/how-the-alt-right-was-decimated-after-charlottesville/.

5. Shane Burley, "Anti-fascist organizing explodes on US college campuses," *Waging Nonviolence*, February 15, 2018, https://wagingnonviolence.org/2018/02/antifascist-organizing-explodes-college-campuses/. Susan Svrluga, "Michigan State agrees to let Richard Spencer give a speech on campus," *Washington Post*, January 18, 2018, https://www.washingtonpost.com/news/grade-point/wp/2018/01/18/michigan-state-agrees-to-let-richard-spencer-give-a-speech-on-campus/.

6. Martin Slagter, "University of Michigan students stage walk-out in protest of Richard Spencer," *MLive*, November 19, 2017, https://www.mlive.com/news/ann-arbor/2017/11/university_of_michigan_student_125.html.

7. Phil Helsel and The Associated Press, "Hundreds Protest Speech by White Nationalist Richard Spencer at Texas A&M," *NBC News*, December 6, 2016, https://www.nbcnews.com/news/us-news/hundreds-protest-speech-white-nationalist-richard-spencer-texas-m-n692871.

25 Theses on Fascism

1. Robert O. Paxton, "The Five Stages of Fascism," *The Journal of Modern History* 70, No. 1 (March 1998): 1–23.

The Kult of Kek

1. Saint Obamas MomJeans, *Deus Kek: The Kek and the Dead* (Charleston: CreateSpace, 2017), 12.

2. Berman, Marshall, *All That Is Solid Melts Into Air: The Experience of Modernity* (London: Verso, 1982), 15.

3. The most plainly expounded of these texts is the aptly named *Against the Modern World, Fascism Viewed from the Right, and Men Among the Ruins*, all of which are translated and republished by the Alt Right-allied *Arktos Media*, which also publishes many books common inside of pagan and occult circles.

4. It should be noted that this racialized and nationalist interpretations of the Vedas are not shared by the predominance of Hindus, though may be shared by some authoritarian Hindu nationalist sects.
5. Richard Spencer, "Become Great Again." National Policy Institute Conference 2016. November 18, 2016.
6. "Perennial Decay: Decadent Politics." *Graceless: A Journal of the Radical Gothic*, Issue 1 (2011): 6.

The "Free Speech" Cheat

1. Sawyer Click, "Allegations against President Boreing Reveal Student Government Trend of TPUSA affiliations," *University Star*, August 31, 2018, https://www.universitystar.com/25470/news/allegations-against-president-boreing-reveal-student-government-trend-of-tpusa-affiliation/.
2. Charlie Kirk, @charliekirk11, *Twitter*, April 10, 2019, https://twitter.com/charliekirk11/status/1116182851563577344.
3. Alison G. Castillo, April 11th, 2019, Office of Student Government at Texas State University, "SUBJECT: Senate Resolution 20 "The Faculty and Student Safety Resolution of 2019," https://gato-docs.its.txstate.edu/jcr:dc7aedc6-f4a7-47e8-b3c4-48244abe3100/Memorandum%20of%20Ve.
4. Charlie Kirk, @charliekirk11, *Twitter*, April 10, 2019, https://twitter.com/charliekirk11/status/1116182851563577344.
5. Brianna Stone, "This is why — and how — a conservative club was rejected at Santa Clara University," *USA Today*, February 8, 2017, https://www.usatoday.com/story/college/2017/02/08/this-is-why-and-how-a-conservative-club-was-rejected-at-santa-clara-university/37427207/.
6. Pennsylvania Power Network, onepa.org/pa-student-power-network.
7. Shane Burley and Kristina Khan, "Young Fascists on Campus: Turning Point USA and Its Far-Right Connection," *Truthout*, February 5, 2018, https://truthout.org/articles/young-fascists-on-campus-turning-point-usa-and-its-far-right-connections/.

We're Being Played

1. Shane Burley, "Massive Anti-Fascist Coalition Rebuffs Far-Right Proud Boys in Portland, *Truthout*, July 3, 2019, https://truthout.org/articles/massive-anti-fascist-coalition-rebuffs-far-right-proud-boys-in-portland/.
2. Shane Burley, "The Proud Boys Have Revived Far-Right Gang Terror With GOP Support," *Truthout*, October 18, 2018, truthout.org/articles/

the-proud-boys-have-revived-far-right-gang-terror-with-gop
-support/; Jason Wilson, "Riot in Portland as far-right marchers clash
with anti-fascists," *The Guardian*, July 1, 208, https://www.theguardian
.com/us-news/2018/jul/01/riot-in-portland-as-far-right-marchers
-clash-with-anti-facists.

3. Shane Burley and Alexander Reid Ross, "A Popular Mobilization Is
Forming in Portland to Stop the Growth of Hate Groups," *Truthout*,
August 1, 2018, truthout.org/articles/popular-mobilization-forming-
in-portland-to-stop-growth-of-hate-groups/.

4. Shane Burley, "Massive Anti-Fascist Coalition Rebuffs Far-Right Proud
Boys in Portland, *Truthout*, July 3, 2019, https://www.truthout.org
/articles/massive-anti-fascist-coalition-rebuffs-far-right-proud-boys
-in-portland/.

5. Andy Ngô, "Fired for Reporting the Truth," *National Review*,
May 12, 2017, https://www.nationalreview.com/2017/05/free-speech
-islam-portland-state-vanguard-editor-fired-tweets/.

6. Andy Ngô, "A Visit to Islamic England," *Wall Street Journal*, August 29,
2018, https://www.wsj.com/articles/a-visit-to-islamic-england-15355
81583.

7. After writing this essay, on August 29, 2020, we saw the killing of
Patriot Prayer member Aaron Danielson by Michael Reinoehl, who
had been attending the protests. Video later released by Oregon Public Broadcasting shows Danielson charging after Reinoehl with bear
spray, and Reinoehl responding by firing his gun. Reinoehl was later
killed by federal authorities.

8. Lexi McMenamin, "How cars became a deadly anti-protest weapon," *Mic*, December 30, 2020, https://www.mic.com/p/how-cars
-became-a-deadly-anti-protest-weapon-53291831.

Wolf Age

1. William Isaac Thomas and Dorothy Swaine Thomas, *The Child in
America: Behavior Problems and Programs* (New York: Knopf, 1938), 572.

Contested Space

1. "At Daggers Drawn: An Interview with Alsarath," A Blaze Ansuz,
May 5, 2020, antifascistneofolk.com/2020/05/05/at-daggers-drawn
-an-interview-with-alsarath/.

2. Margaret Killjoy, "Cede No Ground to Fascists," Birds Before the
Storm, May 11th, 2017, http://birdsbeforethestorm.net/2017/05/cede
-no-ground-to-fascists/.

3. Author interview with Kieran Knutson, October 30, 2019.

4. Nigel Copsey, *Anti-Fascism in Britain* (London: Routledge, 2017), 126–44; David Renton, *Never Again: Rock Against Racism and the Anti-Nazi League* (London: Routledge, 2019).

5. Matthew N. Lyons, *Insurgent Supremacists: The U.S. Far Right's Challenge to State and Empire* (Montreal: Kersblebedeb and PM Press, 2018), 58.

6. Cynthia Miller-Idriss, *Hate in the Homeland: The New Global Far Right* (Princeton, NJ: Princeton University Press, 2020), 129.

7. Shane Burley, *Fascism Today*, 136–39.

8. Tamir Bar-On, *Where Have All the Fascists Gone?* (New York: Routledge, 2007); *Against Democracy and Equality: The European New Right* (Budapest: Arktos Media, 2011); Alain de Benoist and Charles Champetier, *Manifesto for a European Renaissance* (Budapest: Arktos Media, 2012).

9. Author interview with Richard Spencer, September 14, 2016.

10. Benjamin Teitelbaum, "Daniel Friberg and Metapolitics in Action," in *Key Thinkers of the Radical Right: Behind the New Threat to Liberal Democracy*, Mark Sedgwick, ed. (New York: Oxford University Press, 2019), 261–73.

11. Anton Shekhovtsov, "Apoliteic music: Neo-Folk, Martial Industrial and 'Metapolitical Fascism,'" *Patterns of Prejudice* 43, No. 5 (2009): 431–57.

12. Roger Griffin, "The Palingenetic Core of Fascism," in A. Campi, ed., *Che cos'è il fascismo? Interpretazioni e prospecttive di richerche* (Rome: Ideazione editrice, 2003), 98.

13. Nancy C. Love, *Trendy Fascism: White Power Music and the Future of Democracy* (Albany: State University of New York Press, 2016), 8–13.

14. Alexander Reid Ross, *Against the Fascist Creep* (Chico: AK Press, 2017).

15. It should be noted that European clubs are fundamentally different than in the U.S., and entire teams can have a fascist fanbase, not just supporters' groups of any team.

16. The Football Faculty, "Political Football Clubs Part Two: The Right," November 13, 2018, http://www.thefootballfaculty.com/2018/11/13/political-football-clubs-part-2-the-right/; Jack Beville, "Fascism in Football: The Ugly Side of the Beautiful Game," World Football Index, June 13, 2020, https://worldfootballindex.com/2020/06/fascism-in-football-the-ugly-side-of-the-beautiful-game/.

17. Shane Burley, "Stick it to Sports," *The Baffler*, October 17, 2019, https://thebaffler.com/latest/stick-it-to-sports-burley.

18. Lee Marsh, "Football: Top Ten Antifa Ultras," *Freedom News*, January 28 (no year listed), https://freedomnews.org.uk/football-top-ten-antifa-ultras/.

19. Hank Shteamer, "Brooklyn Anti-Fascist Metal Fest Was a Beacon for a Troubled Scene," *Rolling Stone*, January 28, 2019, https://

www.rollingstone.com/music/music-live-reviews/black-flags -over-brooklyn-kim-kelly-anti-fascist-metal-fest-785088/.

20. Author interview with Kim Kelly, March 1, 2019.

21. Shane Burley, "Black Metal for the Oppressed," *Protean Magazine*, July 21, 2019, https://proteanmag.com/2019/07/21/black-metal-for-the -oppressed/.

22. Author Interview with Simon B. on February 4, 2019.

23. Quoted in Burley, "Black Metal for the Oppressed," *Protean Magazine*.

24. Ansuz, "A Biocentric Future: Interview with Ecologist," *A Blaze Ansuz*, July 8, 2020, https://antifascistneofolk.com/2020/07/08 /a-biocentric-future-interview-with-ecologist/.

25. Author interview with Kim Kelly, March 1, 2019.

26. Anti-Fascist News, "Under the Radar: The Neo-Folk Band 'Changes' and Their Open Fascism," *Anti-Fascist News*, October 23, 2015, https://antifascistnews.net/2015/10/23/under-the-radar-the-neo -folk-band-changes-and-their-open-fascism/.

27. Ansuz, "Sangre de Muerdago's Galician Neofolk is Resistance to Spain's Fascist History," *A Blaze Ansuz*, April 29, 2019, https:// antifascistneofolk.com/2019/04/29/sangre-de-muerdagos-galician -neofolk-is-resistance-to-spains-fascist-history/.

28. Ansuz, "The Sounds of the Wild: An Interview with Nøkken+The Grim," *A Blaze Ansuz*, April 8, 2019, https://antifascistneofolk.com/2019/04/08/ the-sounds-of-the-wild-an-interview-with-nokken-the-grim/.

29. Ansuz, "A Community-Centered Folk Revival: An Interview With Vael," *A Blaze Ansuz*, April 22, 2020, https://antifascistneofolk.com /2020/04/22/a-community-centered-folk-revival-an-interview-with -vael/.

30. Ansuz, "Apocalyptic Militancy: An Interview with Emerson Dracon," *A Blaze Ansuz*, February 18, 2020, https://antifascistneofolk .com/2020/02/18/apocalyptic-militancy-an-interview-with-emerson -dracon/.

31. Ansuz, "Announcing A Blaze Ansuz, a Chronicle and Playlist of Antifascist Neofolk," *A Blaze Ansuz*, March 27, 2019, https://antifascist neofolk.com/2019/03/27/announcing-a-blaze-ansuz-a-chronicle-and -playlist-of-antifascist-neofolk/.

32. Author interview with Jay Nada on September 28th, 2020.

33. On October 2, 2020, Left/Folk released an 18-track compilation in collaboration with *A Blaze Ansuz* to support the Black Lives Matter National Bail Fund.

34. Ansuz, "Daisies and Gas Masks: An Interview With Blocco-Nero," *A Blaze Ansuz*, September 28, 2020, https://antifascist neofolk.com/2020/09/28/daisies-and-gas-masks-an-interview -with-blocconero/.

35. Matthias Gardell, *Gods of the Blood: The Pagan Revival and White Separatism* (Durham: Duke University Press, 2003).

36. Author interview with Ryan Smith, June 3, 2019.

37. Ibid.

38. Author interview with Sophie Martinez, October 10, 2020.

39. Ibid.

40. Ryan Smith, *The Way of Fire and Ice: The Living Tradition of Norse Paganism* (Woodbury, Mass.: Llewellyn Publishing, 2019), 334–36.

41. Shane Burley and Ryan Smith, "Asatru's Racist Missionary: Stephen McNallen, Defend Europe, and the Weaponization of Folkish Heathery," *Gods & Radicals*, September 14, 2017, https://godsandradicals .org/2017/09/14/asatrus-racist-missionary-stephen-mcnallen-defend -europe-and-the-weaponization-of-folkish-heathery.

42. Shane Burley, *Fascism* Today, 143–44.

43. Author interview with Alexander Reid Ross, October 5, 2020.

44. Enzo Traverso (echoing the critiques of authors like David Renton) argue that the far-right today is a form of "post-fascism" because it negates key features of fascist movements in an effort to find an alliance with the broad political right. While I may not ultimately agree, this point is well illustrated in the number of far-right groups whose public politics is not that distant from the mainstream political parties. Their expression of those politics, however, takes on a form of immediatist violence or revolutionary activity (such as the Proud Boys or militia movement). Enzo Traverso, *The New Faces of Fascism: Populism and the Far Right* (New York: Verso, 2019), 2–7; David Renton, *The New Authoritarians: Convergence on the Right* (Chicago: Haymarket, 2019), 12–19.

45. David Neiwert, *The Eliminationists: How Hate Talk Radicalized the American Right* (New York: Routledge, 2009).

46. Spencer Sunshine, "The Growing Alliance Between Neo-Nazis, Right Wing Paramilitaries and Trumpist Republicans," *Colorlines*, June 9, 2017, https://www.colorlines.com/articles/growing-alliance-between -neo-nazis-right-wing-paramilitaries-and-trumpist-republicans.

47. Shane Burley, "Trump and the GOP are using Kyle Rittenhouse in last-ditch 2020 voter strategy," *NBC News*, October 4, 2020, https:// www.nbcnews.com/think/opinion/trump-gop-are-using-kyle-ritten-house-last-ditch-2020-voter-ncna1241940.

48. See "Chase the Black Sun" in this book.

49. "Local Objectives," The Huey P. Newton Gun Club, https://hueyp newtongunclub.org/about.

50. Grandmaster Jay quoted in, Benjamin Fearnow, "Armed Black Militia Challenges White Nationalists at Georgia's Stone Mountain Park," *Newsweek*, July 5, 2020, https://www.newsweek.com/armed

-black-demonstrators-challenge-white-supremacist-militia-georgias
-stone-mountain-park-1515494.

51. Ibid.

52. Zack Linly, "Armed Black Militia Marches Through Stone Mountain Park Calling for Removal of Nation's Largest Confederate Monument," *The Root*, July 6, 2020, https://www.theroot.com/armed-black-militia-marches-through-stone-mountain-park-1844284200.

53. Antifash Gordon, @AntiFashGordon, *Twitter*, July 4, 2020, https://twitter.com/AntiFashGordon/status/1279587110346002434.

54. Shane Burley, "Amid the coronavirus crisis, mutual aid networks erupt across the country," *Waging Nonviolence*, March 27, 2020, wagingnonviolence.org/2020/03/coronavirus-mutual-aid-networks-erupt-across-country/; Shane Burley, "'A huge difference': Volunteers mobilise in Oregon fire aftermath," *Al Jazeera*, September 25, 2020, https://www.aljazeera.com/news/2020/9/25/a-huge-difference-activists-mobilise-in-oregon-fire-aftermath.

55. Ross, *Against the Fascist Creep*, 3.

56. Anti-Defamation League, "R.A.M.: Rise Above Movement," https://www.adl.org/resources/backgrounders/rise-above-movement-ram.

57. Anti-Fascist News, "Introducing Haymaker, Chicago's New Anti-Fascist Gym," April 18, 2017, *Anti-Fascist News*, https://antifascistnews.net/2017/04/18/introducing-haymaker-chicagos-new-anti-fascist-gym/.

58. Miller-Idriss, *Hate in the Homeland*, 101.

59. Ibid., 93.

60. Hilary Moore, "'We Can Do More Together' How Fighting Sports Build Confidence in European Antifascist Networks," in *¡No pasarán!: Readings in Antifascism*, ed. Shane Burley (Chico: AK Press/Institute for Anarchist Studies, forthcoming).

61. Ella Gilbert. 2018. "Meet the Founders of an Antifa Fight Club," https://www.facebook.com/watch/?v=1929958890428841.

62. Stanislav Vysotsky, *American Antifa: The Tactics, Culture, and Practice of Militant Antifascism* (New York: Routledge, 2020), 122–23.

63. Author interview with Effie Baum, January 21, 2020.

Introduction to Armageddon

1. David Spratt and Ian Dunlop, "Existential climate-related security risk: A scenario approach," *Breakthrough - National Centre for Climate Restoration*, May 2019, https://docs.wixstatic.com/ugd/148cb0_a1406e0143ac4c469196d3003bc1e687.pdf.

2. Slavoj Žižek in *An Examined Life*, dir. Astra Taylor (Toronto: Zeitgeist Films, 2008).

3. Matthew Goodwin and Roger Eatwell, *National Populism: The Revolt Against Liberal Democracy* (London: Pelican Books, 2017).

4. Eric Kaufman, *Whiteshift: Populism, Immigration, and the Future of White Majorities* (New York: Abrams Press, 2019).

5. Chris Begley, "I study collapsed civilizations. Here's my advice for a climate change apocalypse," *Lexington Herald Leader*, September 23, 2019, https://www.kentucky.com/opinion/op-ed/article235384162.html.

6. Michael Hardt and Antonio Negri, *Empire* (Cambridge: Harvard University Press, 1999), 62.

7. This history is discussed by Joshua Clover, *Riot, Strike, Riot: The New Era of Uprisings* (New York: Verso Books, 2019).

Because of Their Violence

1. The Workers Viewpoint Organization only renamed itself as the Communist Workers Party a couple of weeks in advance of the November 3rd anti-Klan demonstration, in an effort to follow through on what the larger organizing body said would be a "five year plan" ending in communist revolution. "The massacre is not reducible to us changing our name. We did not use CWP on our literature until the day of the demonstration. But our name change and our language facilitated the attack against us and helped them to get away with it," said Nelson Johnson, explaining after the fact the ease at which the word "communist" was used to paint the activists as unsympathetic and dangerous.

2. Robert F. Williams, "from Negroes With Guns (1962)," in *The U.S. Anti-fascism Reader*," ed. Bill V. Mullen and Christopher Vials (New York: Verso Books, 2020), 248–52.

3. Sally Avery Bermanzohn, *Through Survivors' Eyes: From the Sixties to the Greensboro Massacre* (Nashville: Vanderbilt University Press, 2003), 185.

4. Ibid., 188.

5. Matthew N. Lyons, *Insurgent Supremacists*, 170–71.

6. Eric Ginsburg, "The Greensboro Massacre of 1979, Explained," *Teen Vogue*, May 18, 2018, https://www.teenvogue.com/story/the-greensboro-massacre-of-1979-explained.

7. James W. McCarthy, "The Embrace of Justice: The Greensboro Truth and Reconciliation Commission, Miroslav Volf, and the Ethics of Reconciliation," *Journal of the Society of Christian Ethics* 33, no. 2 (2013): 115.

8. Lisa Magarrell and Joya Wesley, *Learning from Greensboro: Truth and Reconciliation in the United States* (Philadelphia: University of Pennsylvania Press, 2008), 3–11.

9. Kathleen Belew, *Bring the War Home: The White Power Movement and Paramilitary America* (Cambridge: Harvard University Press, 2018).

10. *Slate* podcast, season 4, *Slow Burn: David Duke* ,

11. David Neiwert, *Alt-America: The Rise of the Radical Right in the Age of Trump* (London: Verso Books, 2017), 222.

12. Shane Burley, "How White Nationalists are Setting Immigration Policy in Trump's White House," *Truthout*, April 27, 2017, https://truthout.org/articles/how-white-nationalists-are-setting-immigration-policy-in-trump-s-white-house/. Matthew N. Lyons, *Insurgent Supremacists*, 65.

13. "Almost Acceptable: The Curious Case of the Council of Conservative Citizens," *Anti-Fascist News*, July 25, 2015, https://antifascistnews.net/2015/07/25/almost-acceptable-the-curious-case-of-the-council-of-conservative-citizens.

14. Tamir Bar-On, *Where Have All the Fascists Gone?*; Tamir Bar-On, *Rethinking the French New Right: Alternatives to Modernity* (London and New York: Routledge, 2016).

15. Zoe Hyman, "Transatlantic white supremacy: American segregationists and international racism after civil rights," in *Global White Nationalism: From Apartheid to Trump*, ed. Daniel Geary, Camilla Schofield, and Jennifer Sutton (Manchester: Manchester University Press, 2020), 197–211.

16. Elinor Langor, *A Hundred Little Hitlers*, 344–50.

17. Shane Burley, "As the alt-right moves to violence, community responses matter," *Waging Nonviolence*, June 1, 2017, https://wagingnonviolence.org/2017/06/alt-right-violence-portland-community-response/.

18. Mike Wendling, *Alt Right: From 4Chan to the White House* (London: Pluto Press, 2018), 190–91.

19. David Neiwert, *Red Pill, Blue Pill: How to Counteract the Conspiracy Theories That Are Killing Us* (Lanham, MD: Prometheus Books, 2020), 43–47.

20. Shane Burley, "Institutionalizing Lone-Wolf Terrorism: How Fascist Organizations Inspire Mass Violence," *The Hampton Institute*, September 21, 2015, https://www.hamptonthink.org/read/institutionalizing-lone-wolf-terrorism-how-fascist-organizations-inspire-mass-violence.

21. Matthew N. Lyons, *Insurgent Supremacists*, 168.

22. Author interview with Vicky Osterweil, September 13, 2020. Osterweil's point was that 2020 was filled with instances of police allowing far-right white vigilantes attack Black Lives Matter, antifascist, and antiracist protesters, which surprised many. It was, however, a "return to history" since that is historically the dominant dynamic rather than police repressing dissidents and marginalized communities all on their own.

23. Elinor Langor, *A Hundred Little Hitlers*, 271–77.

24. *Learning from Greensboro*, 86

25. Greensboro Truth and Reconciliation Committee, "Executive Summary," Greensboro Truth and Reconciliation Commission Report, Presented to the residents of Greensboro, the City, the Greensboro Truth and Community Reconciliation Project and other public bodies on May 25, 2006, https://greensborotrc.org/exec_summary.pdf.

26. Ibid., 16.

27. Alexander Reid Ross, *Against the Fascist Creep*, 284.

28. Extremist Files, "Frazier Glenn Miller," Southern Poverty Law Center, https://www.splcenter.org/fighting-hate/extremist-files/individual/frazier-glenn-miller.

29. The approach of the police with white nationalist groups is complex, and not one that can be sufficiently unpacked here. The Greensboro Massacre shows clear complicity between the police and the Klan, primarily in their absence or unwillingness to see the actual threat the white nationalists presented. The cause can range from support to structural inequality, creating blindspots, but either way it creates a structure of support. This is different, however, when the revolutionary white nationalists turn their guns on the State itself, and then the police suddenly find themselves as effective in dismantling white nationalist organizations. The interplay is inconsistent and always shifting.

30. Martin Durham, *White Rage: The Extreme Right in American Politics* (London: Routledge, 2007), 103–104.

31. Author interview with Jalane Schiller, August 22, 2019.

32. Author interview with Don Gathers, June 28, 2019.

33. Ibid.

34. Author interview with Christian Picciolini, February 19, 2020.

35. Author interview with Susan Bro, August 7, 2020.

36. Shane Burley, "Trump and the GOP are using Kyle Rittenhouse in last-ditch 2020 voter strategy," *NBC News*, October 4, 2020, https://www.nbcnews.com/think/opinion/trump-gop-are-using-kyle-rittenhouse-last-ditch-2020-voter-ncna1241940.

37. Amy Goodman, "Greensboro Massacre: City Apologizes 41 Years After Cops Allowed Klan, Nazis to Kill 5 Antiracists," *Democracy Now!*, October 7th, 2020, democracynow.org/2020/10/7/1979_greensboro_massacre_survivors_city_apology.

38. Bermanzohn, *Through Survivor's Eyes*, 248

39. National Anti-Klan Network "'Call for February 2nd Mobilization, Greensboro, North Carolina' (1980)," collected in *Remaking Radicalism: A Grassroots Documentary Reader of the United States, 1973–2001*, ed. Dan Berger and Emily K. Hobson (Athens: Georgia University Press, 2019), 72–73.

40. Hilary Moore and James Tracy, *No Fascist USA!: The John Brown Anti-Klan Committee and Lessons for Today's Movements* (San Francisco: City Lights Books, 2020).

Living Your Life in a State of War

1. Dan Sabbagh, "Investigation into alleged use of white phosphorus in Syria," *The Guardian*, October 18, 2019, https://www.theguardian.com/world/2019/oct/18/un-investigates-turkey-alleged-use-of-white-phosphorus-in-syria.
2. Author interview with Andrej Grubačić, November 11, 2019.
3. Strangers in a Tangled Wilderness, *A Small Key Can Open A Large Door: The Rojava Revolution* (Strangers in a Tangled Wilderness, 2015).
4. The organization's origins date to 1978, but the years of armed struggle in the Qandil Mountains began in 1984.
5. "Being Part of the Revolution," *The Internationalist Commune*," https://internationalistcommune.com/being-part-of-the-revolution/.
6. This is not to say that the Abraham Lincoln Brigades were fully on the side of the anarchists, and included an element that betrayed them as directed by Stalin's forces.
7. "Kyriarchy is a term that extends patriarchy to encompass and connect to other structures of oppression and privilege, such as racism, ableism, capitalism, etc. Basically, the term kyriarchy recognizes that there are overlapping, complicated power strata." "Identity Politics: isms, privilege, kyriarchy," https://www.mtholyoke.edu/~haydo2os/classweb/world_politics/kyriarchy.html.
8. International Revolutionary People's Guerilla Forces, "Smashing the State in Rojava and Beyond: The Formation and Intentions of the International Revolutionary People's Guerrilla Forces," *The Anarchist Library*, 2017, theanarchistlibrary.org/library/international-revolutionary-people-s-guerrilla-forces-smashing-the-state-in-rojava-and-beyond.
9. Author interview with Debbie Bookchin, November 6, 2019.
10. Michael Staudenmaier and Rami El-Amine, "The Three Way Fight Journal of Social Justice 53 Debate," *Upping the Anti* #5, November 19, 2009, https://uppingtheanti.org/journal/article/05-the-three-way-fight-debate.
11. Murray Bookchin, *To Remember Spain: The Anarchist and Syndicalist Revolution of 1936* (Oakland: AK Press, 2001); Frank Mintz, *Anarchism and Workers' Self-Management in Revolutionary Spain* (Oakland: AK Press, 2013); Danny Evans, *Revolution and the State: Anarchism in the Spanish Civil War, 1936–1939* (Chico: AK Press, 2020).
12. *Pickaxe,* dir. Tim Ream (CrimethInc, 1999), 94 mins.

13. Mihalis Mentinis, *Zapatistas: The Chiapas Revolt and What It Means for Radical Politics* (London: Pluto Press, 2006).
14. George Hagglund, interview by Shane Burley, October 31, 2019.
15. Friedrich Nietzsche, *The Gay Science* (New York: Random House, 1974).
16. Author interview with Berivan Qerecoxy, November 3, 2019.
17. Author interview with Debbie Bookchin, November 6, 2019.

The Continuing Appeal of Antisemitism

1. Savannah Behrmann, "'Sickening': Bernie Sanders campaign condemns protester who unfurled swastika flag at Phoenix rally," *USA Today*, March 6, 2020, https://www.usatoday.com/story/news/politics /elections/2020/03/06/bernie-sanders-campaign-condemns-nazi -swastika-flag-phoenix-rally/4973750002/.
2. Ari Feldman, "Six Nights of Hanukkah, Seven Anti-Semitic Incidents in New York City," *Forward*, December 27, 2019, https://www.forward .com/news/national/437346/anti-semitic-attacks-nyc-brooklyn/.
3. Shaun Walker, "Jews in Germany Warned of Risks of Wearing Kippah Cap in Public," *The Guardian*, May 25, 2019, https://www.theguardian.com/world/2019/may/26/jews-in-germany -warned-of-risks-of-wearing-kippah-cap-in-public.
4. Shane Burley, "Anti-Semitism in the White House: Stephen Bannon, Donald Trump and the Alt-Right," *Truthout*, November 20, 2016, https: //truthout.org/articles/anti-semitism-in-the-white-house-stephen -bannon-donald-trump-and-the-alt-right/.
5. Joan Braune, "Who's Afraid of the Frankfurt School? "Cultural Marxism" as an Antisemitic Conspiracy Theory," *The Journal for Social Justice*, Vol. 9, (2019).
6. The idea that Jews are tribal, ethnocentric, and privately conservative is an incredibly common and bigoted stereotype that many people, even many who would otherwise decry antisemitism, believe is true. Instead, Jewish communities have every range of political and social ideas that the rest of the world does: some are right wing, some are left-wing, some are exclusionary to others, some are inclusive. The fact that we have to correct the record to remind people that Jews are "just like everyone else" is evidence of the problem.
7. Kevin MacDonald, *The Culture of Critique: An Evolutionary Analysis of Jewish Involvement in Twentieth-Century Intellectual and Political Movements* (Bloomington: AuthorHouse, 1998).
8. Kevin MacDonald, "Recently in The Occidental Quarterly: Special Sections on White Pathology," *Occidental Observer*, October 28, 2013, www .theoccidentalobserver.net/2013/10/28/recently-in-the-occidental -quarterly-special-sections-on-white-pathology/.

9. Richard Spencer and Kevin MacDonald, "Origins of the White Man," *Radix Journal Podcast*, January 2, 2016, Archived at https://archive.org/details/TheOriginsOfTheWhiteMan.

10. This current runs through much of society, not just people who are easily identified as antisemites, and exists as a part of the latent antisemitism of a society that trains an inherent skepticism of the Jewish experience.

11. Matthew Yglesias, "The (((echo))), explained," *Vox*, June 6, 2016, https://www.vox.com/2016/6/6/11860796/echo-explained-parentheses-twitter.

12. "The Happy Merchant," *The Anti-Defamation League*, https://www.adl.org/education/references/hate-symbols/the-happy-merchant.

13. And it should go without saying that this has no connection to any actual Jewish person.

14. It should go without saying that this reading of the Talmud is almost entirely from the imagination of the antisemites. In reality, it is filled with instructions about polite kindnesses.

15. Madelein Schwartz, "The Origins of Blood Libel," *The Nation*, January 28, 2016, https://www.thenation.com/article/archive/the-origins-of-blood-libel.

16. *The Believer*, Henry Beam, dir. (New York: Seven Arts Pictures, 2001).

17. Ibid.

18. The word "wicked" always comes to mind when discussing this, which means "to twist" or distort. Antisemitism takes something real, such as class anger, and twists it into an unnatural distortion that becomes a mobilizing bigotry rather than the fuel for a liberatory social movement. The bit of truth, the anger of the economic deprivation, is mixed with the conspiratorial lie to create something monstrous. It likewise brings to mind the warning in William Peter Blattey's novel *The Exorcist*. "The demon is a liar. He will lie to confuse us; but he will also mix lies with the truth to attack us. His attack is psychological, Damien. And powerful."

19. *The Protocols of the Meetings of the Learned Elders of Zion*, trans. by Victor E. Marsden (Escondido, California: The Book Tree, 1999), 159.

20. The Zionist World Congress meeting was convened to form a Jewish state as a protective, and potentially colonial, solution to antisemitism. This is the movement that would become political Zionism, that would form the present State of Israel. The antisemitic mythology of it is that it was a meeting where secretive Jewish elites plotted to control the world.

21. Umberto Eco, foreword to *The Plot: The Secret Story of The Protocols of the Elders of Zion*, Will Eisner (New York: W. W. Norton & Company, 2006), vii.

22. Author interview with Greg Johnson, September 22, 2016.

23. We should acknowledge here that we cannot reduce Jewish separation from surrounding communities as only the result of outside forces, there is also a tradition of Jewish distinctiveness driven from unique folkways that come from halakha and religious requirements. This is what Robert Wistrich described as "unusual social cohesion, compactness and religiously sanctioned exclusiveness." The idea that Jews "self-segregate" is one that is both heavily relied upon by antisemites and is one of the ways that antisemitic narratives have creeped into some discourse around Jewish history, but Jewish distinctiveness should also not be erased. "This does not mean that the cause of antisemitism lay in the Jews themselves, but it can help us to understand how the peculiar brand of social hostility which we call by this name first arose as one possible response (there were of course others, ranging from admiration to indifference) to the reality of Jewish exclusiveness. Jewish distinctiveness despite many millennia of oppression, dispersion, and attempts at destruction has often been identified as one of the possible roots of antisemitism, where this persistence is seen as a threat to those who want to remake the world in their own image. Robert Wistrich, *Antisemitism: The Longest Hatred* (New York City: Pantheon Books, 1991), xviii.

24. Joy Schaverien, "THE SCAPEGOAT TRANSFERENCE—The Holocaust and the Collective Unconscious: Themes and Images Revealed in Art Therapy," *European Judaism: A Journal for the New Europe* 29, no. 1 (1996): 64–74.

25. Jean-Paul Sartre, *Anti-Semite and Jew: An Exploration of the Etiology of Hate* (New York: Schocken, 1995), 20.

26. Max Horkheimer and Theodor W. Adorno, *Dialectic of Enlightenment: Philosophical Fragments* (Stanford: Stanford University Press, 1987), 137–72.

27. There is an entirely other type of antisemitism that is itself elitist and aristocratic, seen mostly in the WASP. This is the antisemitism that is openly contemptuous of difference. I would argue though that it does transfer to the masses less than Jews as agents of capital or cabal of conspiracy.

28. Bodo Kahmann. "Antisemitism and Antiurbanism, Past and Present: Empirical and Theoretical Approaches," in Alvin H. Rosenfeld, ed. *Deciphering the New Antisemitism* (Bloomington: Indiana University Press, 2015), 488.

29. David Nirenberg, *Anti-Judaism: The Western Tradition* (New York: W.W. Norton and Company, 2013), 468.

30. Ibid., 436.

31. He identified this period as 1750–1950, the tail end being the

Holocaust, the loss of public acceptability for antisemitism, and the creation of the State of Israel.

32. Enzo Traverso, *The End of Jewish Modernity* (London: Pluto Press, 2016), 12–16, 20–23.

33. Enzo Traverso, *The Jewish Question: History of a Marxist Debate* (Chicago: Haymarket Books, 2018), 55–58.

34. Moishe Postone, "Anti-Semitism and National Socialism," in Anson Rabinbach and Jack Zipes, eds. *Germans and Jews Since the Holocaust* (New York: Holmes and Meier, 1986), 304.

35. Ibid., 305.

36. Ibid., 306.

37. Werner Bonefeld, "Notes on Anti-Semitism," *Common Sense* 21 (1997): 62.

38. Ibid., 64.

39. Ibid., 69.

40. "On the Jewish Question" offers a complex picture of how the left dealt with antisemitism in the mid-nineteenth century. Marx believes antisemitic stereotypes about Jews and Judaism, and puzzles how to end the oppression against Jews, a question not pondered by those behind the "movement" of antisemitism. The struggle against capital is then represented through the flawed understanding of people, oppression, and the nature of religion, suggesting that Judaism reflects an actual essential role in the market process. Marxists have struggled since to re-interpret antisemitism, yet the essay itself should be seen critically in its historical context and Marx's inability to free himself from antisemitic modalities of deconstruction.

41. David Nirenberg, *Anti-Judaism*.

42. Werner Bonefield, "Antisemitism and the Power of Abstraction: From Political Economy to Critical Theory," in ed. Marcel Stoetzler, *Antisemitism and the Constitution of Modern Sociology* (Lincoln: University of Nebraska Press, 2014), 320.

43. Tomislav Sunic, *Against Democracy and Equality: The European New Right* (London: Arktos Media Ltd., 2011), 107–24.

44. For a more in depth explanation of this see Michael Barkun, *Religion and the Racist Right: The Origins of the Christian Identity Movement* (Chapel Hill: The University of North Carolina Press, 2014), 48–80.

45. Ibid., 136–142. It should be noted that a less demonic presentation of the Khazar Theory is used in some areas of anti-Zionist literature, most notably Israeli author Shlomo Sand. The point of this writing is to prove that Ashkenazi Jews are not of Middle Eastern origin, and therefore have no claim of national indigeneity to Palestine. Shlomo Sand, *The Invention of the Jewish People* (New York City: Verso Books, 2009).

46. Ibid., 161–62.

47. Kathleen Belew, *Bring the War Home*.

48. Jessica Elgot, "Labour suspends party members in 'anti-Semitic' Facebook group," *The Guardian*, March 8, 2018, https://www.theguardian.com/politics/2018/mar/08/labour-suspends-party-members-in-anti-Semitic-facebook-group.

49. Mark Townsend, "UK left activists attended events with far right antisemites," *The Guardian*, February 22, 2020, https://www.theguardian.com/news/2020/feb/22/uk-left-activists-at-far-right-events-antisemites-holocaust-deniers.

50. While more scholarship is necessary on this subject, the Settlement Movement makes is a militant far-right movement in its own right with fascist contingents that call for the ethnic cleansing of Palestine.

51. Spencer Sunshine, "Looking Left at Antisemitism," *The Journal of Social Justice*, vol. 9 (2019).

52. Marilyn Mayo, "Anti-Semitic 9/11 Conspiracy Theorists Thrive 15 Years After Attacks," *Anti-Defamation League*, September 9, 2016.

53. Shane Burley, "Google Jewish Bankers," *The Journal of Social Justice*, Vol. 9 (2019).

54. This is the position offered by authors like Alexander Cockburn, Israel Shamir, and Gilad Atzmon. While people can dismiss them as cranks (and should), there is a significant portion of the international organized left that has politics that back up against this perspective.

55. Quoted in "Holocaust on Trial," documentary transcript, *PBS*, Airdate: October 31, 2000, https://www.pbs.org/wgbh/nova/transcripts/2711holocaust.html.

56. Quoted in Chip Berlet, "'Trumping' democracy: Right-wing populism, fascism, and the case for action," in *Trumping Democracy: From Reagan to the Alt-Right*, ed. Chip Berlet (London: Routledge, 2019), 185–86.

Chase the Black Sun

1. Burley, *Fascism Today*, 136.

2. Paul Waggener, *On Magic: A No-Bullshit Primer on Working the Will* (Lynchburg: Self-Published, 2016), 1–8.

3. While the majority of pagans who follow some form of Nordic paganism (broadly called *heathenry*) are opposed to the racist manifestations, there is still a very sizable group that use it as a proxy for racial identity. The term *Asatru* was coined in the mid-twentieth century, and while it has no specific racial denotation (it was used largely for the more magically focused Icelandic variety of heathenry), it has been used by "folkish" racial pagan groups like the Asatru Folk Assembly and Asatru Alliance. All this is to say that *Asatru* is often a racial religion, which sees the Gods of the North as implicit to white

psyches, and that is how the Waggeners saw it. For more on antiracist heathens, see "Contested Spaces" in this volume.

4. Paul Waggener, "Psychos," Paul-Waggener.com, August 27, 2018, www.paul-waggener.com/2018/08/psychos/.

5. "Greg Johnson Interviews Paul Waggener," Counter-Currents Radio, *Counter-Currents Publishing*, January 7, 2016, https://counter-currents .com/2016/01/greg-johnson-interviews-paul-waggener/.

6. Jack Donovan, "A Time for Wolves," Jack-Donovan.com, June 14, 2014, web.archive.org/web/20140617172729/http://www.jack-donovan .com/axis/2014/06/a-time-for-wolves/. (Now offline.) While I won't spend a lot of time on this here, *folkish* is the defining quality of racialized paganism and is built on the idea that the gods are spiritual archetypes that are owned only by those of Northern European descent. It was the founding principle behind the creation of Odinism, which was a racial religion from the start, and has continued on through the Asatru Folk Assembly, people like Stephen McNallen, and journals like *Tyr*, *Runa*, and the *Journal of Heathen Studies*. Suffice it to say, that "folkish" is a white nationalist concept that is often repackaged as a universal spiritual idea. It is not uncommon to find this idea still floating around heathen circles, except for those who have decided to become actively antiracist.

7. Shane Burley, "Total Life Reform: The Real Consequences of the Far Right's Self-Help Grift," *Political Research Associates*, November 9, 2020, politicalresearch.org/2020/11/09/total-life-reform.

8. Ibid.

9. Paul Waggener, "Might Is Right," *Iron and Blood* 1: 1–2.

10. Paul Waggener and Matthias Waggener, "Operation Werewolf—Balancing Lifting and Jiu Jitsu," YouTube, RT: 6:19, October 16, 2019, https://www.youtube.com/watch?v=V1izkdoArKI.

11. Paul Waggener, *It's Not Enough: Werewolf Elite Program Dispatch #001* (Lynchburg: Amazon CreateSpace, 2018).

12. Paul Waggener, "Operation Werewolf—Antifa, The Joker, and Ancestry," YouTube, October 18, 2019, RT: 14:41, https://www.youtube.com/ watch?v=4ZJZp6C2pcY.

13. Many of these have been short lived, likely built hastily as part of Paul's "temporal" advice of starting small businesses, which led to high-interest loans that eventuated in bankruptcy. Few people want to pay $300 a month to work out in a garage covered in black metal posters. Cari Wade Gervin, "Vengeance Strength Kvlt Gym in East Nashville Has Links to Alt-Right," *Nashville Scene*, July 20, 2017, https:// www.nashvillescene.com/news/pith-in-the-wind/article/20868176/ strength-cult-gym-in-east-nashville-has-ties-to-altright.

14. Betsy Swan, "Inside Virginia's Creepy White-Power Wolf Cult,"

The Daily Beast, April 13, 2017, https://www.thedailybeast.com/inside-virginias-creepy-white-power-wolf-cult.

15. While the "wolf" is a common image of art and mythology, it is not as universal as some claim. There is an effort to create a perennial mythological language (see Joseph Campbell) that often flattens the complex world of religion and folklore and elevates western religious experiences.

16. Operative 413, "The Wolf God and the Ecstatic Host," *Operation Werewolf War Journal*, November 1, 2019, www.operationwerewolf.com/war-journal/2019/11/01/the-wolf-god-and-the-ecstatic-host/.

17. Sedgewick, *Against the Modern World*, 179–85.

18. Paul Waggener, "Operation Werewolf: Steroids," YouTube, October 25, 2019, RT: 24:37, https://www.youtube.com/watch?v=jQkXCPJ3avw&t.

19. Paul Waggener, "Simple Rules for a Savage Existence," *Operation Werewolf War Journal*, April 21, 2016, www.operationwerewolf.com/war-journal/2016/04/21/simple-rules-for-a-savage-existence/.

20. Ibid.

21. Operative 413, "Testosterone" *Operation Werewolf War Journal*, December 16, 2018, www.operationwerewolf.com/war-journal/2018/12/.

22. Ibid.

23. In an effort to really follow their advice I brought my testosterone levels to over 1,000, which is above a recommended high middle, but where they argue it should stay. In other circles, this would be considered "cycling," meaning running anabolic steroids. Like I said in the text, it had little effect other than as a workout aid.

24. Author interview with Katie McHugh, February 21, 2020.

25. Barbara Ehrenreich, foreword to *Male Fantasies* (1987), in *The Antifascism Reader*, ed. Bill V. Mullen and Christopher Vials (New York: Verso, 2020), 308.

26. Ibid., 309–10.

27. Enzo Traverso, *Fire and Blood: The European Civil War, 1914–1945* (New York: Verso Books, 2016), 210,

28. Ibid.

29. Waggener cites the book *The One-eyed God: Odin and the (Indo-)Germanic Männerbünde,* a recent volume that is published by a racist, pseudo-scholarly publishing outfit founded by a eugenicist, and which propagates the same mythology that drove the proto-Nazis. This is an example of the pseudo-scholarship that underskirts their sense of self, couched in neutral language yet reproducing the same white supremacist mythologies that have been used to historically justify atrocities and give the illusion of permanence and depth to a superficial phenomenon.

30. John Stoltenberg, *Refusing to Be a Man: Essays on Sex and Justice* (London: Breitenbush Books, 1989), 9. I want to acknowledge that while there are some meaningful insights in Stoltenberg's work, there are other parts that are both dated and erase the lived experiences of many sex workers.

31. Judith Butler, "Performative Acts and Gender Constitution: An Essay in Phenomenology and Feminist Theory," *Theatre Journal* 40, no. 4 (1988): 526.

32. This is actually literally true since Paul Waggener has a company called Rogue Advertising to offer branding services, and he trains Operation Werewolf recruits on those advertising concepts both through the Werewolf Elite Program and through another company called the Berkano Initiative.

33. Matthew N. Lyons, "Jack Donovan and Male Tribalism," in *Key Thinkers of the Radical Right: Behind the New Threat to Liberal Democracy* (New York City: Oxford University Press, 2019), 254.

34. Shane Burley, "Fascism Against Time: Nationalism, Media Blindness, and the Cult of Augustus Sol Invictus," *Gods & Radicals*, March 24, 2016, https://godsandradicals.org/2016/03/24/fascism-against-time -nationalism-media-blindness-and-the-cult-of-augustus-sol-invictus/.

35. Ibid.

36. Thelema is the spiritual and esoteric tradition created by Aliester Crowley. It has a libertine quality and is not inherently right-wing, but has had far-right members.

37. Author interview with Katy McHugh.

38. Anna Invictus, "Full Statement for Bond Hearing," Document Cloud, February 14, 2019, https://www.documentcloud.org/documents/6777989-Anna-Invictus-Full-Statement-for-Bond-Hearing.html.

39. Nick Martin, "Augustus Invictus gets another shot at release," *The Informant*, February 10, 2020, https://www.informant.news/p/augustus -invictus-gets-another-shot.

40. Pilar Melendez, "White Supremacist Augustus Sol Invictus Back in Jail After Allegedly Stalking Wife," *The Daily Beast*, April 21, 2020, https://www.thedailybeast.com/white-supremacist-augustus-sol -invictus-back-in-jail-after-allegedly-stalking-wife.

41. Andy Ngô, @MrAndyNgo, Twitter, January 16, 2019, https://twitter.com/MrAndyNgo/status/1085599630484750336.

42. His name has been changed out of respect for his family and friends.

43. Jack Donovan, *A Sky Without Eagles* (Milwaukie, Oregon: Dissonant Hum, 2014), 17–24.

44. Paul Waggener, *The Inner Circle (OPWW)* (Lynchburg: Self-Published, 2018), 37.

45. "All the Way Alive" (ATWA) is a phrased popularized by neo-Nazi

serial killer Charles Manson, who is often referenced by the Wolves and is featured in the artwork of one of their prominent members.

46. Krag Maga is explicitly discouraged as one of the fighting styles because they say that you can never train that style at 100% because it is designed to kill people, and you cannot actually test efficacy. No mention of its supposedly Jewish origin is made.

47. The first rule of Conclave is. . .

48. Author interview with Shannon Reid, November 6, 2020.

49. One can only be reminded of John Stoltenberg's words about normalization of violent and victimizing social dynamics in the assignment of "natural" gender roles for men.

50. Jack Donovan, *Becoming a Barbarian* (Portland, Oregon: Dissonant Hum Press, 2016).

51. Jack Donovan, The Way of Men (Portland, Oregon: Dissonant Hum Press, 2013), 150–175.

52. Ibid., 145, Kindle Edition.

53. Ibid., 146, Kindle Edition.

54. Donovan, *Becoming a Barbarian*, 2.

55. Paul Waggener, "Greg Johnson Interviews Paul Waggener," *Counter-Currents*, https://.counter-currents.com/2016/02/greg-johnson-inter views-paul-waggener-2/.

56. Tomislav Sunic, *Against Democracy and Equality: The European New Right* (Budapest: Arktos Media, 2011), 73–89.

57. Jack Donovan, *A Sky Without Eagles* (Portland: Dissonant Hum, 2014), 47.

58. Ibid., 54.

59. Jack Donovan, *Becoming a Barbarian* (Portland, Oregon: Dissonant Hum Press, 2016), 1–3.

60. Ibid., 4–25.

61. Rhyd Wildermuth, "Barbarians in the Age of Mechanical Reproduction Pt. 1," *Gods and Radicals*, June 17, 2017, https://godsandradicals .org/2017/06/17/barbarians-in-the-age-of-mechanical-reproduction/.

62. Ibid.

63. Matthew N. Lyons, "Jack Donovan and Male Tribalism," in *Key Thinkers of the Radical Right*, 248.

64. Jack Donovan, *A Sky Without Eagles*, 17–24.

65. Jack Donovan, "Positions & FAQ," Jack-Donovan, www.jack-donovan .com/sowilo/bio/positions.

66. Donovan, *A Sky Without Eagles*, 45.

67. Jack Donovan, *A More Complete Beast* (Portland, Oregon: Dissonant Hum, 2018). *Might is Right* is an early proto-fascist text that argues against the concept of neutral human rights and instead for a social Darwinist idea that success should be determined by those who have the power to enforce it.

68. When fact checking a 2020 article I wrote about Operation Werewolf, I had to reach out to Donovan for comment. He said he wanted white nationalists to "throw away his books" and that his relationship with them was a "dark time" in his life, but when pressed on his earlier racist statements he equivocated and would not confirm or deny.

69. A default advice in OPWW is that if a workout "sucks more," it is likely better. So the advice is to make your exercises more difficult and painful since suffering is a direct line to both achievement and transcendence.

70. This is actually at the heart of a range of the Alt Right's objections to modernity, and there is an obsessive focus on any form of pleasure that feels as though it is disconnected from suffering. A good example of this is Counter-Currents' Greg Johnson's problem with cannabis, which he says makes inferior art and food more enjoyable, and therefore evil. "Self-actualization requires pain and struggle. Virtue is hard not easy. But why worry about that, when marijuana can make you perfectly content with whatever level of ignorance, immaturity, and bad taste that you happen to be at when you take your first hit?," Greg Johnson, "Against Pot," *Counter-Currents Publishing*, May 22, 2015, https://counter-currents.com/2015/05/against-pot/.

71. Spartan Ownership, "How to Start a Tribe—Interview w/ Paul Waggener," YouTube, September 13, 2016, RT: 1:14:07, https://www.youtube.com/watch?v=DrpD1rIU390&t.

72. Blair Taylor, "Alt-Right Ecology: Ecofascism and Far-Right Environmentalism in the United States," in *The Far-Right and the Environment: Politics, Discourse and Communication*, ed. Bernhard Forchtner (London: Routledge, 2019), 284.

73. "Greg Johnson Interviews Paul Waggener," Counter-Currents Radio, *Counter-Currents Publishing*, January 7, 2016, counter-currents.com/2016/01/greg-johnson-interviews-paul-waggener/.

74. I want to acknowledge the immediate problems with this. This is not exactly "best practices" for dealing with domestic assault. But the idea was that they wanted to hold them accountable, not that they knew how to do it well.

75. Stoltenberg, *Refusing to Be a Man*, xxiv–xxv.

76. adrienne maree brown, "relinquishing the patriarchy," May 28, 2019, http://adriennemareebrown.net/2019/05/28/relinquishing-the-patriarchy/comment-page-1/.

77. Nora Samaran, *Turn This World Inside Out: The Emergence of Nurturance Culture* (Chico: AK Press, 2019), 32.

78. Ibid., 37–38.

79. Ibid., 18.

80. bell hooks, *The Will to Change: Men, Masculinity, and Love* (New York:

Atria Books, 2004), 6.

81. Ibid., 7.

82. Hannah Seligson, "These Men Are Waiting to Share Some Feelings With You," *New York Times*, December 8, 2018, https://www.nytimes.com/2018/12/08/style/men-emotions-mankind-project.html.

83. Owen Marcus, *Grow Up: A Man's Guide to Masculine Emotional Intelligence* (USA: New Tribe Press, 2013).

84. "About CMS," *Challenging Male Supremacy*, challengingmalesupremacy.org/about-cms/.

85. Samantha Schmidt, "No game days. No bars. The pandemic is forcing some men to realize they need deeper friendships.," *Washington Post*, November 30, 2020, https://www.washingtonpost.com/road-to-recovery/2020/11/30/male-bonding-covid/.

86. Paul Waggener, "Might Is Right," *Iron and Blood, Issue 1*: 1–2. Inequality is a key tent-pole for my definition of fascism. Shane Burley, *Fascism Today*, 49–50.

87. Paul Waggener, "You Are Not Equal," *Operation Werewolf War Journal*, January 7, 2016, www.operationwerewolf.com/war-journal/2016/01/07/you-are-not-equal.

88. Paul Waggener, "The Pressure Project Podcast #145: OPERATION WEREWOLF—GRIMNIR RETURNS!" YouTube, July 3,2015, 1:47:44, https://www.youtube.com/watch?v=n8y6zTjTdqM.

89. Rhyd Wildermuth, Barbarians in the Age of Mechanical Reproduction Pt. 1, *Gods and Radicals*, June 17, 2017, https://godsandradicals.org/2017/06/17/barbarians-in-the-age-of-mechanical-reproduction/.

90. Paul Waggener, "The Pressure Project Podcast #145: OPERATION WEREWOLF—GRIMNIR RETURNS!" YouTube, July 3,2015, 1:47:44, https://www.youtube.com/watch?v=n8y6zTjTdqM.

91. Paul and Matthias Waggener, "Barbarian Brothers—Pagans Stole Christmas from Jesus," YouTube, December 11, 2019, RT: 32:04, https://www.youtube.com/watch?v=JSAYWUXv8hg&t=146s.

92. The essays were published as a book: Peter Kropotkin, *Mutual Aid: A Factor of Revolution* (London: Freedom Press, 1987), also available at *The Anarchist Library*, www.theanarchistlibrary.org/library/petr-kropotkin-mutual-aid-a-factor-of-evolution.

93. Operative 413, "Conquerors Don't Apologize," *Operation Werewolf War Journal*, January 30, 2020, https://www.operationwerewolf.com/war-journal/2020/01/30/conquerors-dont-apologize/.

94. The Stanford Prison Experiment was a 1971 psychological study trying to determine what affect power has on a person's behavior and outlook. The study found that when a person was given power over another, such as a guard in a prison, they shift easily to authoritarian controls over their subjects and will even sanction torture.

95. Silvia Federici, "In Praise of the Dancing Body," *Gods & Radicals*, August 22, 2016, https://godsandradicals.org/2016/08/22/in-praise-of-the-dancing-body.
96. hooks, *The Will to Change*, 12.
97. Ibid., xvii.
98. Robert O. Paxton, *The Anatomy of Fascism*, 41.
99. Ibid., 16.

Index

AK PRESS is small, in terms of staff and resources, but we also manage to be one of the world's most productive anarchist publishing houses. We publish close to twenty books every year, and distribute thousands of other titles published by like-minded independent presses and projects from around the globe. We're entirely worker run and democratically managed. We operate without a corporate structure—no boss, no managers, no bullshit.

The **FRIENDS OF AK PRESS** program is a way you can directly contribute to the continued existence of AK Press, and ensure that we're able to keep publishing books like this one! Friends pay $25 a month directly into our publishing account ($30 for Canada, $35 for international), and receive a copy of every book AK Press publishes for the duration of their membership! Friends also receive a discount on anything they order from our website or buy at a table: 50% on AK titles, and 30% on everything else. We have a Friends of AK ebook program as well: $15 a month gets you an electronic copy of every book we publish for the duration of your membership. *You can even sponsor a very discounted membership for someone in prison.*

Email **friendsofak@akpress.org** for more info, or visit the website: **https://www.akpress.org/friends.html**.

There are always great book projects in the works—so sign up now to become a Friend of AK Press, and let the presses roll!